BAYLOR'S REGIMENT

The Third Continental Light Dragoons

Christine L. Langner

HERITAGE BOOKS
2015

HERITAGE BOOKS
AN IMPRINT OF HERITAGE BOOKS, INC.

Books, CDs, and more—Worldwide

For our listing of thousands of titles see our website
at
www.HeritageBooks.com

Published 2015 by
HERITAGE BOOKS, INC.
Publishing Division
5810 Ruatan Street
Berwyn Heights, Md. 20740

Copyright © 2015 Christine L. Langner

All rights reserved. No part of this book may be reproduced or transmitted in any form or by any means, electronic or mechanical, including photocopying, recording or by any information storage and retrieval system without written permission from the author, except for the inclusion of brief quotations in a review.

International Standard Book Numbers
Paperbound: 978-0-7884-5624-4
Clothbound: 978-0-7884-6132-3

*This book is dedicated to William Langley,
one of Baylor's men.*

Contents

Preface..vii

Acknowledgments...xi

The Men of the 3rd Regiment of

    Light Dragoons..1

Bibliography..191

Index..195

About the Author...207

Preface

In December 1776, while the Revolutionary War was being waged in Delaware, George Washington saw the action of a company of what he termed "Volunteer Horse from Connecticut" under the command of Major Elisha Sheldon. While Washington relied on the units of foot soldiers who could move more fluidly through the countryside, he had begun to realize the advantage of having a mounted, mobile, and certainly more intimidating unit. On December 11, 1776, he wrote to John Hancock, who was serving as President of the Second Continental Congress:

> *From the Experience I have had this Campaign of the Utility of Horse, I am convinced there is no carrying on the War without them, and I would therefore recommend the Establishment of one or more Corps, (in proportion to the Number of Foot) in Addition to those already raised in Virginia.*[1]

One regiment of horse had been raised in June 1776 in Virginia, and was under the command of Colonel Theodorick Bland, but by January of 1777, after Washington's recommendation, Congress had resolved to raise three more regiments of light dragoons, and put all four regiments on Continental pay. The existing regiment under Colonel Bland was designated the 1st Regiment of Light Dragoons. Elisha Sheldon, of Connecticut, became colonel of the 2nd Regiment,

---

[1] Chase, Philander D. 1985. *The Papers of George Washington. Revolutionary War Series.* University Press of Virginia, Charlottesville. Vol. 7, page 297.

and Stephen Moylan was assigned to the 4th Regiment on January 5th, 1777. In regards to the 3rd Regiment, John Hancock wrote back to Washington on January 1, 1777:

> From the enclosed Resolve you will percieve Congress have determined, that a Horse, properly caparisoned, be presented to your Aid de Camp Colo. Baylor, and to recommend it to you to promote him to be a Colonel of a Regiment of Light Horse.[2]

Under the newly-appointed Colonel George Baylor, six troops were established:

1st Troop   Captain George Lewis
(this troop served as the commander-in-chief's life guard)

2nd Troop   Captain Cadwallader Jones
3rd Troop   Captain John Swan
4th Troop   Captain Chiswell Barrett
5th Troop   Captain Churchill Jones
6th Troop   Captain Presley Thornton[3]

The troops were accepted into Continental pay on January 14, 1777 and recruitment went on throughout the summer of 1777 for the Third Regiment of Continental Light Dragoons, which would always be known as "Baylor's Regiment."

The first troop, assigned to be Washington's Life Guards, is not included in this book, but is covered in Carlos E. Godfrey's book, *The Commander-in-Chief's Guard*. The scope of this book is the men of the remaining troops, who were almost entirely recruited from Virginia, with some men from North Carolina, but who, after the war, settled and raised families not only in Virginia, but in surrounding states, including Kentucky, Tennessee, North Carolina, and South Carolina.

The officers of the Third Regiment have been well documented, based on regimental returns, but the one surviving muster roll of the troops gives us only a snapshot of the men, so in

---

2   Ibid., page 506.
3   Sanchez-Saavedra, E. M. 1978. *A Guide to Virginia Military Organizations in the American Revolution, 1774-1787*. Virginia State Library, Richmond, page 105.

order to identify them, it has been necessary to search letters written to and from the regimental officers, quartermaster records, and post-war sources, such as state and federal pension records, rejected pension applications, and bounty land warrants. Due to this scarcity of documentation, it is not possible to compile a complete listing of the men of the Third Continental Light Dragoons, but the men and their accounts summarized here give us insight into their service and the hardships suffered during the war, the battles they fought in, their families, the friendships they made, and quite often, the poverty resulting from their inability to work after the war due to their wounds.

A detailed history of the Third Continental Light Dragoons, including their movements, battles, and hardships can be found in C. F. William Maurer's *Dragoon Diary: The Third Continental Light Dragoons*, and will not be covered here. However, one event in the history of the Third Light Dragoons is worth mentioning, which shaped not only the men and the regiment, but seems to have served as the basis for their life-long loyalty to George Baylor. This event, known variously as "the surprise of the regiment at Tappan" or "Baylor's Massacre" came in September 1778, when the regiment was ordered to move to new quarters near Old Tappan, New Jersey, and were billeted one night in a number of barns and houses in the area. They were betrayed to the British troops stationed in the area by some of the loyalist townspeople, and were attacked in the night by men serving under General "No Flint" Grey. More than sixty of the men of the Third Regiment were bayoneted and died in the attack, and the death toll would have been higher, except that one of the British officers disobeyed his orders, and took the entire 4th troop prisoner, instead of killing them. Among the dead was Major Alexander Clough, and Colonel George Baylor was wounded and taken prisoner.

During an investigation of the events leading up to the massacre, the surviving men described the attack, including the brutality and unmerciful actions taken by the British troops, and spoke of their wounds, and of their friends who died. George Baylor, although he still maintained contact with the regiment during his recovery, was never again able to return to active command, so in November 1778, field command passed to Lt. Col. William Washington, and the regiment soon moved into winter quarters near Fredericktown, Maryland.

In November 1779, William Washington received orders to

begin preparations to move to Charleston, South Carolina, and it was there, early in 1781, that the remaining troops from Baylor's Dragoons were combined with troops from the First Continental Dragoons, which had been reduced due to casualties. This combined regiment was re-named the First and Third Continental, under Lt. Col. William Washington. The combined regiments saw action throughout the south, and served there until the end of the war.

Perhaps because of the hardships they had suffered together, especially during the attack at Tappan, the men shared a loyalty to George Baylor, such that even while serving under Lt. Col. William Washington, and in later years when describing their service in their pension applications, many of the men still referred to themselves as part of "Baylor's Dragoons."

Acknowledgments

I would like to thank the many historians, librarians, and archivists who recognize the value of historic documents and work to preserve and digitize them. This gratitude also extends to those who helped locate sources for Baylor's men, especially the staff at the Library of Virginia.

The Men of the 3rd Regiment of Light Dragoons

Spelling, punctuation and/or grammar have been corrected in some instances for ease of reading. Some references have been divided into paragraphs, also to be easier to read, so sources are noted at the end of each reference.

Adams, Francis

Francis Adams, W8313. Resident of Fauquier County, Virginia until 1791. In 1780 he enlisted under Capt. Eslond or Eslong, then marched to Philadelphia where he was attached to Col. Washington's regiment of horse as a trumpeter, and served two years. Nancy Adams, of Mercer County, Kentucky, stated in October 1838 that she married Francis Adams in Fredericksburg, Virginia, about two months before the capture of Cornwallis, and that Francis died 11 January 1837. Susannah Cummins, age 48 in October 1838, stated that she was the fifth child of Francis and Nancy Adams. (Revolutionary War Pension and Bounty-Land Warrant Application Files. National Archives Microfilm Publication M804, roll 10; also Dorman, John Frederick. 1958. Virginia Revolutionary Pension Applications, 46:19.)

Adams, John

"John Adams in my Company of Militia from Orange County enlisted under Capt. Thornton in the light horse, Sep. 19, 1781." Voucher of Robert Stubblefield, undated.

"I Certify the within mentioned John Adams was enlisted by me in the 3d Regiment Light Dragoons to serve during the war." Presley Thornton, former Captain 3rd Regiment, 17 November 1785.

(Virginia Governor's Office. Bounty Warrants, 1779-1860. Accession 41429, The Library of Virginia, Richmond, Va.)

Allen, Daniel

Daniel Allen, S37657. While in service as an 18-month soldier, he enlisted on 1 July 1781 in Col. Baylor's Regiment of Dragoons, by an officer named Randall, marched to Petersburg, and from there was under the command of Major Call to Charleston, South Carolina. He was discharged at the end of the war at Nelson's Ferry, South Carolina. William Barret, Captain in Baylor's Regiment, stated on 20 December 1784 that Daniel Allen served his full term.

On 1 August 1820, in Rockbridge, Virginia, Daniel Allen stated he was about 60 years old, his wife was about 80, and he had no children. Bounty land warrant 11867-100, issued 29 May 1792 to Francis Graves, assignee. (Revolutionary War Pension and Bounty-Land Warrant Application Files. National Archives Microfilm Publication M804, roll 34; also Dorman, John Frederick. 1958. Virginia Revolutionary Pension Applications, 1:62.)

"It appears from the Size Roll of 4 Troop that Danl. Allen Enlisted for the war in Baylor's Dragoons 1st July 1781 & Served faithfully the full term of his Enlistment." William Barret, former Captain, Baylor's Dragoons, December 20, 1784. (Virginia Governor's Office. Bounty Warrants, 1779-1860. Accession 41429, The Library of Virginia, Richmond, Va.)

Amey, James

James Amey, 5th troop. James Amey was one of the forage guards at the attack at Tappan, and received seven wounds. (David Griffith. Letter, 20 October 1778. Accession 22789. Personal papers collection. The Library of Virginia, Richmond, Va.)

Anderson, David

David Anderson, W5625. David Anderson, aged 76, of Prince Edward County, Virginia, in August 1832, volunteered in June or July 1776 as a minute man under Captain Frank Goode of Chesterfield, and was stationed in Portsmouth, Virginia six months, to 20 December 1776. In May 1777 he enlisted for three years with Captain Cadwallader Jones and served under Colonel George Baylor, Captain Cadwallader Jones, 1st Lieutenant John Stith, and 2nd Lieutenant William Barret. They were at Fredericksburg,

Virginia until November 1777, then went to Fredericktown, Maryland, and Lancaster, Pennsylvania, and then to Readingtown where he had smallpox. After crossing the Delaware, he went to Princeton and Trenton where he was discharged in June 1778.

In March 1781, David Anderson was living in Prince Edward County, Virginia, and was pressed into military service by the commissary stationed at the court house, as a wagoner, after which he acted as a guard over military stores and as a collector of provisions for the army at Yorktown. David Anderson was born in Cumberland County, Virginia, 16 July 1756, married 21 September 1785 to Lucy Horsley, and he died 5 August 1835. (Revolutionary War Pension and Bounty-Land Warrant Application Files. National Archives Microfilm Publication M804, roll 54; also Dorman, John Frederick. 1958. Virginia Revolutionary Pension Applications, 2:22.)

On February 24, 1819, Joel Bragg, now of Chesterfield County, Virginia, and formerly of Colonel Baylor's Regiment, affirmed that David Anderson was a soldier of Captain Cad Jones' company, and enlisted for three years. (Virginia Governor's Office. Bounty Warrants, 1779-1860. Accession 41429, The Library of Virginia, Richmond, Va.)

Anderson, Jordan

Jordan Anderson, S6504. On 10 September 1832 in Chesterfield County, Virginia, Jordan Anderson, who would be age about 73 in December, stated that he enlisted in 1777 with Lieutenant Baylor for three years in Col. Baylor's Regiment of Cavalry, in Captain Cadwallader Jones' company, with Major Clough in command. They marched from Chesterfield County through Hanover, Henrico, and Fredericksburg, then Georgetown, Maryland, and Lancaster, Pennsylvania, where he was inoculated for smallpox. He was examined by Dr. George Evans and was discharged due to inability to perform his duty. He was then drafted into the militia in October 1780, and marched to South Carolina where he remained for some time, receiving his discharge at Guilford, having served five months.

On 10 June 1831, David Anderson of Prince Edward County, Virginia stated that Jordan Anderson enlisted in Continental service in 1777 and served three years in Col. Baylor's Regiment. (Revolutionary War Pension and Bounty-Land Warrant Application Files. National Archives Microfilm Publication M804, roll 57; also

Dorman, John Frederick. 1958. Virginia Revolutionary Pension Applications, 2:31.)

On February 24, 1819, Joel Bragg, now of Chesterfield County, Virginia, and formerly of Colonel Baylor's Regiment, affirmed that Jordan Anderson was a soldier of Captain Cad Jones' company, and enlisted for three years. (Virginia Governor's Office. Bounty Warrants, 1779-1860. Accession 41429, The Library of Virginia, Richmond, Va.)

Anderson, Leonard

Leonard Anderson, W8329. He substituted in 1776 or 1777 in Captain Morris Wolf's company for three years. They marched to Fredericksburg, Virginia where he was placed in Captain Baylor's company of Dragoons, under Colonel William Washington. After escorting General Washington in Virginia, they marched south to several places in Georgia, then to Charleston, South Carolina, where they remained until the British took the city, at which point his company retreated to Camden, South Carolina. He was wounded and captured at Waxhaws, but escaped the next night and joined a company of militia commanded by Captain Foss. After several skirmishes, they marched toward Camden, and at Lynch's Creek he was appointed a Lieutenant under Captain Carter of Baylor's Dragoons. He was again taken prisoner near Camden, and kept at Charleston for six months. He was eventually taken to Virginia and after being exchanged, went to join Colonel William Washington on the Broad River in South Carolina. Leonard Anderson was born in Augusta County, Virginia, in 1755.

Rosanna Anderson, aged 71 in Logan County, Kentucky, stated she was married to Leonard Anderson in March 1791 in South Carolina, and that he died 16 April 1838. (Revolutionary War Pension and Bounty-Land Warrant Application Files. National Archives Microfilm Publication M804, roll 57; also Dorman, John Frederick. 1958. Virginia Revolutionary Pension Applications, 2:33.)

Andrews, Adam

"Adam Andrews, Private in the third Regiment of Dragoons having faithfully Served the Period for which he was Enlisted as appears in a Certificate from Colonel Baylor is hereby discharged from the Said Regiment. General head Quarters, South Carolina Oct. 29 1782." Discharge signed by Nathaniel Greene. (Virginia

Governor's Office. Bounty Warrants, 1779-1860. Accession 41429, The Library of Virginia, Richmond, Va.)

Adam Andrews, S37674. Adam Andrews, of Botetourt County, Virginia in 1818, stated that he enlisted in August 1777 with Captain Fielding Lewis in the 3rd Regiment of Light Dragoons commanded by Col. George Baylor, serving until 1783. Lieutenant Henry Bowyer vouched for the service of Adam Andrews. Adam Andrews was born about 1750, was living in Botetourt County, Virginia in 1818 and 1820, and died 11 July 1835. (Revolutionary War Pension and Bounty-Land Warrant Application Files. National Archives Microfilm Publication M804, roll 60; also Dorman, John Frederick. 1958. Virginia Revolutionary Pension Applications, 2:48-49.)

Adam Andrews, Soldier Cavalry. Certificate for £118.6.11 received by George Rice, September 13, 1783. (Numbered Record Books Concerning Military Operations and Service, Pay and Settlement of Accounts, and Supplies in the War Department Collection of Revolutionary War Records. National Archives Microfilm Publication M853. Volume 176: Record of Pay and Service of Officers and Men of Virginia, New York and Georgia, 1775-1856, page 80.)

Aplin, John

John Aplin had pistol and belt; his arms and accouterments were given to Ct. Smith's servant. The pistol, belt, and cartridge box of Snelling King, who was deceased, were given to John Aplin. Return, dated 1 March 1778, of arms and accouterments in the Third Troop belonging to Colonel George Baylor's Regiment of Light Dragoons. (Virginia Office of the Quartermaster General, Fredericksburg. Returns of Colonel George Baylor's Regiment, 1778-1779. Access 22547, The Library of Virginia, Richmond, Va.)

Arnold, John

"This is to Certify that John Arnold Served the term of three years as Sergeant in the Continental Virginia Line being the term for which he was enlisted and was regularly discharged from the same." Discharge signed by Captain Samuel Tapsley of Colonel Nathaniel Gist's Regiment, August 1, 1783. (Virginia Governor's Office. Bounty Warrants, 1779-1860. Accession 41429, The Library of Virginia, Richmond, Va.)

John Arnold, S37682. John Arnold enlisted in August 1778 for eighteen months under Captain John Benam, as a substitute for his father, serving for a few months in the 3rd Virginia Regiment commanded by Colonel Matthews. He next served in the 7th Virginia Regiment commanded by Colonel James Innis, then in the 17th Virginia Regiment of Colonel William Dangerfield, under Captain John Browning. Near the end of his term of service, they marched to Savannah, and he re-enlisted in Washington's Corps of horse in the company of Captain John Lightfoot. He was wounded at the battle of Cowpens, and discharged by Colonel William Washington after eighteen months. John Arnold was born in Caroline County, Virginia, 24 June 1758, the son of Anthony Arnold. He lived in Spotsylvania County until the fall of 1803, when he moved to Clark County, Kentucky. He died 15 July 1840 in Clark County, Kentucky. (Revolutionary War Pension and Bounty-Land Warrant Application Files. National Archives Microfilm Publication M804, roll 78; also Dorman, John Frederick. 1958. Virginia Revolutionary Pension Applications, 2:98-99.)

Bachelor, Cornelius

"Know all men by these presents that I Cornelius Bachelor private & wagoner in the Third Regiment Light Dragoons do hereby nominate & constitute and appoint Richd Call Esqr my lawful attorney to transact and receive all the Pay due me from the United States for my Services in Said Regiment Given under my hand this 3rd Day of July 1786." Voucher signed by Cornelius Bachelor, of Richmond County, Georgia, 3 July 1786. (Virginia Governor's Office. Bounty Warrants, 1779-1860. Accession 41429, The Library of Virginia, Richmond, Va.)

Bailey, Peirce

"It appears from the Size Roll of 3 Troop that Peirce Bailey Enlisted for the War in 3 Regiment Dragoons Octr 10th 1781 & served the term of his Enlistment." Voucher signed by William Barret, former Captain of Baylor's Dragoons, November 1, 1784. (Virginia Governor's Office. Bounty Warrants, 1779-1860. Accession 41429, The Library of Virginia, Richmond, Va.)

Ball, William

"For Value Recd I do assign to Henry Stringfellow the Balance of pay Gratuity & bounty of land due me as a Serjt &

Trumpeter in 3d Regiment L.D. who enlisted for & served to the end of the war." Signed by William Ball, October 31, 1784. (Virginia Governor's Office. Bounty Warrants, 1779-1860. Accession 41429, The Library of Virginia, Richmond, Va.)

"I do Certify that Wm Ball enlisted in Baylor's Dragoons June 1777 for three years; in 79 he reenlisted for the war and was appointed Trumpeter the last year 1780 & served as a good Soldier until the Mutiny May 1783. He was pay'd to 1st Aug 1780." William Barret, formerly a Captain in Baylor's Dragoons, December 15, 1784. (Virginia Governor's Office. Bounty Warrants, 1779-1860. Accession 41429, The Library of Virginia, Richmond, Va.)

"I do hereby certify that William Ball was a Trumpeter in the third Regiment of Dragoons in the service of the United States in the Revolutionary war, and that he continued in the said Regiment to the end of the war." George Hite, Winchester, Virginia, October 1, 1800. (Virginia Governor's Office. Bounty Warrants, 1779-1860. Accession 41429, The Library of Virginia, Richmond, Va.)

"I do hereby Certify that when I Rec^d my commission in the third regiment of dragoons William Ball was then a trumpeter in the regiment and belonged to the troop to which I was attached. That in the muster rolls made out for the troop he was returned as a trooper for during the war the three years for which he was enlisted (or during the war) having expired." George Hite, late Lieutenant of the 3rd Regiment of Dragoons, Charleston, January 22, 1807. (Virginia Governor's Office. Bounty Warrants, 1779-1860. Accession 41429, The Library of Virginia, Richmond, Va.)

"I do hereby certify that William Ball now of the Town of Winchester in the County of Frederick in the State of Virginia belonged to the third Regiment of Light Dragoons in the Revolutionary war, which Regiment was incorporated with the first Regiment and thereafter was called the first Regiment that he served to the end of the war, and was regularly discharged. I further think that he acted in the capacity of Trumpeter to the said Regiment." George Hite, 16 January 1815. (Virginia Governor's Office. Revolutionary War Rejected Claims, 1779-1860. Accession 41986, State government records collection, The Library of Virginia, Richmond, Va.)

William Ball, W3376. William Ball served as a trumpeter and sergeant in the 4th troop, under Captain Cadwallader Jones, in Colonel William Washington's Regiment, and served to the end of the war. He married Elizabeth Riley 25 March 1785 in Frederick County, Virginia and had one son, Samuel H. Ball. William Ball died 7 July 1829. (Revolutionary War Pension and Bounty-Land Warrant Application Files. National Archives Microfilm Publication M804, roll 128; also Dorman, John Frederick. 1958. Virginia Revolutionary Pension Applications, 4:38-399.)

Ballew or Ballieu, David

In a deposition made by George Hood in December 1828, he stated that after his term expired, he went to Philadelphia, where he met Lieutenant David Ballieu, of Col. Washington's cavalry, whom he knew from Virginia, and enlisted with him. (Revolutionary War Pension and Bounty-Land Warrant Application Files. National Archives Microfilm Publication M804, roll 1320.)

George Hood stated that at the end of his enlistment in October 1779, he was in Philadelphia, with no friends or money, and he came across David Ballew, a friend of his father's and an officer of William Washington's regiment, who was recruiting there. (Virginia Governor's Office. Bounty Warrants, 1779-1860. Accession 41429, The Library of Virginia, Richmond, Va.)

Barnes, John

"I do certify that Jno Barnes enlisted for the war March 81 in Baylor's Dragoons, served the full term of his Enlistment." Voucher signed by William Barret, formerly a Captain in Baylor's Dragoons, March 1, 1785. (Virginia Governor's Office. Bounty Warrants, 1779-1860. Accession 41429, The Library of Virginia, Richmond, Va.)

John Barnes, W8338. John Barnes enlisted in Spotsylvania County, Virginia in Captain Oliver Towles' company in the 6th Virginia infantry and served for two years, then enlisted in Captain Page's company in Colonel George Baylor's regiment of horse. He was in the battles of Trenton, Brandywine, Germantown, and Princeton, and was discharged by Colonel William Washington. John Barnes was born about 1758, married Milly (last name not given) in Culpeper County, Virginia on 27 November 1784. In 1818 he stated that he had four children, but depositions made in 1841 by Haman Million and James Baird mentioned an eldest son named James. The family moved to Bourbon County, Kentucky, and then to Harrison County, Kentucky, where John Barnes died 5 August 1840. (Revolutionary War Pension and Bounty-Land

Warrant Application Files. National Archives Microfilm Publication M804, roll 148; also Dorman, John Frederick. 1958. Virginia Revolutionary Pension Applications, 4:84-85.)

Barret, William

Alexander Clough recommended "Wm. Barrt" as replacement for William Parsons in the first troop, as "I look upon him to be steady, and such a person is wanted for that troop." (University of Virginia. Alderman Library Special Collections. Accession 2257, Papers of the Baylor Family of Newmarket, Caroline County, Va, in part transcripts: [manuscript], 1653-1915. Box 4: the folder is labeled "1756, 1777-1781; Military Papers," item 8: "Letter from Alexander Clough to George Baylor, 4 Feb 1778 at Millsone.")

Will Barrett, Lieutenant, Date of Commission April 10, 1778. Arrangement of Light Dragoons, 3^d Regiment, undated. (Revolutionary War Rolls, 1775-1783. National Archives Microfilm Publication M246. Roll 115, folder 13, 3^d Regiment Light Dragoons, 1779, item 3.)

Lieutenant Barret mentioned as having William Jesse with him. (University of Virginia. Alderman Library Special Collections. Accession 2257, Papers of the Baylor Family of Newmarket, Caroline County, Va, in part transcripts: [manuscript], 1653-1915. Box 4: the folder is labeled "1756, 1777-1781; Military Papers," item 14: "A list of the men's names absent belonging to Colonel Baylor's Regiment, Fredericksburg, June 27, 1778.")

William Barrett, Lieutenant April 10, 1778. A Return of Officers in the 3rd Regiment of Light Dragoons with the Dates of their Commissions, Sept. 18, 1777. (Revolutionary War Rolls, 1775-1783. National Archives Microfilm Publication M246. Roll 115, folder 13, 3^d Regiment Light Dragoons, 1779, item 6.)

William Barrett, mentioned on a roster of officers of the 3rd Regiment. (University of Virginia. Alderman Library Special Collections. Accession 2257, Papers of the Baylor Family of Newmarket, Caroline County, Va, in part transcripts: [manuscript], 1653-1915. Box 4: the folder is labeled "1756, 1777-1781; Military Papers," item 21: "ca. 1780 Continental Troops, roster of Officers, 1st & 3rd Regiments.")

"I certify upon my honor I have served as an officer in Colonel Baylor's Regiment L Dragoons from Spring 1777 until this time." Voucher dated July 16, 1783, and signed by William Barret,

Captain, 1st Regiment Light Dragoons. (Virginia Governor's Office. Bounty Warrants, 1779-1860. Accession 41429, The Library of Virginia, Richmond, Va.)

William Barret, pay due him for 1782 and 1783. (Miscellaneous Numbered Records [The Manuscript File] in the War Department Collection of Revolutionary War Records, 1775-1790's. National Archives Microfilm Publication M859. Manuscript 17629, "The United States in Account with Cap. William Barret," dated 29 October 1784.)

"I do certify that William Barret was in Service in the Continental army in Colonel Baylor's Regiment of Light Dragoons, early in the Spring of the year 1777, and continued in Service until the termination of the war in November 1783, and that he was promoted before that time, to the Rank of Captain." Voucher, dated 23 May 1809, and signed by James Wood, former Brigadier General of the Continental Army. (Virginia Governor's Office. Bounty Warrants, 1779-1860. Accession 41429, The Library of Virginia, Richmond, Va.)

Barrett, Chiswell

Chiswell Barrett, Cornet, February 6, 1777. A Return of Officers in the 3rd Regiment of Light Dragoons with the Dates of their Commissions, Sept. 18, 1777. (Revolutionary War Rolls, 1775-1783. National Archives Microfilm Publication M246. Roll 115, folder 13, 3d Regiment Light Dragoons, 1779, item 6.)

Chiswell Barrett, Cornet, February 6, 1777, commission granted March 4, 1778. (Revolutionary War Rolls, 1775-1783. National Archives Microfilm Publication M246. Roll 115, folder 13, 3d Regiment Light Dragoons, 1779, item 2.)

Cornet Barret, mentioned as receiving a set of bridle bits on 5 January 1778. (University of Virginia. Alderman Library Special Collections. Accession 2257, Papers of the Baylor Family of Newmarket, Caroline County, Va, in part transcripts: [manuscript], 1653-1915. Box 4: the folder is labeled "1756, 1777-1781; Military Papers," item 19: "Continental Troops, Itemized Account, September 1777 to June 1779.")

Chiswell Barret signed an oath of allegiance 10 June 1778 at Radnor, as Cornet in Colonel Baylor's Regiment. (Numbered Record Books Concerning Military Operations and Service, Pay and Settlement of Accounts, and Supplies in the War Department Collection of Revolutionary War Records. National Archives

Microfilm Publication M853. Roll 12: Oaths of allegiance and fidelity and oaths of office 1778-1781. Book 166, page 39.)

Chiswell Barrett wrote to Col. Baylor in January 1782 to accept his resignation, saying he was "sorry to leave a Regiment In such high estimation...." (University of Virginia. Alderman Library Special Collections. Accession 2257, Papers of the Baylor Family of Newmarket, Caroline County, Va, in part transcripts: [manuscript], 1653-1915. Box 4: the folder is labeled "Military Papers, 1782, 1814, & n.d.," item 2: "1782 Jan 28, Chiswell Barrett to Col. George Baylor.")

"Capt. Chiswell Barret has served as an officer in Colonel Baylor's Regiment L Dragoons From April 1777 until Febry 82." Voucher signed by William Barret, Captain of Baylor's Dragoons, July 16, 1783. (Virginia Governor's Office. Bounty Warrants, 1779-1860. Accession 41429, The Library of Virginia, Richmond, Va.)

Chiswell Barret, Captain; pay due him for January 1782. (Miscellaneous Numbered Records [The Manuscript File] in the War Department Collection of Revolutionary War Records, 1775-1790's. National Archives Microfilm Publication M859. Manuscript 17682, "The United States to Cap[t] C. Barret," dated 1 December 1784.)

Barrett, Churchill

Churchill Barrett, Lieutenant. Arrangement of Light Dragoons, 3[d] Regiment, undated. (Revolutionary War Rolls, 1775-1783. National Archives Microfilm Publication M246. Roll 115, folder 13, 3[d] Regiment Light Dragoons, 1779, item 3.)

Barry, Michael

Michael Barry, "Surgeon 3rd Cont. Dragoons Nov. 1, 1779." (Gwathmey, John Hastings. 1938. Historical register of Virginians in the Revolution: Soldiers, sailors, marines, 1775-1783. Dietz Press, Richmond, Va.)

Bassett, William

William Bassett, former Captain in Baylor's Dragoons, affirmed David Sheppard's service in the 1st Regiment of Light Dragoons, on August 25, 1784. (Virginia Governor's Office. Bounty Warrants, 1779-1860. Accession 41429, The Library of Virginia, Richmond, Va.)

William Bassett, W9739. William Bassett enlisted for two years and nine months under Colonel George Baylor, Captain John Stith and Lieutenant Custis. He was in the battle of Monmouth Court House, and was wounded at the massacre at Tappan, and gave a detailed record of the attack. William Bassett was discharged in May 1779, by Captain John Stith. He was born in the county of Surrey, in England, 18 April 1755, and was living in Botetourt County, Virginia at the time of his service. He married Peggy (last name not given) on 27 November 1780, and their Bible record shows eleven children. After the war he and his family moved to Kentucky, and then to Ripley County, Indiana. William Bassett died 6 February 1840. (Revolutionary War Pension and Bounty-Land Warrant Application Files. National Archives Microfilm Publication M804, roll 171; also Dorman, John Frederick. 1958. Virginia Revolutionary Pension Applications, 5:29-31.)

Baylor, George

George Baylor, Colonel, Date of Commission January 9, 1777. Arrangement of Light Dragoons, 3^d Regiment, undated. (Revolutionary War Rolls, 1775-1783. National Archives Microfilm Publication M246. Roll 115, folder 13, 3^d Regiment Light Dragoons, 1779, item 3.)

George Baylor, Colonel, January 9, 1777; also signed return. A Return of Officers in the 3rd Regiment of Light Dragoons with the Dates of their Commissions, Sept. 18, 1777. (Revolutionary War Rolls, 1775-1783. National Archives Microfilm Publication M246. Roll 115, folder 13, 3^d Regiment Light Dragoons, 1779, item 6.)

Provisions issued to a detachment of Colonel Baylor's regiment, 13 September to 30 September 1777, at Fredericksburg were 560 rations, 695 lbs. beef, 695 lbs. flour, 10 lbs. salt. (Miscellaneous Numbered Records [The Manuscript File] in the War Department Collection of Revolutionary War Records, 1775-1790's. National Archives Microfilm Publication M859. Manuscript 22156, "Return of Provisions, 13 to 30 September 1777.")

Provisions issued to a detachment of Colonel Baylor's Regiment of Light Horse at Fredericksburg, Virginia, October 1777, were 3,328 rations; 643 lbs. bacon; 3,263 lbs. beef; 4,132 lbs. flour; 59 lbs. of salt. (Miscellaneous Numbered Records [The Manuscript File] in the War Department Collection of Revolutionary War

Records, 1775-1790's. National Archives Microfilm Publication M859. Manuscript 22149, "Provision return for the Southern District of America.")

Colonel Baylor, a return of new, and broken, arms and other equipment, showing clothing (coats, breeches, stockings, mittens, boots, caps), saddles and other gear, and equipment such as oil cloths, canteens, curry combs, tent cloths, swords, pistols, sword belts, iron pots and axes. (University of Virginia. Alderman Library Special Collections. Accession 2257, Papers of the Baylor Family of Newmarket, Caroline County, Va, in part transcripts: [manuscript], 1653-1915. Box 4: the folder is labeled "1756, 1777-1781; Military Papers," item 10: "A Return of Clothing arms and Accouterments now in Store belonging to Col. Baylor's Regiment Light Dragoons Feb 6th 1778.")

George Baylor, letter to Colonel Harrison; signed by George Baylor. (Revolutionary War Rolls, 1775-1783. National Archives Microfilm Publication M246. Roll 115, folder 13, 3d Regiment Light Dragoons, 1779, item 2.)

Col. George Baylor, cash received, March 1778. (Miscellaneous Numbered Records [The Manuscript File] in the War Department Collection of Revolutionary War Records, 1775-1790's. National Archives Microfilm Publication M859. Manuscript 17560, "Lt. Col. Jno. Jameson To Col. George Baylor," undated.)

George Baylor, while in Fredericksburg, Virginia, in June 1778, received two letters from Colonel Theodorick Bland. The first was in regards to some regimental money Colonel Baylor loaned him, the prices he was expected to pay for horses, and asking if Baylor could acquire blankets, shirts, spurs, bridles, uniforms, and arms for him. The second concerned recruiting money, bridles, and horse prices. (University of Virginia. Alderman Library Special Collections. Accession 2257, Papers of the Baylor Family of Newmarket, Caroline County, Va, in part transcripts: [manuscript], 1653-1915. Box 4: the folder is labeled "1756, 1777-1781; Military Papers," item 12: "1778 June 6, Theodorick Bland to Col. George Baylor," and item 13: "June 12, 1778, Theodorick Bland to Col. George Baylor.")

Account of monies to be charged Colonel Baylor, which indicates that there were about 232 men mustered in 1777, but only enough horses to support three troops. In 1778 there were 266 officers and men, and that all were mounted. (Miscellaneous

Numbered Records [The Manuscript File] in the War Department Collection of Revolutionary War Records, 1775-1790's. National Archives Microfilm Publication M859. Manuscript 20380, undated.)

Colonel Baylor. "...and besides Major Clough who died of his wounds, there were wounded of the Officers, Colonel Baylor, Lieutenant Morrow and Mr. Evans the Surgeon." (David Griffith. Letter, 20 October 1778. Accession 22789. Personal papers collection. The Library of Virginia, Richmond, Va.)

George Baylor, W5966. George Baylor, of Caroline County, Virginia, was Colonel of the 3rd Regiment of Light Dragoons. He married Lucy Page 30 May 1778, in Spotsylvania County, Virginia, and had one son, John W. Baylor. George Baylor received a wound in one of the engagements in New Jersey from which he never recovered, and which caused his death. He died 19 November 1784, on the island of Bermuda, where he had gone due to his health. (Revolutionary War Pension and Bounty-Land Warrant Application Files. National Archives Microfilm Publication M804, roll 183; also Dorman, John Frederick. 1958. Virginia Revolutionary Pension Applications, 5:60-61.)

George Baylor, pay due him as a Colonel of Light Dragoons from 1 January 1782 to 15 November 1783; also a statement by William Barret regarding Colonel Baylor's chest of vouchers being left at the Quartermaster General's office in Fredericksburg in the summer of 1778. (Miscellaneous Numbered Records [The Manuscript File] in the War Department Collection of Revolutionary War Records, 1775-1790's. National Archives Microfilm Publication M859. Manuscript 17568, "The United States in Account with George Baylor," dated 8 February 1786.)

George Baylor, payments for horses and saddles from January 9, 1778 to September 8, 1778; his pay for service from January 1, 1777. (Miscellaneous Numbered Records [The Manuscript File] in the War Department Collection of Revolutionary War Records, 1775-1790's. National Archives Microfilm Publication M859. Manuscript 17569, "George Baylor in account current with the United States," undated.)

George Baylor, expenses and payments to various men of the regiment from July 10, 1779 to March 4, 1780. (Miscellaneous Numbered Records [The Manuscript File] in the War Department Collection of Revolutionary War Records, 1775-1790's. National

Archives Microfilm Publication M859. Manuscript 17589, "George Baylor's Regiment of Horse," undated.)

On 27 November 1786, Chiswell Barrett certified that Colonel George Baylor had a considerable sum of public money which was taken at the "Surprise of the Regiment at Tappan." (Miscellaneous Numbered Records [The Manuscript File] in the War Department Collection of Revolutionary War Records, 1775-1790's. National Archives Microfilm Publication M859. Manuscript 20309, dated 27 November 1786.)

George Baylor reported that after he was taken prisoner by the British at Tappan, more than $13,000 United States money was missing. This report was made to Colonel John Jameson and witnessed by William Barret. (Miscellaneous Numbered Records [The Manuscript File] in the War Department Collection of Revolutionary War Records, 1775-1790's. National Archives Microfilm Publication M859. Manuscript 17988, dated 4 April 1787.)

George Baylor settled payments for saddlery furnished the cavalry by Edward Simpson in September 1779. (Miscellaneous Numbered Records [The Manuscript File] in the War Department Collection of Revolutionary War Records, 1775-1790's. National Archives Microfilm Publication M859. Manuscript 18056, dated 4 December 1786.)

George Baylor, deceased. On 28 September 1786, Mann Page and the other executors of the estate of Colonel George Baylor wrote the Commissioner of Army Accounts regarding public monies that George Baylor had not turned in vouchers for, due to the loss of the vouchers in 1781, and which monies the commissioner wished to receive from George Baylor's estate. (Miscellaneous Numbered Records [The Manuscript File] in the War Department Collection of Revolutionary War Records, 1775-1790's. National Archives Microfilm Publication M859. Manuscript 20325, dated 28 September 1786.)

On 9 March 1787, Martin Hawkins, assistant to Mr. Young, stated that George Baylor deposited a chest with Mr. Richard Young, Quartermaster at Fredericksburg, Virginia and that the chest contained several books and a large number of papers belonging to Colonel George Baylor. (Miscellaneous Numbered Records [The Manuscript File] in the War Department Collection of Revolutionary War Records, 1775-1790's. National Archives

Microfilm Publication M859. Manuscript 20328, dated 9 March 1787.)

Minutes from an inquiry into monies handled by George Baylor, with questions to be put to William Barret regarding Baylor's accounts, and his corresponding answers. William Barret locked the account books and vouchers of Colonel Baylor in a strong chest which was then left in the care of Richard Young, Quartermaster. After Baylor's death in the winter of 1784, William Barret was informed that the chest, along with the Quartermaster's stores, had been sent "to the Country QMs, for safety in 1781 when the British Army was in Virginia & moving towards Fredericksburg," and he requested that the chest be returned. Mr. Herndon, an assistant in Mr. Young's department, informed him that the chest had been broken open, and the books and papers destroyed. William Barret went to Fredericksburg to examine the chest and found no papers or vouchers of any importance. (Miscellaneous Numbered Records [The Manuscript File] in the War Department Collection of Revolutionary War Records, 1775-1790's. National Archives Microfilm Publication M859. Manuscript 20369, "George Baylor, accounts with the United States," dated 4 January 1786.)

George Baylor, sketch of a report of monies he was to be charged accountable for, by the Commissioner of Army Accounts. (Miscellaneous Numbered Records [The Manuscript File] in the War Department Collection of Revolutionary War Records, 1775-1790's. National Archives Microfilm Publication M859. Manuscript 20370, undated.)

"George Baylor stands charged with the following sums, and from which his Executors want to be exonerated...." (Miscellaneous Numbered Records [The Manuscript File] in the War Department Collection of Revolutionary War Records, 1775-1790's. National Archives Microfilm Publication M859. Manuscript 20372, undated.)

Baylor, John

John Baylor, Lieutenant, Date of Commission February 15, 1777. Arrangement of Light Dragoons, 3^d Regiment, undated. (Revolutionary War Rolls, 1775-1783. National Archives Microfilm Publication M246. Roll 115, folder 13, 3^d Regiment Light Dragoons, 1779, item 3.)

John Baylor, Lieutenant, February 15, 1777. A Return of Officers in the 3rd Regiment of Light Dragoons with the Dates of their Commissions, Sept. 18, 1777. (Revolutionary War Rolls, 1775-1783. National Archives Microfilm Publication M246. Roll 115, folder 13, 3ᵈ Regiment Light Dragoons, 1779, item 6.)

J. Baylor, mentioned as receiving a pair of pistols on 3 December 1777. (University of Virginia. Alderman Library Special Collections. Accession 2257, Papers of the Baylor Family of Newmarket, Caroline County, Va, in part transcripts: [manuscript], 1653-1915. Box 4: the folder is labeled "1756, 1777-1781; Military Papers," item 19: "Continental Troops, Itemized Account, September 1777 to June 1779.")

Baylor, Walker

Walker Baylor, Lieutenant, June 1, 1777, commission granted March 4, 1778. (Revolutionary War Rolls, 1775-1783. National Archives Microfilm Publication M246. Roll 115, folder 13, 3ᵈ Regiment Light Dragoons, 1779, item 2.)

Walker Baylor, Lieutenant, Date of Commission July 1, 1777. Arrangement of Light Dragoons, 3ᵈ Regiment, undated. (Revolutionary War Rolls, 1775-1783. National Archives Microfilm Publication M246. Roll 115, folder 13, 3ᵈ Regiment Light Dragoons, 1779, item 3.)

Lieutenant Baylor, June 28, 1777. Arrangement of part of Colonel Baylor's Regiment, showing the date of Lieutenant Colonel Byrd's, Captain Smith's, Lieutenant Page's, Lieutenant Randolph's, and Lieutenant Baylor's commissions, undated. (Revolutionary War Rolls, 1775-1783. National Archives Microfilm Publication M246. Roll 115, folder 13, 3ᵈ Regiment Light Dragoons, 1779, item 4.)

Walker Baylor, Lieutenant, July 1, 1777. A Return of Officers in the 3rd Regiment of Light Dragoons with the Dates of their Commissions, Sept. 18, 1777. (Revolutionary War Rolls, 1775-1783. National Archives Microfilm Publication M246. Roll 115, folder 13, 3ᵈ Regiment Light Dragoons, 1779, item 6.)

Walker Baylor, brother of Colonel George Baylor. Alexander Clough wrote Colonel Baylor and asked to be remembered to his brother Walker. (University of Virginia. Alderman Library Special Collections. Accession 2257, Papers of the Baylor Family of Newmarket, Caroline County, Va, in part transcripts: [manuscript], 1653-1915. Box 4: the folder is labeled

"1756, 1777-1781; Military Papers," item 8: "Letter from Alexander Clough to George Baylor, 4 Feb 1778 at Millsone.")

Walker Baylor, Major, declared he had been a captain and commanded the 1ˢᵗ troop of light dragoons in the 3ʳᵈ Virginia Regiment. (Revolutionary War Pension and Bounty-Land Warrant Application Files. National Archives Microfilm Publication M804, roll 183; also Dorman, John Frederick. 1958. Virginia Revolutionary Pension Applications, 21:34.)

"Dear Sir Your letter of an old date came lately to hand. Your Inquiries Relative to Capt. Walker Baylor, I can not ever come of them, as we served in the same Regiment during the Revolution. Capt. Baylor was appointed a Cornet in the 3d Regiment of Light Dragoons in January 1777. He was wounded at German Town. His appointment as Capt. I do not recollect; but that fact may be appertained by application to the war office; also as to his Resignation, every thing you wish may be had at the war office, therefore I would recommend it to you to apply there.... I am very Respectfully your Obdt. Servt. C. Jones, Chatham May 17th: 1822." (Virginia Governor's Office. Bounty Warrants, 1779-1860. Accession 41429, The Library of Virginia, Richmond, Va.)

"I Walker Baylor a Captain in the third Regiment of Light dragoons in the Virginia line on Continental establishment do declare that I in the month of January 1777 was appointed a Cornet in the 3d Regiment and was at the battle of Germantown in 1777 severely wounded by having my left foot & ankle very much fractured by a cannon ball which rendered me unable to do duty for about sixteen months. While I was confined by my wound I was advance to a Lieutenancy in the same Regiment as soon as I got able to do duty I joined my Regiment which was in the latter part of 1778 then quartered at Fredericktown, Maryland and was advanced to a Captaincy in the same Regiment. I served through the campaigns at the Southward until the surrender of Charleston in 1780 when my health had become so infirm in consequence of my wound that I was unable to do duty and there being a sufficient number of officers in the Regiment I was by Colonel Washington who then commanded the Regiment sent home as supernumerary and was never after called into service but never resigned my commission... but was in service at the close of the war in 1783. My wound has ever since been very troublesome to me and has rendered me almost incapable of doing any business which required me to walk. I do further certify that I have received from the State of Virginia but four thousand acres of military land warrants. Given under my hand this 20th day of February 1822." Walker Baylor, formerly a Captain in the 3rd Regiment of Light Dragoons. (Virginia Governor's Office. Bounty Warrants, 1779-1860. Accession 41429, The Library of Virginia, Richmond, Va.)

"I do hereby certify that Walker Baylor was appointed a Cornet in the late 3d Regiment of Light Dragoons by me, the 27th of January 1777 & that he was promoted to a first Lieutenancy the 1st of June 1777 & also that he was promoted to a Captaincy in February 1779. Capt. Baylor resigned the 10th of May 1780." George Baylor, in Caroline County, April 13, 1783. (Virginia Governor's Office. Bounty Warrants, 1779-1860. Accession 41429, The Library of Virginia, Richmond, Va.)

Beall, Nathaniel

"This will certify that in the spring of 1779 I enlisted Nathaniel Beall to serve as a trooper in the third troop of the third Regiment of Cavalry commanded by Col: George Baylor of the Virginia line, for three years, which he served until the expiration, & then enlisted during the war in the same regiment; & during the whole of his service he conducted himself as a good & faithful soldier receiving sundry wounds both at Stono & Lanew's [Lenud's] Ferry." Presley Thornton, formerly a Captain in the 3d Regiment of Light Dragoons, September 27, 1809. (Virginia Governor's Office. Bounty Warrants, 1779-1860. Accession 41429, The Library of Virginia, Richmond, Va.)

"I do certify that Nathaniel Beall served as a Soldier in the 3 Regiment of Light Dragoons to the end of the war - which will appear by the Muster Rolls of said Regiment." Voucher signed by Churchill Jones, formerly a Captain in Baylor's Regiment, March 13, 1809. (Virginia Governor's Office. Bounty Warrants, 1779-1860. Accession 41429, The Library of Virginia, Richmond, Va.)

Nathaniel Beall or Beal was enlisted by Captain Presley Thornton in the spring of 1779, in the 3rd Troop of the 3rd Regiment of Cavalry commanded by Colonel George Baylor. He was wounded at Stono and Lenud's Ferry, and served three years. In 1809, Nathaniel Beall gave power of attorney to Major Hezekiah Rogers to receive his land warrant for services in the 3rd Regiment. (Revolutionary War Pension and Bounty-Land Warrant Application Files. National Archives Microfilm Publication M804, roll 187; also

Dorman, John Frederick. 1958. Virginia Revolutionary Pension Applications, 5:76.)

Belfield, John

John Belfield, Major, Third Dragoons 1780 to 9 November 1782. (Francis B. Heitman, 1982. Historical Register of Officers of the Continental Army during the War of the Revolution, April 1775, to December 1783.)

"I do hereby certify that John Belfield late of the county of Richmond, deceased, was appointed in June 1776 a Lieutenant in my troop of cavalry... & that he served to the end of the war, being promoted to a Captaincy & afterwards to the best of my recollection to a Majority." Henry Lee, September 24, 1807. (Virginia Governor's Office. Bounty Warrants, 1779-1860. Accession 41429, The Library of Virginia, Richmond, Va.)

John Belfield, BLWt 254-400-Major, issued 11 Dec 1797. (Revolutionary War Pension and Bounty-Land Warrant Application Files. National Archives Microfilm Publication M804, roll 204; also Dorman, John Frederick. 1958. Virginia Revolutionary Pension Applications, 6:29.)

Bell, Henry

Henry Bell, mentioned on a roster of officers of 3rd Regiment. (University of Virginia. Alderman Library Special Collections. Accession 2257, Papers of the Baylor Family of Newmarket, Caroline County, Va, in part transcripts: [manuscript], 1653-1915. Box 4: the folder is labeled "1756, 1777-1781; Military Papers," item 21: "ca. 1780 Continental Troops, roster of Officers, 1st & 3rd Regiments.")

"I do certify that Lieut. Hary Bell was appointed an officer in 3 Reg L Dragoons by Lt Col Washington sometime in the spring 1779 & has continued to the end of the war & that he was a native of this state." Voucher signed by Will Barret, Captain of Baylor's Dragoons, January 21, 1784. (Virginia Governor's Office. Bounty Warrants, 1779-1860. Accession 41429, The Library of Virginia, Richmond, Va.)

Henry Bell, Lieutenant. On 13 December 1784, Captain William Barret certified that Henry Bell enlisted in Baylor's Dragoons in March 1777, was appointed Quartermaster-Sergeant 18 June 1777, Sergeant-Major 1 September, Cornet 1 February 1779, Lieutenant in May 1779 and continued in service until December

1782. (Miscellaneous Numbered Records [The Manuscript File] in the War Department Collection of Revolutionary War Records, 1775-1790's. National Archives Microfilm Publication M859. Manuscript 18050, dated 13 December 1784.)

Henry Bell, pay as Lieutenant of Dragoons from 1 January to 31 December 1782. (Miscellaneous Numbered Records [The Manuscript File] in the War Department Collection of Revolutionary War Records, 1775-1790's. National Archives Microfilm Publication M859. Manuscript 17530, "The United States in Account with Henry Bell," dated 23 December 1784.)

"I do Certify that Henry Bell entered into Col. George Baylor's Regiment of Light Dragoons in the year 1776 and served until the disbanding of the said army in the year 1783 as a Lieutenant given under my hand this 11th day of August 1807." Signed by John Watts, former Captain in the 3rd Regiment of Light Dragoons. (Virginia Governor's Office. Bounty Warrants, 1779-1860. Accession 41429, The Library of Virginia, Richmond, Va.)

Henry Bell, Lieutenant, gave Captain William Barret the power of attorney to settle accounts for pay and depreciation. (Miscellaneous Numbered Records [The Manuscript File] in the War Department Collection of Revolutionary War Records, 1775-1790's. National Archives Microfilm Publication M859. Manuscript 20368, undated.)

Henry Bell, BLWt 623-200. Henry Bell entered Colonel George Buford's regiment in 1776 and served as Lieutenant until the end of the war, as certified by Captain John Watts. (Revolutionary War Pension and Bounty-Land Warrant Application Files. National Archives Microfilm Publication M804, roll 205; also Dorman, John Frederick. 1958. Virginia Revolutionary Pension Applications, 6:30.)

Bell, Serj't

"Serj't Bell" was disinherited by his father for entering the service in the capacity of a private, and Alexander Clough recommended that he be appointed as Cornet. (University of Virginia. Alderman Library Special Collections. Accession 2257, Papers of the Baylor Family of Newmarket, Caroline County, Va, in part transcripts: [manuscript], 1653-1915. Box 4: the folder is labeled "1756, 1777-1781; Military Papers," item 11: "1778 Spring, Maj. Alexander Clough to Col. [George] Baylor.")

Bell, William

William Bell, private, enlisted February 22, 1777, on command. Muster Roll of the 2nd Troop in the 3^d Regiment Light Dragoons in the Service of the United States commanded by Lieutenant Colonel William Washington for the Months of May, June, July, August, September, October, 1779. (Revolutionary War Rolls, 1775-1783. National Archives Microfilm Publication M246. Roll 115, folder 13, 3^d Regiment Light Dragoons, 1779, item 1.)

"I do certify that William Bell was Enlisted by me to serve three years in the Army of the United States and that his time of service Expired Feby 20th 1780." "I do certify that William Bell served his full term of three years as a soldier in Colonel Baylor's Dragoons Signed 12 Aug 1784." Vouchers signed by C. Page, formerly a Captain of Light Dragoons. (Virginia Governor's Office. Bounty Warrants, 1779-1860. Accession 41429, The Library of Virginia, Richmond, Va.)

Bennett, Caleb P.

Caleb Bennett declared that he enlisted in March 1776 under General Mercer, was appointed an officer in the Delaware Regiment, and in April 1780 the regiment was commanded to join the southern army. While in the south, two companies of the Delaware Regiment were ordered to join Col. Washington's Light Dragoons, and Caleb served in that regiment until 1783 when the regiment was disbanded. He received wounds at Germantown, and at the Pee Dee River in North Carolina.

Peter Jacquet of New Castle, Delaware stated in October 1830 that Caleb P. Bennett entered the army in the spring of 1776 and continued to the end of the war in 1783, at which time he was in Col. Washington's Regiment of Cavalry, to which he was transferred after the battle of Camden. (Virginia Governor's Office. Bounty Warrants, 1779-1860. Accession 41429, The Library of Virginia, Richmond, Va.)

Caleb P. Bennett, S35779. In March 1818, Caleb P. Bennett of Wilmington, Delaware, aged 60 years, said he was appointed an Ensign in April 1777 in the 5th Company of the Delaware Regiment under Captain Thomas Holland, then on Continental establishment, and that he remained in service during the remainder of the war. He received two wounds, one in the knee in October 1777 at the battle of Germantown, and the other in the foot on the Pee Dee River in South Carolina in August 1780, "the scars of which my shattered frame still exhibits." (Revolutionary War Pension and Bounty-Land Warrant Application Files. National Archives Microfilm Publication M804, roll 217)

Benson, Thomas

Thomas Benson, private in the fourth troop of Baylor's regiment. In his deposition regarding the attack on the regiment at Tappan, he stated that he was quartered with the second troop in a barn in Herring town when the British attacked in the night. Thomas Benson was stabbed twelve times before making his escape over a fence in the barnyard. This deposition was taken by William Livingston, Governor of New Jersey, and sent to Henry Laurens; see the letter dated Morris Town, 22 October 1778, in Papers of the Continental Congress. (David Griffith. Letter, 20 October 1778. Accession 22789. Personal papers collection. The Library of Virginia, Richmond, Va.)

Betsill, John

John Betsill, S39194. John Betsill enlisted in Virginia in Colonel George Baylor's regiment of cavalry for three years on 1 January 1779. He served in the 5th troop under Captain William Barret and Colonel William Washington. His discharge was left in the Auditor's Office in Virginia by the man who purchased his land. He served in battles at Monk's Corner and Lenud's Ferry in 1780, and at Tarleton's defeat at Cowpens. Afterwards he was sent by Captain Parsons to Virginia, to deliver dispatches to Major Call. William Dangerfield affirmed that John Betsill served with him in the 3rd Regiment for three years and was discharged by Colonel George Baylor. John Betsill was born about 1761, and was living in Charleston, South Carolina in August 1820, in Christ Church Parish on land belonging to his wife, Sarah. (Revolutionary War Pension and Bounty-Land Warrant Application Files. National Archives Microfilm Publication M804, roll 230; also Dorman, John Frederick. 1958. Virginia Revolutionary Pension Applications, 6:79-80.)

Bidgood, Philip

"This is to Certify & make known that I Nathanl Wills of the Town of Petersburg & State of Virginia do perfectly remember Philip Bidgood dec'd who Enlisted in the year 1780 as a Private in the 3rd Regiment of Dragoons afterwards incorporated in the 1st

Virginia Regiment of Light Dragoons to which I also belong'd and served with the said Bidgood to the end of the late war with England. And that his representative the widow Margaret Bidgood (now old and infirm) is an inhabitant of Petersburg and was to my knowledge his lawful wife and as such is entitled to the Bounty of land as promised her husband on entering the service for the said war and also one Hundred acres granted by a Law of Congress some time after the war ended to all who served to the end of the war. Given under my hand 18th April 1810, Nathaniel Wills." (Virginia Governor's Office. Bounty Warrants, 1779-1860. Accession 41429, The Library of Virginia, Richmond, Va.)

"I do certify that Philip Bidgood a private in the Continental cavalry enlisted the 20th August 1781 to serve during the war and continued during that period. Given under my hand this 4th of March 1784." Will Parsons, Captain 1st Regiment. (Virginia Governor's Office. Bounty Warrants, 1779-1860. Accession 41429, The Library of Virginia, Richmond, Va.)

Bird, Benjamin (see Francis Otway Byrd)

Bishop, Robert

Robert Bishop "Dead and armes Lost." Return, dated 1 March 1778, of arms and accouterments in the Third Troop belonging to Colonel George Baylor's Regiment of Light Dragoons. (Virginia Office of the Quartermaster General, Fredericksburg. Returns of Colonel George Baylor's Regiment, 1778-1779. Accession 22547, The Library of Virginia, Richmond, Va.)

Bishop, Stephen

Stephen Bishop of Buckingham, Virginia stated that he enlisted for two years under Nathaniel Mason of Sussex County in March 1776, marched to Chatham, New Jersey and joined the northern army under the command of General Stephens. He served until 24 December 1777 when a furlough was offered for the balance of the two years to all those who would enlist under Colonel William Washington, so he enlisted and continued in the Cavalry three years, and was honorably discharged by Churchill Jones at Harrisburg in North Carolina. His discharge was filed in the War office in Richmond, Virginia by Charles Gee of Prince George County; subsequently the papers were moved to Washington and were burned in the fire there. Voucher dated December 9, 1820, in

Richmond, Virginia. (Virginia Governor's Office. Bounty Warrants, 1779-1860. Accession 41429, The Library of Virginia, Richmond, Va.)

Stephen Bishop, S37770. He enlisted in March 1776 in the 4th Virginia Regiment under Captain Nathaniel Mason and served two years. He next enlisted under Colonel William Washington for three years, under Captain William Barret, and was discharged at Harrisburg, North Carolina. He was in the battles of Princeton, Trenton, Brandywine, and others. He was born about 1755, and in 1820 was living in Buckingham County, Virginia, along with his wife Charlotte. (Revolutionary War Pension and Bounty-Land Warrant Application Files. National Archives Microfilm Publication M804, roll 247; also Dorman, John Frederick. 1958. Virginia Revolutionary Pension Applications, 7:20.)

Biswell, John

"I do Certify that Corpl. John Biswell enlisted in the first Regiment Dragoons from the State of Virginia the 10th day of July One thousand seven hundred & Eighty for the War & that he served in the said Regiment till the date hereof." Voucher signed J. Belfield, Major of Cavalry, dated November 7, 1783. (Virginia Governor's Office. Bounty Warrants, 1779-1860. Accession 41429, The Library of Virginia, Richmond, Va.)

John Biswell, S35191. On 18 May 1818, John Biswell of Jessamine County, Kentucky, claimed that he first enlisted in Pittsylvania County, Virginia, in the 6th Virginia Regiment, with Captain Thomas Hudgins, and served two years. In 1778 he again enlisted, this time at Hillsborough in the 1st Virginia Regiment, under Captain Griffin Fauntleroy, and served until the end of the war. During this enlistment, he was annexed to Colonel William Washington's regiment of light dragoons, where he served about three and a half years. He was in the battles of Guilford Court House, Camden, the Siege of Ninety-Six Six, the taking of Colonel Rugely and Eutaw Springs. In May 1818, John Biswell was living in Fayette County, Kentucky, and in 1820, in Jessamine County, Kentucky, age about 60 years. (Revolutionary War Pension and Bounty-Land Warrant Application Files. National Archives Microfilm Publication M804, roll 249; also Dorman, John Frederick. 1958. Virginia Revolutionary Pension Applications, 7:22-23.)

Blanks, Jesse

Jesse Blanks, with Cornet Washington. (University of Virginia. Alderman Library Special Collections. Accession 2257, Papers of the Baylor Family of Newmarket, Caroline County, Va, in part transcripts: [manuscript], 1653-1915. Box 4: the folder is labeled "1756, 1777-1781; Military Papers," item 14: "A list of the men's names absent belonging to Colonel Baylor's Regiment, Fredericksburg, June 27, 1778.")

Bloxom or Blocksome, Arthur

Arthur Blocksome is listed as a prisoner on a report of the Guards, May 10, 1782, confined for two days for "Neglect of Duty." (University of Virginia. Alderman Library Special Collections. Accession 2257, Papers of the Baylor Family of Newmarket, Caroline County, Va, in part transcripts: [manuscript], 1653-1915. Box 4: the folder is labeled "Military Papers, 1782, 1814, & n.d.," item 14: "1782 May 10, Continental Troops, report of the Guards, 1st & 3rd Regiments Light Dragoons, signed by James Meriwether, officer of the Day.")

"It appears from the size Roll of the first Troop of Baylor's Dragoons, that Arthur Bloxom enlisted for the war March 1781, and served until his death 1782 or 1783." William Barret, December 28, 1785. (Virginia Governor's Office. Bounty Warrants, 1779-1860. Accession 41429, The Library of Virginia, Richmond, Va.)

Bowers, George

George Bowers, pay due him for 1782 and from 1 January 1783 to 16 November 1783. (Miscellaneous Numbered Records [The Manuscript File] in the War Department Collection of Revolutionary War Records, 1775-1790's. National Archives Microfilm Publication M859. Manuscript 17694, "The United States in Account with George Bowers private late 3rd Light Dragoons," dated 26 May 1794.)

Bowmer, _____

Henry Roberts of Frankfurt, Kentucky in 1823, stated that a man named Bowmer deserted with John Casey from William Washington's Light Dragoons in November 1777. This claim may not be true, as John Casey stated that Henry Roberts lied regarding his desertion. See Casey, John. (Revolutionary War Pension and

Bounty-Land Warrant Application Files. National Archives Microfilm Publication M804, under John Casey, S30308, roll 493.)

Bowyer, Henry

Henry Bowyer, Lieutenant, pay due him for 1782 and 1783. (Miscellaneous Numbered Records [The Manuscript File] in the War Department Collection of Revolutionary War Records, 1775-1790's. National Archives Microfilm Publication M859. Manuscript 17630, "The United States in account with Henry Bowyer," dated 14 December 1784.)

Henry Bowyer, W5859. In October 1838, Agatha, widow of Henry Bowyer, stated that he was commissioned as a Lieutenant and commanded a troop of cavalry attached to the corps of Colonel William Washington, and served to the end of the war. Henry Bowyer was paid as Lieutenant and Adjutant in the 1st Regiment of Light Dragoons from October 1777 to 31 December 1781. Henry Bowyer and Agatha were married 8 August 1792, in Botetourt County, and were still living there when Henry died on 13 June 1832. (Revolutionary War Pension and Bounty-Land Warrant Application Files. National Archives Microfilm Publication M804, roll 306; also Dorman, John Frederick. 1958. Virginia Revolutionary Pension Applications, 9:14-15.)

"I do certify that Lieutenant Henry Bowyer of the first regiment of Light Dragoons was appointed an Officer in May 1777 in the 12th Virginia Regiment of foot, and was transferred to the Cavalry the 7th May 1780; and has been in actual service successively ever since...." Major Samuel Finley, Richmond, August 23, 1783. (Virginia Governor's Office. Bounty Warrants, 1779-1860. Accession 41429, The Library of Virginia, Richmond, Va.)

Boyd, William

William Boyd, of Fleming County, Kentucky, in May 1822 stated that he enlisted in 1777 for three years in Captain John Stith's troop of horse under Colonel George Baylor, and served until he was taken prisoner at Hackensack in the fall of 1779. He was freed on a parole of honor not to bear arms during the war unless legally exchanged, which exchange never happened, and he remained under that parole until the end of the war. (Virginia Governor's Office. Revolutionary War Rejected Claims, 1779-1860. Accession 41986,

State government records collection, The Library of Virginia, Richmond, Va.)

William Boyd, S35197. In September 1818, William Boyd, of Fleming County, Kentucky, said he enlisted in July 1776 under Col. George Baylor and served until 1780, when he was discharged. In 1821, William Boyd was about 67 years old, and while he was formerly a shoemaker, he was no longer able to labor at any kind of work, and had no home or family; a letter in the pension file dated January 1821 refers to Thomas Boyd, son of William Boyd. (Revolutionary War Pension and Bounty-Land Warrant Application Files. National Archives Microfilm Publication M804, roll 308)

Bragg, Joel

Joel Bragg had sword, pistol, belt, and cartridge box; "Present." Return, dated 1 March 1778, of arms and accouterments in the Third Troop belonging to Colonel George Baylor's Regiment of Light Dragoons. (Virginia Office of the Quartermaster General, Fredericksburg. Returns of Colonel George Baylor's Regiment, 1778-1779. Accession 22547, The Library of Virginia, Richmond, Va.)

"Joel Bragg having faithfully served Three years is hereby Discharged from the third Regiment of Light Dragoons." Discharge signed by Lt. Col. William Washington, April 2, 1780. (Virginia Governor's Office. Bounty Warrants, 1779-1860. Accession 41429, The Library of Virginia, Richmond, Va.)

On February 24, 1819, Joel Bragg, now of Chesterfield County, Virginia, and formerly of Colonel Baylor's Regiment, affirmed that both David and Jordan Anderson were soldiers of Captain Cad Jones' company. (Virginia Governor's Office. Bounty Warrants, 1779-1860. Accession 41429, The Library of Virginia, Richmond, Va.)

Branham, William

William Branham, private. Muster Roll of the 2nd Troop in the 3[d] Regiment Light Dragoons in the Service of the United States commanded by Lieutenant Colonel William Washington for the Months of May, June, July August, September, October 1779. (Revolutionary War Rolls, 1775-1783. National Archives Microfilm Publication M246. Roll 115, folder 13, 3[d] Regiment Light Dragoons, 1779, item 1.)

"Know all men by these presents that I William Branham Soldier belonging to the third Regiment Light Dragoons Commanded by Col. George Baylor for divers causes by these presents do make Constitute and appoint my true friend Benjamin Hawkins my true and lawful attorney...." Voucher dated March 5, 1784. (Virginia Governor's Office. Bounty Warrants, 1779-1860. Accession 41429, The Library of Virginia, Richmond, Va.)

"I do Certify Will: Branham enlisted for the war in Colonel Baylor's Dragoons 1778 & has faithfully served the term of his enlistment." Certificate signed by William Barret, former Captain of Baylor's Dragoons, August 27, 1784. (Virginia Governor's Office. Bounty Warrants, 1779-1860. Accession 41429, The Library of Virginia, Richmond, Va.)

William Branham was of Virginia. (M859, Miscellaneous Numbered Records [The Manuscript file] of the War Department Collection of Revolutionary War Records, 1775-1790's. Manuscript number 17449.)

Bridgeman, Boswell

"I do Certify that Boswell Bridgeman enlisted as a Soldier for the war in Baylor's Regiment Light Dragoons August 10th 1780 & that he has never Rec'd any part of his pay, and has serv'd the time of his enlistment as witness my hand." Voucher signed by William Barret, Captain Baylor's Dragoons, April 30, 1784. (Virginia Governor's Office. Bounty Warrants, 1779-1860. Accession 41429, The Library of Virginia, Richmond, Va.)

Bridges, John

"This is to certify that John Bridges enlisted as a Soldier in the 3d Regiment of Light Dragoons com'd by Col Wm Washington for the war the 20 day of May one Thousand Seven hundred Eighty one." Voucher signed by Cornet John Perry and Captain William Barret, October 12, 1789. (Virginia Governor's Office. Bounty Warrants, 1779-1860. Accession 41429, The Library of Virginia, Richmond, Va.)

John Bridges, 3 Reg. L.D. (M859, Miscellaneous Numbered Records [The Manuscript file] of the War Department Collection of Revolutionary War Records, 1775-1790's. Manuscript number 29360.)

John Bridges, W4904. John Bridges enlisted in the fall of 1777, in Virginia under Captain William Washington in the regiment of Colonel Heth and served three years, until discharged in Pennsylvania. In 1779 he enlisted under Lieutenant Linton, in the 3rd Regiment of horse of Colonel William Washington, and was discharged at Guilford Court House. John Bridges was born about 1755 or 1756, married Jane (last name not given) on 12 March 1785 in Stafford County, Virginia, and he died 20 March 1838. In August of 1822 they were living in Boone County, Kentucky, and in 1833 they were in Scott County, Kentucky. (Revolutionary War Pension and Bounty-Land Warrant Application Files. National Archives Microfilm Publication M804, roll 333; also Dorman, John Frederick. 1958. Virginia Revolutionary Pension Applications, 10:22-24.)

Bridges, Richard

Richard Bridges had cartridge box; "Sword Belt and Pistol Broke and lost." Return, dated 1 March 1778, of arms and accouterments in the Third Troop belonging to Colonel George Baylor's Regiment of Light Dragoons. (Virginia Office of the Quartermaster General, Fredericksburg. Returns of Colonel George Baylor's Regiment, 1778-1779. Accession 22547, The Library of Virginia, Richmond, Va.)

Brooking, Samuel

Samuel Brooking, Corporal, enlisted 13 March 1777, on duty. Muster Roll of the 2nd Troop in the 3d Regiment Light Dragoons in the Service of the United States commanded by Lieutenant Colonel William Washington for the Months of May, June, July, August, September, October, 1779. (Revolutionary War Rolls, 1775-1783. National Archives Microfilm Publication M246. Roll 115, folder 13, 3d Regiment Light Dragoons, 1779, item 1.)

Samuel Brooking, Private in Baylor's Regiment. Samuel Brooking was lodged with nineteen others of his regiment in a barn in Herring Town near Tappan, when they were surrounded by the British. He said that some men tried to get out of the barn, but were stabbed in the attempt, whereupon the rest cried out for quarters. The British troops told them to come out, but as the men came out, the British stabbed them. Samuel Brooking was stabbed in his arm when he came near the barn door, and while trying to disengage the bayonet from his arm, the bayonet came off the soldier's gun. Samuel Brooking made his escape through another door of the barn, and with the bayonet sticking out of his arm, traveled close to four miles to reach the place where Colonel Baylor was lodged, only to find it surrounded by more British troops. This deposition was taken by William Livingston, Governor of New Jersey, and sent to Henry Laurens; see the letter dated Morris Town, 22 October 1778, in Papers of the Continental Congress. (David Griffith. Letter, 20 October 1778. Accession 22789. Personal papers collection. The Library of Virginia, Richmond, Va.)

"Samuel Brooking, Corporal having faithfully served three years in the 3rd Regmt of Light Dragoons is hereby discharged the said Brooking has conducted himself with the greatest propriety being a good officer & of great integrity." Signed by William Washington, Lt. Col., Dorchester, March 19, 1780. (Virginia Governor's Office. Bounty Warrants, 1779-1860. Accession 41429, The Library of Virginia, Richmond, Va.)

Brown, Samuel

Samuel Brown, S32138. Samuel Brown enlisted in the fall of 1780 at Hillsborough, North Carolina, with Captain Barret in the 3rd Regiment of Cavalry of Colonel William Washington. He was in the battles of Rugely's Farm, and Cowpens, and then was detached with a recruiting officer. He joined the regiment again at the Siege of Ninety-Six, but came down with small pox; after recovery he met them again near Camden and fought at Eutaw Springs, and served until the war ended. Samuel Brown was born in Pittsylvania County, Virginia, in 1764, and married Berthena Groves in Illinois about 10 September 1838. He died in Morgan County, Illinois about 20 August 1851, according to his widow. (Revolutionary War Pension and Bounty-Land Warrant Application Files. National Archives Microfilm Publication M804, roll 377; also Dorman, John Frederick. 1958. Virginia Revolutionary Pension Applications, 11:66-67.)

Brumback or Bumback, Peter

"It appears from the Size Roll of 3 Troop that Peter Bumback Enlisted for the war in Baylor's Dragoons March 1781 & Cont. to serve until the Mutiny May 83." Signed by William Barret, former Captain Baylor's Dragoons, April 8, 1785. (Virginia Governor's Office. Bounty Warrants, 1779-1860. Accession 41429, The Library of Virginia, Richmond, Va.)

Peter Brumback, W8400. In September 1818, Peter Brumback of Shelby County, Kentucky, stated that he first entered the war in South Carolina, and was taken prisoner at Sunbury. After he escaped from the British, he enlisted in the Third Regiment of Light Dragoons under Col. William Washington, served to the close of the war, and was discharged at Winchester, Virginia. He fought in the battles at Guilford Court House and Camden, and was wounded in both battles. Seth Stratton, also of Shelby County, affirmed Peter Brumback's service.

In 1820, Peter Brumback was about 66 years old, was unable to work, and had his wife and four children living with him. In 1833, he was 79, of Scott County, Kentucky, and said he enlisted under Lieutenant John Linton, was honorably discharged, but had lost or mislaid his discharges. In June 1835, John Jacobs of Georgetown, Kentucky, John Casey, and John Bridges, all former soldiers in the same regiment, affirmed his service.

In 1848, Elizabeth Brumback, nee Simpson, of Boone County, Kentucky, age 82, said she was born in Fairfax County, Virginia. She married Peter Brumback a few years after the war ended, they had twelve children, and he died April 6, 1846. (Revolutionary War Pension and Bounty-Land Warrant Application Files. National Archives Microfilm Publication M804, roll 385.)

Brumbly or Brumly, Robert

Robert Brumbly had a sword, pistol, belt, and cartridge box; "Sick absent and his arms with him." Return, dated 1 March 1778, of arms and accouterments in the Third Troop belonging to Colonel George Baylor's Regiment of Light Dragoons. (Virginia Office of the Quartermaster General, Fredericksburg. Returns of Colonel George Baylor's Regiment, 1778-1779. Accession 22547, The Library of Virginia, Richmond, Va.)

"Robt Brumly having faithfully Served three years in the 3rd Regiment of Light Dragoons is hereby Discharged." Signed by William Washington, August 1, 1780. (Virginia Governor's Office. Bounty Warrants, 1779-1860. Accession 41429, The Library of Virginia, Richmond, Va.)

Bryant, John

John Bryant, Virginia, private, 3rd Regiment Light Dragoons. (General Index to Compiled Military Service Records of Revolutionary War Soldiers. National Archives Microfilm Publication M860, Card 1901.) Sargent, 3rd Regiment Light Dragoons. (Card 1902.)

"I do Certify that Jno Bryant enlisted himself to serve as soldier in 3 Regiment L Dragoons for three years, which time he serv'd from March 1777. I do also Certify that Bryant was a native of this state." Signed by William Barret, 14 December 1783. (Virginia Governor's Office. Bounty Warrants, 1779-1860. Accession 41429, The Library of Virginia, Richmond, Va.)

"I do Certify that John Bryen Served as a Soldier in the 3 Regiment of Light Dragoons from early in the year one thousand Seven hundred & Seventy Seven, Until the end of the war." Signed by Churchill Jones, January 19, 1808. (Virginia Governor's Office. Bounty Warrants, 1779-1860. Accession 41429, The Library of Virginia, Richmond, Va.)

John Bryant, S38570. John Bryant stated that he enlisted 10 March 1777 as a private under Lieutenant Gresham of the light dragoons commanded by Colonel George Baylor for three years. He eventually served five years, part of that time under Captain Churchill Jones, and was discharged after the siege of York. (Revolutionary War Pension and Bounty-Land Warrant Application Files. National Archives Microfilm Publication M804, roll 391; also Dorman, John Frederick. 1958. Virginia Revolutionary Pension Applications, 12:29.)

Bryant, William

"I do hereby certify that William Bryant enlisted himself a soldier in 3d Regiment of light dragoons the 19th Sep. 1777." Signed Presley Thornton, former Captain of 3rd Regiment, December 27, 1783. "William Bryant a private in 3d Regiment of light dragoons, his term of enlistment having expired is hereby discharged from said Regiment, 12th August 1781." Signed Richard Call, Major, 3rd Regiment Light Dragoons. (Virginia Governor's Office. Bounty Warrants, 1779-1860. Accession 41429, The Library of Virginia, Richmond, Va.)

Buckley, Abrim

Abrim Buckley, sick absent. (University of Virginia. Alderman Library Special Collections. Accession 2257, Papers of the Baylor Family of Newmarket, Caroline County, Va, in part transcripts: [manuscript], 1653-1915. Box 4: the folder is labeled "1756, 1777-1781; Military Papers," item 14: "A list of the men's names absent belonging to Colonel Baylor's Regiment, Fredericksburg, June 27, 1778.")

Bunn, Daniel

"I do Certify that Danel Bunn enlisted as a soldier for the war in the 3d Regiment of Light Dragoons the 20 day of December 1777." Signed by John Perry, Cornet, August 21, 1783. (Virginia Governor's Office. Bounty Warrants, 1779-1860. Accession 41429, The Library of Virginia, Richmond, Va.)

Byrd, Francis Otway

Lieutenant Colonel Byrd, March 14, 1777, commission granted March 4, 1778. Arrangement of part of Colonel Baylor's Regiment, showing the date of Lieutenant Colonel Byrd's, Captain Smith's, Lieutenant Page's, Lieutenant Randolph's, and Lieutenant Baylor's commissions, undated. (Revolutionary War Rolls, 1775-1783. National Archives Microfilm Publication M246. Roll 115, folder 13, 3[d] Regiment Light Dragoons, 1779, item 4.)

Probably the "Lieutenant Colonel Benjamin Bird, March 14, 1777 – November 20, 1778" listed under the 3rd Regiment of Continental Light Dragoons, 1777-1783. (Sanchez-Saavedra, E.M. 1978. A Guide to Virginia Military Organizations in the American Revolution, 1774-1787. Library of Virginia, Richmond, Virginia.)

Francis Otway Byrd, W6219. Anna Munford Byrd, the widow of Francis Otway Byrd, declared that her husband was appointed a cadet by the Convention of Delegates in Richmond, 17 July 1775. He served as aide-de-camp to General Lee during 1775 and 1776, and after that as Lieutenant Colonel of cavalry until he resigned his commission in the fall of 1781. She further stated that they were married in Mecklenberg County, Virginia, 6 April 1781, and first settled in Charles City County, where he was High Sheriff. They later moved to Norfolk, Virginia where he was Collector of the Port until his death in September 1800.

On 26 August 1775, at the Convention of Delegates at the Town of Richmond, it was recorded that the convention strongly recommended Otway Byrd, Esqr., as a cadet in the Continental Army. Journals of Congress on 20 November 1778 resolved that Major Washington be promoted to the rank of Lieutenant Colonel in place of Lieutenant Colonel Byrd, of Baylor's dragoons, who had resigned. On 18 June 1784 in the Journal of the House of Delegates of Virginia, it was recorded that Otway Byrd resigned his commission in the British service and in September 1775 was appointed aide-de-camp to General Lee, and on 1 January 1777 he was appointed Lieutenant Colonel of Light Dragoons and acted in that capacity until 15 July 1778.

A petition made by Otway Byrd to Congress stated that at an early age he was entered as a midshipman in the British Navy by his father, the late William Byrd, Esq. of Westover in Virginia. He served on board several ships of war, especially the Fowey, which was then commanded by George Montague, Esq. In 1774, Francis Otway Byrd upon learning that his native country might come into conflict with the British crown, left the British service despite his father's objections, and entered the service previously described. He stated that, in 1778, upon finding that his pay, upon depreciation, was inadequate to support him, he resigned his commission. (Revolutionary War Pension and Bounty-Land Warrant Application Files. National Archives Microfilm Publication M804, roll 444; also Dorman, John Frederick. 1958. Virginia Revolutionary Pension Applications, 14:30-32.)

Byrns, Thomas

"Thomas Byrns a soldier in the 3d Virginia Regiment of Light Dragoons is hereby discharged after having served three years the term of his enlistment. Given under my hand this 15 June 1781." Discharge signed by Presley Thornton, Captain 3rd Regiment. (Virginia Governor's Office. Bounty Warrants, 1779-1860. Accession 41429, The Library of Virginia, Richmond, Va.)

Caffrey or Calfrey, Charles

Charles Calfry had pistol, "C.B. top off and Deserted with Sword and Belt and John Smith." Return, dated 1 March 1778, of arms and accouterments in the Third Troop belonging to Colonel George Baylor's Regiment of Light Dragoons. (Virginia Office of the Quartermaster General, Fredericksburg. Returns of Colonel George Baylor's Regiment, 1778-1779. Accession 22547, The Library of Virginia, Richmond, Va.)

"I do hereby Certify that Chas Caffrey was enlisted in the late 3rd Regiment of Light Dragoons the 1st of May 1777 & that he served three years in the Regiment as a private soldier." Discharge signed by George Baylor, Colonel of the 1st Regiment of Cavalry, Caroline County, April 9, 1783. (Virginia Governor's Office. Bounty Warrants, 1779-1860. Accession 41429, The Library of Virginia, Richmond, Va.)

Call, Richard

Richard Call signed an oath of allegiance 18 August 1778 at White Plains, as Captain of Light Dragoons. (Numbered Record Books Concerning Military Operations and Service, Pay and Settlement of Accounts, and Supplies in the War Department Collection of Revolutionary War Records. National Archives Microfilm Publication M853. Roll 12: Oaths of allegiance and fidelity and oaths of office 1778-1781. Book 166, page 106.)

Richard Call wrote from Richmond, Virginia, to Col. Baylor regarding his settling some personal accounts, and his progress in obtaining supplies for the Regiment. He also asked the Colonel to let him know where the Regiment had been ordered to in the south. (University of Virginia. Alderman Library Special Collections. Accession 2257, Papers of the Baylor Family of Newmarket, Caroline County, Va, in part transcripts: [manuscript], 1653-1915. Box 4: the folder is labeled "1756, 1777-1781; Military Papers," item 24: "1781 Oct 26, Maj. Richard Call to Col. [George] Baylor.")

Major Richard Call, cash advanced him by the Paymaster General, 1781. (Miscellaneous Numbered Records [The Manuscript File] in the War Department Collection of Revolutionary War Records, 1775-1790's. National Archives Microfilm Publication M859. Manuscript 17559, "Major Richard Call," dated 22 April 1786.)

Major Call, cash paid him by Mr. Harrison, for expenses of collecting horses, 29 July 1781. (Miscellaneous Numbered Records [The Manuscript File] in the War Department Collection of Revolutionary War Records, 1775-1790's. National Archives Microfilm Publication M859. Manuscript 17584, "George Baylor's Regiment of Horse," undated.)

Major Call, mentioned as being in Colonel Baylor's Regiment. (Miscellaneous Numbered Records [The Manuscript File] in the War Department Collection of Revolutionary War Records, 1775-1790's. National Archives Microfilm Publication M859. Manuscript 20379, "Particulars referred to Colonel Baylor's Regiment," undated.)

Richard Call, BLWt 354-400 issued 19 Aug 1807 by John Smith for the Continental service of Richard Call, major. (Revolutionary War Pension and Bounty-Land Warrant Application Files. National Archives Microfilm Publication M804, roll 451; also

Dorman, John Frederick. 1958. Virginia Revolutionary Pension Applications, 14:57.)

Callaway, Captain

Payment voucher #3683, dated 31 July 1839, and signed by Captain Callaway of Colonel Baylor's Regiment records payment to the widow of Stephen Jones. (Revolutionary War Pension and Bounty-Land Warrant Application Files. National Archives Microfilm Publication M804, roll 1445. Stephen Jones, W7916.)

Camp, Marshall

"I do Certify that Marshall Camp Enlisted in Col. Baylor's Dragoons September 1780 for the War & served as a good Soldier until the action of Waxhaws where he was Killed." Signed by William Barret, December 25, 1784. Also a certificate naming Thomas Camp as heir-at-law of Marshall Camp, dated June 28, 1785. (Virginia Governor's Office. Bounty Warrants, 1779-1860. Accession 41429, The Library of Virginia, Richmond, Va.)

Canaday, _____

"Canaday Deserted with Pistol Belt & C Box." Return, dated 1 March 1778, of arms and accouterments in the Third Troop belonging to Colonel George Baylor's Regiment of Light Dragoons. (Virginia Office of the Quartermaster General, Fredericksburg. Returns of Colonel George Baylor's Regiment, 1778-1779. Accession 22547, The Library of Virginia, Richmond, Va.)

Carden, Edwin or Youen

E. Carden listed as a prisoner on a report of the Quarter Guard, May 2, 1782, confined for two days and nights for "Loseing Currycomb." (University of Virginia. Alderman Library Special Collections. Accession 2257, Papers of the Baylor Family of Newmarket, Caroline County, Va, in part transcripts: [manuscript], 1653-1915. Box 4: the folder is labeled "Military Papers, 1782, 1814, & n.d.," item 13: "1782 May 2, Continental Troops, report of Quarter Guard, 3rd Regiment Light Dragoons, Report signed by James Meriwether, Lt. Officer of the Day.")

Edwin Carden, S8178. Edwin or Youen Carden of Fluvanna County, Virginia, stated on March 23, 1835 that he was age 73, and that he was enlisted in the spring of 1781 in Cumberland County by Lt. Benjamin Garnett of the 7th Regiment in a troop of cavalry under Captain Baylor. He was in the Siege of Yorktown, and then ordered to Charleston, South Carolina, where he stayed until the war ended. He left Charleston in August 1783, on foot, to return to Virginia. William Moody of Fluvanna County stated on July 31, 1835 that Carden was a private in Col. Washington's regiment of horse and remained in service until discharged at Charleston.

Edwin or Youen Carden died March 21, 1850 in Greene County, Virginia, with William Carden of the same county being his only surviving child. There were two daughters, Judith and Mary Carden, whose whereabouts were unknown at the time of his death. (Revolutionary War Pension and Bounty-Land Warrant Application Files. National Archives Microfilm Publication M804, roll 467; also Dorman, John Frederick. 1958. Virginia Revolutionary Pension Applications, 15:59.)

Cardwell, William

"I Certify that Wm Cardwell enlisted as a soldier in the 3d Regiment of Dragoons sometime in April one thousand seven hundred and eighty one & served until the Mutiny May 1783." Voucher signed by Charles Yarborough, Lieutenant 1st Regiment, October 19, 1785. (Virginia Governor's Office. Bounty Warrants, 1779-1860. Accession 41429, The Library of Virginia, Richmond, Va.)

"I William Cardwell of the County of Bullitt & State of Kentucky do declare that I was a Quarter Master's Sergeant in the third Virginia Continental Regiment of Light Dragoons commanded by Col. Baylor...." Dated 28 July 1819. (under Charles Neal. Virginia Governor's Office. Bounty Warrants, 1779-1860. Accession 41429, The Library of Virginia, Richmond, Va.)

William Cardwell, W8590. In 1819, William Cardwell stated that he enlisted for the first time in September 1780 in Spotsylvania County, Virginia, for eighteen months under Captain Crane, and was attached to Colonel Campbell's regiment. In June 1781 he obtained leave of his officers to enlist in the cavalry, and did so at Pee Dee, South Carolina, under Captain Ambrose Gordon in the 3rd Regiment of Dragoons. At some point during his service he was promoted to Sergeant. He served until discharged in the summer of 1783 by Captain Robert Monroe about three miles from Winchester, Virginia. He was in the battles of Guilford under Colonel Campbell, and was at the battles of Cowpens, Guilford

Court House, and Camden as a dragoon. William Cardwell was born about 1760, married Famariah (surname not given) in 1781 in Culpeper County, Virginia, and they had five sons and four daughters living. He died 1 March 1838, in Bullitt County, Kentucky. (Revolutionary War Pension and Bounty-Land Warrant Application Files. National Archives Microfilm Publication M804, roll 467; also Dorman, John Frederick. 1958. Virginia Revolutionary Pension Applications, 15:68-71.)

William Cardwell of Bullitt County, Kentucky, on 2 September 1823, aged 62, declared he was born in Williamsburg, Virginia, and raised in Culpeper County. In September 1779, he enlisted as a private in Colonel Campbell's regiment of foot, and was wounded in the battle of Guilford. He then enlisted on the Big Pee Dee River in South Carolina, with Colonel Washington's 3rd Regiment of Light Dragoons, and was in the battle of Camden. (Dorman, John Frederick. 1958. Virginia Revolutionary Pension Applications, 16:73.)

"This officiant states that he was acquainted with William Cardwell and served with him in the army of the Revolution in the third Virginia Regiment of Light Dragoons under the command of Col. Wm. Washington...." John Story affirmed William Cardwell's service at the battles of the Cowpens, Guilford Court House, and Camden, and that Cardwell was promoted to Sergeant. Voucher dated 21 October 1833. (Virginia Governor's Office. Bounty Warrants, 1779-1860. Accession 41429, The Library of Virginia, Richmond, Va.)

In Franklin County, Kentucky, on October 14, 1833, William Cardwell, age 75, stated that he enlisted in September 1779 in Captain Armistead's Company under Col. Campbell, for eighteen months. Then, when near Petersburg in January 1780, he enlisted in Captain Robert Morrow's Company of Light Dragoons, under Col. Washington, for the war, and that he served as Sergeant until June 1, 1783, when he was discharged. He arrived at his mother's house in Culpeper County, Virginia, June 6, 1783. Voucher dated October 14, 1833. (Virginia Governor's Office. Bounty Warrants, 1779-1860. Accession 41429, The Library of Virginia, Richmond, Va.)

Carrol, Joseph

Joseph Carrol, Private in the 6th troop of Baylor's regiment. Joseph Carrol got dressed after hearing the alarm, and took his saddle to the barn door to get his horse, saw that he was surrounded by the British, and asked for quarters. The British immediately stabbed him, and left him lying in the barnyard. They came back to examine him with a candle to determine if he was dead, and stripped him except for his shirt and waistcoat. This deposition was taken by William Livingston, Governor of New Jersey, and sent to Henry Laurens; see the letter dated Morris Town, 22 October 1778, in Papers of the Continental Congress. (David Griffith. Letter, 20 October 1778. Accession 22789. Personal papers collection. The Library of Virginia, Richmond, Va.)

"I do Certify that Jos: Cerrel served Three years faithfully as a soldier in 3 Regiment L Dragoons, (enlisted into the 28th Decr. 1778) as witness my hand." Signed William Barret, Captain 3rd Regiment, Richmond, August 4, 1783. (Virginia Governor's Office. Bounty Warrants, 1779-1860. Accession 41429, The Library of Virginia, Richmond, Va.)

Carter, John Hill

John H. Carter, Lieutenant, October 12, 1777, commission granted March 4, 1778. (Revolutionary War Rolls, 1775-1783. National Archives Microfilm Publication M246. Roll 115, folder 13, 3d Regiment Light Dragoons, 1779, item 2.)

Hill Carter, Lieutenant. Arrangement of Light Dragoons, 3d Regiment, undated. (Revolutionary War Rolls, 1775-1783. National Archives Microfilm Publication M246. Roll 115, folder 13, 3d Regiment Light Dragoons, 1779, item 3.)

Hill Carter, Lieutenant. A Return of Officers in the 3rd Regiment of Light Dragoons with the Dates of their Commissions, Sept. 18, 1777. (Revolutionary War Rolls, 1775-1783. National Archives Microfilm Publication M246. Roll 115, folder 13, 3d Regiment Light Dragoons, 1779, item 6.)

Carter, Obadiah

Obadiah Carter, after horses. (University of Virginia. Alderman Library Special Collections. Accession 2257, Papers of the Baylor Family of Newmarket, Caroline County, Va, in part transcripts: [manuscript], 1653-1915. Box 4: the folder is labeled "1756, 1777-1781; Military Papers," item 14: "A list of the men's names absent belonging to Colonel Baylor's Regiment, Fredericksburg, June 27, 1778.")

"Obadiah Carter Sergeant in the 3d Regiment of Light Dragoons having served three years in the 3d Regiment of Light

Dragoons is hereby Discharged. The said Carter is a man of bravery & has conducted himself with propriety." Discharge signed by Lt. Col. W. Washington, December 24, 1780. (Virginia Governor's Office. Bounty Warrants, 1779-1860. Accession 41429, The Library of Virginia, Richmond, Va.)

On August 3, 1818, Obadiah Carter, age 64, stated that he was a resident of Lexington, Kentucky, and that he enlisted in Caroline County, Virginia, in the 2nd Virginia regiment in 1775, and served in that regiment until 1777 when he was transferred to the 3rd Regiment of Cavalry under Colonel George Baylor. He was discharged in December 1780 by Col. William Washington in South Carolina. (Virginia Governor's Office. Bounty Warrants, 1779-1860. Accession 41429, The Library of Virginia, Richmond, Va.)

Obadiah Carter, W8585. Obadiah Carter entered service in 1775 with Captain Samuel Hawes in the 2nd Virginia Regiment, and after serving his time with that regiment, enlisted in Colonel Baylor's Regiment of Light Dragoons for three years, and was discharged at the Catawba River and returned home to Virginia. He was then called into the militia and was discharged after the capture of Cornwallis at Little York. He was in the battles of Brandywine, Germantown, and Stono, besides many smaller engagements. He was not at the massacre of the regiment at Tappan, having been detached from his company during that time. Obadiah Carter was born in 1755, married Judy Seigncourt on 13 March 1781 probably in Essex County, Virginia, and he died 28 July 1820. He and his family were living in Lexington County, Kentucky in 1818. (Revolutionary War Pension and Bounty-Land Warrant Application Files. National Archives Microfilm Publication M804, roll 486; also Dorman, John Frederick. 1958. Virginia Revolutionary Pension Applications, 16:42-44.)

Carter or Carster, William

William Carster had pistol, cartridge box; "his Sword given to Shope and Shope Broke it." Return, dated 1 March 1778, of arms and accouterments in the Third Troop belonging to Colonel George Baylor's Regiment of Light Dragoons. (Virginia Office of the Quartermaster General, Fredericksburg. Returns of Colonel George Baylor's Regiment, 1778-1779. Accession 22547, The Library of Virginia, Richmond, Va.)

"William Carter a Soldier in the 3 Regiment Light Dragoons was Enlisted in said Regiment the 27th of December 1777

& Discharged the first day of June 1780 during which time he was wounded." Signed by Presley Thornton, Captain 3d Regiment, dated April 1784. (Virginia Governor's Office. Bounty Warrants, 1779-1860. Accession 41429, The Library of Virginia, Richmond, Va.)

Casey, John

"I Do Certify that John Casey enlisted for the War Sept 1780 in Colonel Baylor's Regiment Dragoons & has never rec'd any part of his Pay. I further Certify he has served as a Good & faithful soldier to the End of the War as witness my hand." Voucher signed by William Barret, Captain Baylor's Dragoons, September 14, 1784. (Virginia Governor's Office. Bounty Warrants, 1779-1860. Accession 41429, The Library of Virginia, Richmond, Va.)

John Casey of Casey County, Kentucky, in October 1818 stated that he was a soldier in Captain William Barret's troop, and knew John Story. (under John Story. Virginia Governor's Office. Bounty Warrants, 1779-1860. Accession 41429, The Library of Virginia, Richmond, Va.)

John Casey, S30308. John Casey enlisted at Hillsborough, North Carolina, in 1779 in Captain William Barret's troop in William Washington's Light Dragoons, and was discharged at the Santee River in South Carolina. He was in the battles at Cowpens, Guilford, Camden, Ninety-Six, and Eutaw Springs. John Casey was born about 1763, possibly in Culpeper County, Virginia, and died sometime after September 1834. In 1818 he was listed as being of Casey County, Kentucky; in 1821 he was in Fayette County, Kentucky, and in 1834, he was in Franklin County, Kentucky.

John Story of Franklin County, Kentucky, Charles Neal of Scott County, and William Cardwell of Bullitt County, Kentucky, all of the 3rd Regiment of Light Dragoons, affirm John Casey's claim to be in the same regiment. John Story "further states that the charge of Desertion against Said Casey He Verily Believes to be totally false & without any foundation as he never heard any such charge Alleged against said Casey before the Charge here alluded to, & feels fully confident if ever such Desertion had happened that he would certainly have heard of it. It is here reported that a Mr Henry Roberts of this county propagated the account of the Desertion & wrote on to the war office on that subject" and that it was a personal act of revenge on Henry Roberts' part. Henry

Roberts of Frankfurt Kentucky, had stated that John Casey deserted in November 1777 with a man named Bowmer. (Revolutionary War Pension and Bounty-Land Warrant Application Files. National Archives Microfilm Publication M804, roll 493; also Dorman, John Frederick. 1958. Virginia Revolutionary Pension Applications, 16:72-74.)

Chambers, Francis

"Fras. Chambers, Serjt" signed a return of the 3rd Regiment of Light Dragoons, April 15, 1782. (University of Virginia. Alderman Library Special Collections. Accession 2257, Papers of the Baylor Family of Newmarket, Caroline County, Va, in part transcripts: [manuscript], 1653-1915. Box 4: the folder is labeled "Military Papers, 1782, 1814, & n.d.," item 7: "1782 April 15, Continental Troops, Detachment Return 3rd Regiment Light Dragoons.")

Chambers, James alias James Burges

"I do Certify that James Chambers Enlisted for the War in Baylor's L Dragoons Apl. 1781 & is entitled his Bounty of land for serving to End of the war." Signed William Barret, Baylor's Dragoons, December 14, 1784. (Virginia Governor's Office. Bounty Warrants, 1779-1860. Accession 41429, The Library of Virginia, Richmond, Va.)

James Chambers, S37838. James Chambers, alias Burges, enlisted in 1779 with Catesby Jones in the Virginia line, was marched with other recruits to Chesterfield Court House in Virginia, and placed under Captain Scott, and afterwards under Captain Lawson, both with Colonel Davis. He was in the battle of Guilford Court House, and after the battle enlisted in the first troop of Light Dragoons, under Captain Jones, in the regiment of Colonel William Washington. He was discharged at the end of the war in Charleston, South Carolina. James Chambers was born about 1759, and was living in Westmoreland County, Virginia when he first enlisted, and was there in 1818. He married and had three children, but they are not named in his statement. (Revolutionary War Pension and Bounty-Land Warrant Application Files. National Archives Microfilm Publication M804, roll 509; also Dorman, John Frederick. 1958. Virginia Revolutionary Pension Applications, 19:46-48.)

Chandler, Jesse

"It appears from the Size Roll of the 3rd Troop that Jessey Chandler enlisted for the War in Baylor's Dragoons 20th Sept 1785." Signed Will Barret, Captain Baylor's Dragoons, December 3, 1785. Enlistment date of 1785 on voucher is probably incorrect. (Virginia Governor's Office. Bounty Warrants, 1779-1860. Accession 41429, The Library of Virginia, Richmond, Va.)

"Jesse Chandler - The bearer hereof belonging to the third Troop of the first Regiment of Dragoons commanded by Colonel George Baylor has leave of absence from his said Regiment till called for...." Voucher signed by Henry Bowyer, Lieutenant and C. Jones, Captain 1st Regiment L. Dragoons, Nelson's Ferry, June 12, 1783. (Virginia Governor's Office. Bounty Warrants, 1779-1860. Accession 41429, The Library of Virginia, Richmond, Va.)

Jesse Chandler, pay due him as a private from 1782 and 1783. (Miscellaneous Numbered Records [The Manuscript File] in the War Department Collection of Revolutionary War Records, 1775-1790's. National Archives Microfilm Publication M859. Manuscript 17673, "The United States in a/c with Jesse Chandler late private 3d Reg. Light Dragoons," dated 14 December 1792. Also Manuscript 17676, dated 5 May 1794.)

Chapman, John

John H. Chapman of Brunswick County, Virginia, affirmed William Chapman, of Rowan County, North Carolina, served "as a Soldier in the foot and acted as a Cornet under Col. Washington in the Horse in the Continental army of Virginia for I was with him while in both...." Voucher dated October 24, 1823. (Virginia Governor's Office. Bounty Warrants, 1779-1860. Accession 41429, The Library of Virginia, Richmond, Va.)

Chapman, William

William Chapman of Salisbury, North Carolina in October 1822 wrote about obtaining bounty land, mentioning his "enlisting in Washington's Troop of Horse during the war" and that he was honorably discharged and that he was a native of Brunswick County, Virginia. On February 20, 1823, while living in Rowan County, North Carolina, he declared that he enlisted in 1778 or 1779 for 18 months, and in 1780 enlisted as a soldier in Washington's regiment for during the war and was honorably discharged by Col. George Baylor at the ford on the Meherrin River in Virginia.

(Virginia Governor's Office. Bounty Warrants, 1779-1860. Accession 41429, The Library of Virginia, Richmond, Va.)

John H. Chapman of Brunswick County, Virginia, affirmed the service of William Chapman of Rowan County, North Carolina. Voucher dated October 24, 1823. (Virginia Governor's Office. Bounty Warrants, 1779-1860. Accession 41429, The Library of Virginia, Richmond, Va.)

William Chapman, S41474. William Chapman entered service in Virginia in about 1779 with Captain Culverson, under Colonel Davis, for eighteen months. He served less than a year and then enlisted under Colonel William Washington's 3rd Regiment. He was discharged a short time before the war ended, having served at the Siege of Ninety-Six, the battles of Camden, Guilford, and others. In 1820, William Chapman was living in Rowan County, North Carolina. (Revolutionary War Pension and Bounty-Land Warrant Application Files. National Archives Microfilm Publication M804, roll 522; also Dorman, John Frederick. 1958. Virginia Revolutionary Pension Applications, 17:87-88.)

Charles, Fred

Fred Charles had "Sword Pistol Belt Cartridge Box on Command." Return, dated 1 March 1778, of arms and accouterments in the Third Troop belonging to Colonel George Baylor's Regiment of Light Dragoons. (Virginia Office of the Quartermaster General, Fredericksburg. Returns of Colonel George Baylor's Regiment, 1778-1779. Accession 22547, The Library of Virginia, Richmond, Va.)

Clack, Moses

"I do Certify that Moses Clack Served as a Soldier in the 3d Regiment Dragoons three years is now on furlough. And was enlisted for the war 26 Decr 1777." Robert Morrow, October 10, 1783. (Virginia Governor's Office. Bounty Warrants, 1779-1860. Accession 41429, The Library of Virginia, Richmond, Va.)

Moses Clack, W2921. Moses Clack enlisted in the Continental Line and served to the end of the war, at which time he was a private in Captain William Barret's company in the 3rd Regiment of Light Dragoons. He married Ann Deadman on 19 October 1792, in Albemarle County, Virginia, and died 25 September 1842, probably in Fleming County, Kentucky. (Revolutionary War Pension and Bounty-Land Warrant Application

Files. National Archives Microfilm Publication M804, roll 546; also Dorman, John Frederick. 1958. Virginia Revolutionary Pension Applications, 19:4-5.)

Clearwater, Benjamin

Benjamin Clearwater, W4925. Benjamin Clearwater claimed to have enlisted as a private about February 1776 for three years in Virginia, in Captain William Barret's company in the 3rd Regiment of Cavalry, commanded by Colonel Baylor. He served under Captain Cad Jones, Captain Jack Linton, and Captain Henry Boyer, until June 1782 or 1783 when he was discharged. He was in the battles of Brandywine, Germantown, Camden, Ninety-Six, Cowpens, and Eutaw Springs, and was wounded several times, including a sword wound to the head.

He was born about 1749 and married Elenor or Elender Robbins 25 December 1786 or 1788, possibly in Randolph County, North Carolina. Benjamin Clearwater died in Dickson County, Tennessee, on 7 March 1848. Affidavits included in his pension application file indicate that he may have had mental problems, and possibly married another woman in Tennessee. (Revolutionary War Pension and Bounty-Land Warrant Application Files. National Archives Microfilm Publication M804, roll 573; also Dorman, John Frederick. 1958. Virginia Revolutionary Pension Applications, 19:77-80.)

Clemens, John

"I do Certify that John Clemens enlisted as a soldier in the first Virginia State Regiment in March 1777 and served three years after which he enlisted in the 3d Regiment of Light Dragoons and served til the Close of the war." Signed by Charles Yarbrough. (Virginia Governor's Office. Bounty Warrants, 1779-1860. Accession 41429, The Library of Virginia, Richmond, Va.)

Clift, William

Wm Clift, on furlough. (University of Virginia. Alderman Library Special Collections. Accession 2257, Papers of the Baylor Family of Newmarket, Caroline County, Va, in part transcripts: [manuscript], 1653-1915. Box 4: the folder is labeled "1756, 1777-1781; Military Papers," item 14: "A list of the men's names absent belonging to Colonel Baylor's Regiment, Fredericksburg, June 27, 1778.")

"I Certify that Wm Clift a soldier enlisted in the 3d Regiment of Light Dragoons for the war in Augt 76." Signed John Perry, Cornet, August 21, 1783. (Virginia Governor's Office. Bounty Warrants, 1779-1860. Accession 41429, The Library of Virginia, Richmond, Va.)

Clough, Alexander

Alexander Clough, Major, appointed January 7, 1777, commission granted March 4, 1778. (Revolutionary War Rolls, 1775-1783. National Archives Microfilm Publication M246. Roll 115, folder 13, 3ᵈ Regiment Light Dragoons, 1779, item 2.)

Alexander Clough, Major, January 8, 1777. A Return of Officers in the 3ʳᵈ Regiment of Light Dragoons with the Dates of their Commissions, Sept. 18, 1777. (Revolutionary War Rolls, 1775-1783. National Archives Microfilm Publication M246. Roll 115, folder 13, 3ᵈ Regiment Light Dragoons, 1779, item 6.)

Alexander Clough congratulated Colonel Baylor on his approaching marriage, and wrote that he had the chance to get one hundred pair of breeches, and two or three hundred pairs of shoes, and asked the Colonel's permission to acquire them. He also wrote that it would be beneficial to collect the regiment together at Millsone, because of the abundance of forage and the convenient quarters. (University of Virginia. Alderman Library Special Collections. Accession 2257, Papers of the Baylor Family of Newmarket, Caroline County, Va, in part transcripts: [manuscript], 1653-1915. Box 4: the folder is labeled "1756, 1777-1781; Military Papers," item 8: "Letter from Alexander Clough to George Baylor, 4 Feb 1778 at Millsone.")

Alexander Clough wrote to Colonel Baylor recommending Sergeant Bell for the next cornet, and letting the Colonel know that the horses arrived. (University of Virginia. Alderman Library Special Collections. Accession 2257, Papers of the Baylor Family of Newmarket, Caroline County, Va, in part transcripts: [manuscript], 1653-1915. Box 4: the folder is labeled "1756, 1777-1781; Military Papers," item 11: "1778 Spring, Maj. Alexander Clough to Col. Baylor.")

Major Clough. "…and besides Major Clough who died of his wounds, there were wounded of the Officers, Colonel Baylor, Lieutenant Morrow and Mr. Evans the Surgeon." (David Griffith. Letter, 20 October 1778. Accession 22789. Personal papers collection. The Library of Virginia, Richmond, Va.)

Colbert, Elisha

"I do Certify that Elisha Colbert enlisted a soldier in 3 Regiment L Dragoons for Three Years Janry 1779 & that he was killed at the U. Town action 81 & that he did not draw any pay after 31st July 81." Signed by William Barret, Captain, Baylor's Dragoons, February 3, 1784. (Virginia Governor's Office. Bounty Warrants, 1779-1860. Accession 41429, The Library of Virginia, Richmond, Va.)

Colgan, William

"William Colgin having Served faithfully three years in the 3rd Regiment of Light Dragoons is hereby Discharged." Signed by W. Washington, Lt. Col., August 1, 1780. John Kerney stated that William Colgan was a citizen of Virginia when he enlisted. (Virginia Governor's Office. Bounty Warrants, 1779-1860. Accession 41429, The Library of Virginia, Richmond, Va.)

William Colgan, S42652. William Colgan enlisted August 1, 1777 for three years in Captain Cad W. Jones' company of the 3rd Regiment, near Martinsburg, Berkeley County, Virginia. He was taken prisoner at Tappan, was sent to New York City and confined in the Sugar House for one month. He was then conducted by a British guard to Elizabethtown and exchanged. He re-joined his regiment and served until discharged at Halifax, North Carolina, on 1 August 1780. He was in the battle of Monmouth and several other skirmishes. William Colgan was born about 1760, and in May 1818, he was living in Mad River Township in Champaign County, Ohio. In August 1820, he said he was a reed maker by trade, but had not followed it by reason of his remote location. His family consisted at that time of his wife, a son and a daughter. William Colgan died 4 November 1837. (Revolutionary War Pension and Bounty-Land Warrant Application Files. National Archives Microfilm Publication M804, roll 610; also Dorman, John Frederick. 1958. Virginia Revolutionary Pension Applications, 21:23-24.)

Colley, Charles

Charles Colley, S34702. Charles Colley enlisted as a private in 1776 with Captain Thomas Johnson of the 3rd Virginia Regiment of Colonel Mercer, and served two years with that regiment. He then enlisted in the cavalry under Major William Washington and served for three years, until he was discharged in

1781. He was born about 1753, lived in Madison County, Kentucky, in 1818, and on 4 June 1825 was in St. Louis County, Missouri. (Revolutionary War Pension and Bounty-Land Warrant Application Files. National Archives Microfilm Publication M804, roll 611; also Dorman, John Frederick. 1958. Virginia Revolutionary Pension Applications, 21:27-28.)

Collins, John

"John Collins enlisted as a Private in the 3d Regiment of Light Dragoons in the Spring of '77 for the war, and served to the end thereof." Signed by J. Swan, May 1, 1781. (Virginia Governor's Office. Bounty Warrants, 1779-1860. Accession 41429, The Library of Virginia, Richmond, Va.)

John Collins, W9813. John Collins enlisted in Captain John Swan's company, the 5th troop of the 3rd Virginia Regiment of Light Dragoons under Colonel George Baylor. He claimed to have served from 1776 to the close of the war, being under Captain John Hughes at the time of his discharge. He was born on 28 August 1758, married Margaret (surname not given) in Westmoreland County, Pennsylvania, on 7 March 1786, and had at least eight children. John Collins died 21 Jan 1828. In 1818 and 1820, he was of Fleming County, Kentucky, and in 1839 his widow was living in Rush County, Indiana. (Revolutionary War Pension and Bounty-Land Warrant Application Files. National Archives Microfilm Publication M804, roll 613; also Dorman, John Frederick. 1958. Virginia Revolutionary Pension Applications, 21:34-36.)

Connor, Edward

Edward Connor, Cornet, Date of Commission July 27, 1778. Arrangement of Light Dragoons, 3^d Regiment, undated. (Revolutionary War Rolls, 1775-1783. National Archives Microfilm Publication M246. Roll 115, folder 13, 3^d Regiment Light Dragoons, 1779, item 3.)

Edward Connor, P. Master, October 1, 1777. A Return of Officers in the 3rd Regiment of Light Dragoons with the Dates of their Commissions, Sept. 18, 1777. (Revolutionary War Rolls, 1775-1783. National Archives Microfilm Publication M246. Roll 115, folder 13, 3^d Regiment Light Dragoons, 1779, item 6.)

"I do hereby certify that Edward Conner was enlisted a Sergeant in the 3d regiment Light dragoons in March '77 & that the said Conner was promoted to a cornet in the said regiment between the 1st day of Aug. & 10th Sept. 1779 & that he died in the service of the United States in Aug or Sept 1780." Voucher signed by Presley Thornton, December 15, 1784. (Virginia Governor's Office. Bounty Warrants, 1779-1860. Accession 41429, The Library of Virginia, Richmond, Va.)

Cookers or Cookes, Michael

"This may Certify the Michael Cookes private in the 3d Regiment of Dragoons has served his full term of enlistment agreeable to a Certificate Given by Major Calo of this date and he is hereby Discharg'd. Given at head Quarters. S Carolina. Apr 9th 1782." Discharge signed by Nathaniel Greene. "Richmond May 4th 82 I do Certify that Michael Cookes has served as a private in the above mentioned Regiment for three years." Voucher signed by William Barret, Captain 3d Regiment. (Virginia Governor's Office. Bounty Warrants, 1779-1860. Accession 41429, The Library of Virginia, Richmond, Va.)

Michael Cookers, W6722. In September 1838, Elizabeth, the widow of Michael Cookers, stated that he was a soldier of cavalry in Colonel William Washington's regiment of horse, mostly in the southern campaign. Michael Cookers and Elizabeth Kile were married in Frederick County, Maryland, on 12 May 1783, and moved to Berkeley County, Virginia. Michael Cookers died 28 May 1829, probably in Berkeley County, Virginia. (Revolutionary War Pension and Bounty-Land Warrant Application Files. National Archives Microfilm Publication M804, roll 642; also Dorman, John Frederick. 1958. Virginia Revolutionary Pension Applications, 22:58-59.)

Cooper, Samuel

Samuel Cooper, Private, enlisted Oct. 17, 1777. Muster Roll of the 2nd Troop in the 3d Regiment Light Dragoons in the Service of the United States commanded by Lieutenant Colonel William Washington for the Months of May, June, July August, September, October 1779. (Revolutionary War Rolls, 1775-1783. National Archives Microfilm Publication M246. Roll 115, folder 13, 3d Regiment Light Dragoons, 1779, item 1.)

Samuel Cooper, pay due him from 17 October 1779 to 17 October 1782. (Miscellaneous Numbered Records [The Manuscript File] in the War Department Collection of Revolutionary War Records, 1775-1790's. National Archives Microfilm Publication

M859. Manuscript 17672, "The United States in Account with Samuel Cooper late a Priv^t in 3rd Regiment L.D.," dated 27 June 1792.)

Corning, Richard

Richard Corning, Private, enlisted March 8, 1777, on command. Muster Roll of the 2nd Troop in the 3^d Regiment Light Dragoons in the Service of the United States commanded by Lieutenant Colonel William Washington for the Months of May, June, July August, September, October 1779. (Revolutionary War Rolls, 1775-1783. National Archives Microfilm Publication M246. Roll 115, folder 13, 3^d Regiment Light Dragoons, 1779, item 1.)

Cosby, Sydnor

"Sydnor Cosby Serjt 3 Regiment LD" signed an account of clothing and supplies delivered to part of the 3rd Regiment on April 3, 1782 in Petersburg, Virginia. (University of Virginia. Alderman Library Special Collections. Accession 2257, Papers of the Baylor Family of Newmarket, Caroline County, Va, in part transcripts: [manuscript], 1653-1915. Box 4: the folder is labeled "Military Papers, 1782, 1814, & n.d.," item 6: "1782 April 3, Continental Troops Clothing & Accoutrement Issue Slip of 3rd Regiment Lt. Dragoons by Lydnor [Sydnor] Cosby.")

Sydnor Cosby, who "is at present a Soldier in your Regiment" is recommended for promotion in a letter from Captain John Minor to Colonel George Baylor, April 29, 1782, as a "person of unblemish'd reputation" and "a young Gentleman, the son of worthy & reputable" parents. (University of Virginia. Alderman Library Special Collections. Accession 2257, Papers of the Baylor Family of Newmarket, Caroline County, Va, in part transcripts: [manuscript], 1653-1915. Box 4: the folder is labeled "Military Papers, 1782, 1814, & n.d.," item 12: "1782 Apr 29, John Minor to Col. George Baylor.")

"I do certify that Sydnor Cosby was a Sergeant in the Continental Cavalry, that he enlisted in June 1781 for the War & Served during that period." Will Parsons, Captain 1st Regiment Light Dragoons, Petersburg, Virginia, December 15, 1783. (Virginia Governor's Office. Bounty Warrants, 1779-1860. Accession 41429, The Library of Virginia, Richmond, Va.)

Cosby, William

"I do Certify William Cosby Enlisted May 20th 1780 for the war in Colonel Baylor's Dragoons & was Appointed Serjt 1st March 1782 he was Payed 1st August 1780 Served faithfully the term of his Enlistment." Voucher signed by William Barret, September 8, 1784. In September 1787, William Cosby was in Petersburg, Virginia. (Virginia Governor's Office. Bounty Warrants, 1779-1860. Accession 41429, The Library of Virginia, Richmond, Va.)

Cox, Presley

Presley Cox, "sick absent." (University of Virginia. Alderman Library Special Collections. Accession 2257, Papers of the Baylor Family of Newmarket, Caroline County, Va, in part transcripts: [manuscript], 1653-1915. Box 4: the folder is labeled "1756, 1777-1781; Military Papers," item 14: "A list of the men's names absent belonging to Colonel Baylor's Regiment, Fredericksburg, June 27, 1778.")

"I hereby Certify that Presley Cox has served the term of three years and eight months in the 3d Regiment L Dragoons... ." Voucher signed by Presley Thornton, September 1, 1780. (Virginia Governor's Office. Bounty Warrants, 1779-1860. Accession 41429, The Library of Virginia, Richmond, Va.)

Crenshaw, Nathaniel

According to Bartlett Cox in 1837, Nathaniel Crenshaw enlisted in 1777 in Lunenberg County, Virginia under Captain Samuel Hopkins for three years, was promoted to Sergeant, and was honorably discharged. He then enlisted under Col. William Washington, was wounded at Guilford Court House, served to the close of the war and was honorably discharged. (Virginia Governor's Office. Bounty Warrants, 1779-1860. Accession 41429, The Library of Virginia, Richmond, Va.)

Nathaniel Crenshaw, W6772. Bartlett Cox of Mecklenberg County, Virginia, stated that Nathaniel Crenshaw, of Lunenberg County, Virginia enlisted first with Captain Samuel Hopkins for three years. After he was discharged, Nathaniel Crenshaw enlisted as a soldier of cavalry under Col. William Washington, was in the battle at Guilford where he was wounded, and served to the end of the war.

In July, 1838, Unity Crenshaw, nee Pamplin, age 78, of Charlotte County, Virginia, said she was the widow of Nathaniel

Crenshaw, who was a soldier of the Virginia Line on Continental establishment. She married Nathaniel Crenshaw on December 26, 1780, and he died November 7, 1793. (Revolutionary War Pension and Bounty-Land Warrant Application Files. National Archives Microfilm Publication M804, roll 690.)

Cross, John

"It Appears from the Size Roll of the 4th Troop that John Cross Enlisted for the war in Baylor's Dragoons June 5th, 1781, & served until the mutiny May 1783." Voucher signed by William Barret, Captain Baylor's Dragoons, December 20, 1784. (Virginia Governor's Office. Bounty Warrants, 1779-1860. Accession 41429, The Library of Virginia, Richmond, Va.)

John Cross, S39382. John Cross enlisted as a private at Point of Fork in Virginia, in the summer of 1782, in Captain Parsons' company in Colonel William Washington's 3rd regiment of cavalry, and served until May 1783 when he was discharged near Winchester, Virginia. John Cross was born about 1768, married, and in 1820 stated that he had four daughters and two sons. In 1818 and 1820 they were living in Jefferson County, Virginia, then moved to Berkeley County, Virginia for several years. In 1829 they were living in Fairfield County, Ohio. According to his son-in-law, John Cross died in 1847. (Revolutionary War Pension and Bounty-Land Warrant Application Files. National Archives Microfilm Publication M804, roll 699; also Dorman, John Frederick. 1958. Virginia Revolutionary Pension Applications, 25:16-17.)

William Ball of Frederick County, Virginia, in September 1818, declared he was in the 3rd Regiment of Cavalry and affirmed John Cross' service in that regiment. (Revolutionary War Pension and Bounty-Land Warrant Application Files. National Archives Microfilm Publication M804, roll 699; also Dorman, John Frederick. 1958. Virginia Revolutionary Pension Applications, 25:16.)

Curtis, James

James Curtis, Private, enlisted June 30, 1777, on command. Muster Roll of the 2nd Troop in the 3^{d} Regiment Light Dragoons in the Service of the United States commanded by Lieutenant Colonel William Washington for the Months of May, June, July August, September, October 1779. (Revolutionary War Rolls, 1775-1783.

National Archives Microfilm Publication M246. Roll 115, folder 13, 3^d Regiment Light Dragoons, 1779, item 1.)

"I do Certify that Mr. James Curtis a young Gentleman who served in Colonel Baylor's Cavalry of horse afterwards Commanded by Colonel Washington was & is still an Inhabitant of Virginia in Loudoun County when recruited in the Horse Service... ." Voucher signed by Thomas Warman, Captain 3rd Virginia Regiment, April 13, 1784.

"James Curtis having faithfully served three years in the 3d Regiment of Light Dragoons is hereby Discharged." Signed by William Washington, Lt. Col. July 1, 1780. (Virginia Governor's Office. Bounty Warrants, 1779-1860. Accession 41429, The Library of Virginia, Richmond, Va.)

Custis, Lieutenant

William Bassett stated that he enlisted for two years and nine months under Colonel George Baylor, Captain John Stith and Lieutenant Custis. (Revolutionary War Pension and Bounty-Land Warrant Application Files. National Archives Microfilm Publication M804, roll 171; also Dorman, John Frederick. 1958. Virginia Revolutionary Pension Applications, 5:29-31.)

Dade, Baldwin

Baldwin Dade, Cadet, Date of Commission May 10, 1778. Arrangement of Light Dragoons, 3^d Regiment, undated. (Revolutionary War Rolls, 1775-1783. National Archives Microfilm Publication M246. Roll 115, folder 13, 3^d Regiment Light Dragoons, 1779, item 3.)

Baldwin Dade, Cadet, May 10, 1778. A Return of Officers in the 3rd Regiment of Light Dragoons with the Dates of their Commissions, Sept. 18, 1777. (Revolutionary War Rolls, 1775-1783. National Archives Microfilm Publication M246. Roll 115, folder 13, 3^d Regiment Light Dragoons, 1779, item 6.)

Mr. B. Dade is mentioned as having John Wood with him. (University of Virginia. Alderman Library Special Collections. Accession 2257, Papers of the Baylor Family of Newmarket, Caroline County, Va, in part transcripts: [manuscript], 1653-1915. Box 4: the folder is labeled "1756, 1777-1781; Military Papers," item 14: "A list of the men's names absent belonging to Colonel Baylor's Regiment, Fredericksburg, June 27, 1778.")

Mr. Dade, "Volunteer Taken Prisoner." A Return of the 3^d Regiment of L. D. Commanded by Captain Stith, October 23, 1778. (Revolutionary War Rolls, 1775-1783. National Archives Microfilm Publication M246. Roll 115, folder 13, 3^d Regiment Light Dragoons, 1779, item 5.)

B. Dade wrote to Colonel Baylor requesting that he use his greatest endeavors to get Colonel Beatty to exchange Dade after he was captured by the British. (University of Virginia. Alderman Library Special Collections. Accession 2257, Papers of the Baylor Family of Newmarket, Caroline County, Va, in part transcripts: [manuscript], 1653-1915. Box 4: the folder is labeled "1756, 1777-1781; Military Papers," item 17: "1779 Feb, B. Dade to Col. George Baylor.")

Dade, Francis

Francis Dade, Cornet, Date of Commission May 1, 1778. Arrangement of Light Dragoons, 3^d Regiment, undated. (Revolutionary War Rolls, 1775-1783. National Archives Microfilm Publication M246. Roll 115, folder 13, 3^d Regiment Light Dragoons, 1779, item 3.)

Francis Dade, Cornet, May 1, 1778. A Return of Officers in the 3rd Regiment of Light Dragoons with the Dates of their Commissions, Sept. 18, 1777. (Revolutionary War Rolls, 1775-1783. National Archives Microfilm Publication M246. Roll 115, folder 13, 3^d Regiment Light Dragoons, 1779, item 6.)

F. Dade received a sword, scabbard, belt and a pair of pistols August 27, 1778. (University of Virginia. Alderman Library Special Collections. Accession 2257, Papers of the Baylor Family of Newmarket, Caroline County, Va, in part transcripts: [manuscript], 1653-1915. Box 4: the folder is labeled "1756, 1777-1781; Military Papers," item 19: "Continental Troops, Itemized Account, September 1777 to June 1779.")

"There are, besides, Prisoners in New York, A Captain (Swan) two subalterns, (Randolph and Dade) a volunteer, (Kilty) and the Surgeons Mate...." (David Griffith. Letter, 20 October 1778. Accession 22789. Personal papers collection. The Library of Virginia, Richmond, Va.)

"I do hereby Certify that Capt. Francis Dade was appointed an officer in the late 3d Regiment of Light Dragoons the 10th day of April 1778. Capt. Dade in the last arrangement was left out through mistake. Capt. Fitzhugh & Kilty who were younger officers were arrayed before him: one of the above mentioned Gentlemen is only entitled to a Lieutenancy." Voucher signed by George Baylor, Fredericksburg, October 9, 1783. (Virginia Governor's Office. Bounty Warrants, 1779-1860. Accession 41429, The Library of Virginia, Richmond, Va.)

Francis Dade, BLWt 606-200, for service as Lieutenant, issued 5 July 1799 to Laurence Dade, Francis Dade, Polly Dade, surviving children and heirs. (Revolutionary War Pension and Bounty-Land Warrant Application Files. National Archives Microfilm Publication M804, roll 728; also Dorman, John Frederick. 1958. Virginia Revolutionary Pension Applications, 26:27.)

Dailey, Dennis

In Fayette County, Kentucky, in April 1823, Dennis Dailey made oath that in the year 1780 he enlisted in Captain William Barret's company of the Third Regiment of cavalry, and served until the war closed, at which time he was honorably discharged in South Carolina. (Virginia Governor's Office. Revolutionary War Rejected Claims, 1779-1860. Accession 41986, State government records collection, The Library of Virginia, Richmond, Va.)

Dennis Dailey or Dayley, S30375. Dennis Dailey enlisted in Hillsborough, North Carolina, on 6 November 1780 in Captain William Barret's 3rd troop of the 3rd regiment of Virginia Dragoons. He served until 11 June 1783, when he was discharged at Nelson's Ferry on the Santee River in South Carolina. He served as trumpeter, and was in the battle of Eutaw Springs in September 1781. In 1844 he stated that he lived in Brunswick County, Virginia when he enlisted, first in the militia, then in Continental service. Dennis Dailey was born in about 1761, married, and was living in Preble County, Ohio, in 1818, in Clark County, Kentucky in 1822, and in Scott County, Kentucky, in 1844. (Revolutionary War Pension and Bounty-Land Warrant Application Files. National Archives Microfilm Publication M804, roll 730; also Dorman, John Frederick. 1958. Virginia Revolutionary Pension Applications, 26:28-30.)

Dangerfield, William

William Dangerfield, Sergeant Major, 3rd Light Dragoons; pay from 1st January 1782 to the 16th November 1783. (Miscellaneous Numbered Records [The Manuscript File] in the

War Department Collection of Revolutionary War Records, 1775-1790's. National Archives Microfilm Publication M859. Manuscript 17512, "The United States in a/c with Wm Dangerfield serj^t major 3^d Regiment light Dragoons," dated 6 May 1794.)

William Dangerfield certified that John Betsill served with him in the 3rd regiment for three years and was discharged by Colonel George Baylor. (Revolutionary War Pension and Bounty-Land Warrant Application Files. National Archives Microfilm Publication M804, John Betsill, roll 230; also Dorman, John Frederick. 1958. Virginia Revolutionary Pension Applications, 6:79-80.)

"I do Certify that Serg't Will. Dangerfield... enlisted for the war in Col. Baylor's Dragoons...." William Barret, former Captain Baylor's Dragoons, September 10, 1784. (Virginia Governor's Office. Revolutionary War Rejected Claims, 1779-1860. Accession 41986, State government records collection, The Library of Virginia, Richmond, Va.)

William Parsons, in a voucher dated September 13, 1784, in Petersburg, Virginia stated that Sargent Dangerfield revolted in May 1783. (Virginia Governor's Office. Bounty Warrants, 1779-1860. Accession 41429, The Library of Virginia, Richmond, Va.)

Davis, Henry

"I do Certify that Henry Davis enlisted into Baylor's Dragoons for Three years December 1776 and Served the full term of his enlistment." Voucher signed by William Barret, Captain, Baylor's Dragoons, October 22, 1787. (Virginia Governor's Office. Bounty Warrants, 1779-1860. Accession 41429, The Library of Virginia, Richmond, Va.)

Davis, Thompson or Thomas

Thomas Davis had sword and belt; "his pistol and Cartridge Box left at the Valley." Return, dated 1 March 1778, of arms and accouterments in the Third Troop belonging to Colonel George Baylor's Regiment of Light Dragoons. (Virginia Office of the Quartermaster General, Fredericksburg. Returns of Colonel George Baylor's Regiment, 1778-1779. Accession 22547, The Library of Virginia, Richmond, Va.)

"I Certify that Thomsand Davis enlisted as a soldier for the war in the 3d Rgt of Light Dragoons 1 day of Febry '77." Voucher signed by John Perry, Cornet, August 22, 1783.

"I do Certify that Thompson Davis was a Soldier in Baylor's Dragoons and was wounded in August 78 at the Surprise of the Regiment in the Jerseys." William Barret, July 11, 1786. "On Examination of Thompson Davis who was a Dragoon formerly of Col. Baylor's regiment.... I find he has been most dangerously wounded particularly about the Head... having received those wounds at Col. Baylor's Surprise...." W. Foushee, May 2, 1786. (Virginia Governor's Office. Bounty Warrants, 1779-1860. Accession 41429, The Library of Virginia, Richmond, Va.)

Davis, William

"It appears from the Size Roll of 1st Troop that Corporal Wm Davis enlisted for the war in Baylor's Dragoons June 81 & Continued until the mutiny May 83." Voucher signed by William Barret, October 18, 1785. (Virginia Governor's Office. Bounty Warrants, 1779-1860. Accession 41429, The Library of Virginia, Richmond, Va.)

William Davis, S35884. William Davis stated that he was enlisted by Colonel Holms of Frederick County, Virginia, in 1781, was transferred to the 3rd Regiment of dragoons under Major Call, and marched to Santee, South Carolina under Captain Churchill Jones. He served to the end of the war, but was on furlough when the army was disbanded. William Davis was born about 1760, and in 1818 and 1828 was living in Fleming County, Kentucky. (Revolutionary War Pension and Bounty-Land Warrant Application Files. National Archives Microfilm Publication M804, roll 769; also Dorman, John Frederick. 1958. Virginia Revolutionary Pension Applications, 28:34.)

Dawson, James

"I hereby Certify that James Dawson Soldier enlisted for the war in the 3d Regiment of Light Dragoons the 20 day of Augt 1779 and served to the end of the war." Signed John Perry, Cornet, August 7, 1784. (Virginia Governor's Office. Bounty Warrants, 1779-1860. Accession 41429, The Library of Virginia, Richmond, Va.)

In Greene County, Tennessee, in June 1823, James Dawson stated that he became acquainted with Richard Porterfield in 1779 at New Providence, North Carolina, enlisted under Col. Washington, and was marched to the taking of Colonel Rugely with a pine log, used in place of a cannon. He was then marched to Pacolet and joined General Morgan's Riflemen and left Col. Washington's regiment. (Deposition by him in the papers for Richard Porterfield: Revolutionary War Pension and Bounty-Land Warrant Application Files. National Archives Microfilm Publication M804, roll 1956.)

James Dawson, S9657. In April 1818, James Dawson, age near 60, a resident of Greene County, Tennessee, stated that he enlisted at New Providence about February 1779, in Captain Watts' company under Col. Washington. He fought in the battles of Eutaw Springs and Camden, but smallpox prevented him from being in the battle of Guilford Court House. He was furloughed at Santee but never called back to service. He resided in North Carolina from the close of the war until about 1815.

James Dawson said he was born in Maryland, but lost his parents at an early age. In October 1820, he said he was about 76 years old. An affidavit made by the former Jane Dawson in July 1870 stated that she married James Dawson 11 March 1823 in Washington County, Tennessee, and that he died in Anderson County, Tennessee 30 June 1838. (Revolutionary War Pension and Bounty-Land Warrant Application Files. National Archives Microfilm Publication M804, roll 771.)

Deal, Joseph

"I do Certify that Joseph Deal enlisted for the War in 3 Regiment L Dragoons Feby 2d 1780 and did not draw any part of his pay from that date till 82." Signed William Barret, Captain, Baylor's Dragoons, October, 1783. (Virginia Governor's Office. Bounty Warrants, 1779-1860. Accession 41429, The Library of Virginia, Richmond, Va.)

Dishman, James

"I do Certify that James Dishman enlisted May 81 for the War which time he has faithfully served & that he is a native of this state." Signed William Barret, January 6, 1784. (Virginia Governor's Office. Bounty Warrants, 1779-1860. Accession 41429, The Library of Virginia, Richmond, Va.)

James Dishman, W9409. In 1851, Jane, the widow of James Dishman, stated that he was a private under Captain William Barret in the Virginia state and Continental line, and also in the militia. She believed that he served three years as a horseman, and at some time during his service was taken prisoner and kept for nine months in the West India Islands. In 1851, Nancy Dishman, age 88, a sister-in-law, declared that James Dishman and his brother first served on the sea, and this was when they were taken prisoner on the West India Islands for six months, then taken to Philadelphia and exchanged. James Dishman then enlisted as a light horseman and served for five years in this capacity. James Dishman married Jane Gunn in Botetourt County, Virginia, in July 1788, and he died 16 October 1820. In 1851 his widow was living in Warren County, Kentucky. (Revolutionary War Pension and Bounty-Land Warrant Application Files. National Archives Microfilm Publication M804, roll 821; also Dorman, John Frederick. 1958. Virginia Revolutionary Pension Applications, 30:23-24.)

Dobbs, Nathan

Nathan Dobbs, S16370. In May 1780, while living in Henry County, Virginia, Nathan Dobbs enlisted in the militia under Captain Roberts. He marched to Hillsborough, North Carolina, then to Rugely's Bridge near Camden, South Carolina. In September 1780 he began service as a substitute in a militia company under Captain Edward Jenkins, in Henry County. When his four months expired, he was at the Pee Dee River in South Carolina, and there joined Captain Jones' company of cavalry under Colonel Washington. He was in the battle of Guilford Court House, was at Eutaw Springs, and the taking of Cornwallis, and the siege of Charleston. He served to the end of the war. Nathan Dobbs was born in Henry County, Virginia, in 1760. In 1831 he was living in Jackson County, Georgia, and in 1833, was in Gwinnett County, Georgia. (Revolutionary War Pension and Bounty-Land Warrant Application Files. National Archives Microfilm Publication M804, roll 823; also Dorman, John Frederick. 1958. Virginia Revolutionary Pension Applications, 30:42-43.)

Drake, Thomas

Thomas Drake, W5264. Thomas Drake enlisted in Amelia County, Virginia and was attached to Captain Parsons' company in Colonel White's regiment, and afterwards put in Colonel William Washington's regiment of horse. After the battle of Guilford, he went to South Carolina and joined General Marion, then went as an escort from General Greene's army to Virginia, and while there, joined an infantry company under Colonel Mathews, and was at the surrender of Cornwallis. Thomas Drake married Catherine Vaughan in Brunswick County, Virginia, on 12 August 1802, and had at least six children. In 1828 they were living in Bedford County, Tennessee, and he died there on 24 March 1835. (Revolutionary War Pension and Bounty-Land Warrant Application Files. National Archives Microfilm Publication M804, roll 851; also Dorman, John Frederick. 1958. Virginia Revolutionary Pension Applications, 31:20-21.)

East, David

David East had sword, pistol, belt, cartridge box; "on command." Return, dated 1 March 1778, of arms and accouterments in the Third Troop belonging to Colonel George Baylor's Regiment of Light Dragoons. (Virginia Office of the Quartermaster General, Fredericksburg. Returns of Colonel George Baylor's Regiment, 1778-1779. Accession 22547, The Library of Virginia, Richmond, Va.)

Ebb or Elb, William

William Elb, Private, enlisted April 1, 1777, on command. Muster Roll of the 2nd Troop in the 3^{d} Regiment Light Dragoons in the Service of the United States commanded by Lieutenant Colonel William Washington for the Months of May, June, July August, September, October 1779. (Revolutionary War Rolls, 1775-1783. National Archives Microfilm Publication M246. Roll 115, folder 13, 3^{d} Regiment Light Dragoons, 1779, item 1.)

"William Ebb is hereby Discharged from the 3d Virginia Regiment of Light Dragoons having served three years faithfully." Signed by William Washington, Lt. Col. March, 1780. (Virginia Governor's Office. Bounty Warrants, 1779-1860. Accession 41429, The Library of Virginia, Richmond, Va.)

Ebbs, John

"This is to Certify that John Ebbs was enlisted by me for during the War in Colonel Baylor's Regiment L Dragoons in the year 1780 Feb: 1st and Served as a Soldier til his Death which was Twelve Months after also never rec^{d} any pay or Land... ." Signed by John Linton, Lieutenant 1st Regiment Light Dragoons. James Ebbs of Prince William County, Virginia, stated in June 1785 that he was the father of John Ebbs, and that John was not married. (Virginia Governor's Office. Bounty Warrants, 1779-1860. Accession 41429, The Library of Virginia, Richmond, Va.)

Emerson, Henry

"Henry Emerson Sergeant in the 3d Regiment of light dragoons having served three years in the 3d Regiment of light dragoons is hereby discharged. The said Emerson is a man of Bravery & has conducted himself with propriety." William Washington, Lt. Col., December 24, 1780. (Virginia Governor's Office. Bounty Warrants, 1779-1860. Accession 41429, The Library of Virginia, Richmond, Va.)

Emet or Emmert, George

George Emet, Private, enlisted September 15, 1777, on command. Muster Roll of the 2nd Troop in the 3^d Regiment Light Dragoons in the Service of the United States commanded by Lieutenant Colonel William Washington for the Months of May, June, July August, September, October 1779. (Revolutionary War Rolls, 1775-1783. National Archives Microfilm Publication M246. Roll 115, folder 13, 3^d Regiment Light Dragoons, 1779, item 1.)

George Emmert, S38680. George Emmert enlisted about September 1777, in Shepherdstown, Berkeley County, Virginia, in Captain John Stith's company of the 3rd Regiment of Dragoons. He served for three years and was discharged 17 September 1781, at Halifax, North Carolina, by Colonel William Washington. He was wounded in the ambush at Tappan, in September 1778. George Emmert was born about 1757; after the war he married and had thirteen children, and in 1818 through 1820, was living in Carter County, Tennessee. (Revolutionary War Pension and Bounty-Land Warrant Application Files. National Archives Microfilm Publication M804, roll 927; also Dorman, John Frederick. 1958. Virginia Revolutionary Pension Applications, 34:8-10.)

Emmons, John

"It appears from the Size Roll 2 Troop that Jno Emmons enlisted for the war July 12th 81 & served until the Mutiny May 1783." William Barret, Captain Baylor's Dragoons, February 28, 1785. (Virginia Governor's Office. Bounty Warrants, 1779-1860. Accession 41429, The Library of Virginia, Richmond, Va.)

English, Charles

Charles English, BLWt 1379-100. Samuel English declared that his brother Charles English enlisted in 1777 in the regiment of Colonel Washington, and served to the close of the war.

(Revolutionary War Pension and Bounty-Land Warrant Application Files. National Archives Microfilm Publication M804, roll 929; also Dorman, John Frederick. 1958. Virginia Revolutionary Pension Applications, 34:19.)

Esbell, Benjamin

Benjamin Esbell, Private, enlisted June 17, 1777, on command. Muster Roll of the 2nd Troop in the 3^{d} Regiment Light Dragoons in the Service of the United States commanded by Lieutenant Colonel William Washington for the Months of May, June, July August, September, October 1779. (Revolutionary War Rolls, 1775-1783. National Archives Microfilm Publication M246. Roll 115, folder 13, 3^{d} Regiment Light Dragoons, 1779, item 1.)

Etter, John

"It appears from the Size Roll of the 1st Troop that John Etter enlisted for the war in Baylor's Dragoons Febry 11th 80 & Served the full term of his enlistment." William Barret, Captain, Baylor's Dragoons, January 18, 1786. (Virginia Governor's Office. Bounty Warrants, 1779-1860. Accession 41429, The Library of Virginia, Richmond, Va.)

John Etter, S46542. John Etter declared that in 1778 he enlisted in the 1st Light Dragoons under Colonel Washington of the Virginia Line and served until discharged by Colonel Washington, at which time he was under Captain Barret. (Revolutionary War Pension and Bounty-Land Warrant Application Files. National Archives Microfilm Publication M804, roll 936; also Dorman, John Frederick. 1958. Virginia Revolutionary Pension Applications, 34:68.)

Evans, George

George Evans, Surgeon, May 20, 1777. A Return of Officers in the 3rd Regiment of Light Dragoons with the Dates of their Commissions, Sept. 18, 1777. (Revolutionary War Rolls, 1775-1783. National Archives Microfilm Publication M246. Roll 115, folder 13, 3^{d} Regiment Light Dragoons, 1779, item 6.)

Mr. Evans, Surgeon. "… and besides Major Clough who died of his wounds, there were wounded of the Officers, Colonel Baylor, Lieutenant Morrow and Mr. Evans the Surgeon." (David Griffith. Letter, 20 October 1778. Accession 22789. Personal papers collection. The Library of Virginia, Richmond, Va.)

Evans, Thomas

Thomas Evans, Surgeon's Mate, June 7, 1777. A Return of Officers in the 3rd Regiment of Light Dragoons with the Dates of their Commissions, Sept. 18, 1777. (Revolutionary War Rolls, 1775-1783. National Archives Microfilm Publication M246. Roll 115, folder 13, 3^d Regiment Light Dragoons, 1779, item 6.)

"There are, besides, Prisoners in New York, A Captain (Swan) two subalterns, (Randolph and Dade) a volunteer, (Kilty) and the Surgeons Mate...." (David Griffith. Letter, 20 October 1778. Accession 22789. Personal papers collection. The Library of Virginia, Richmond, Va.)

Everhart or Everheart, Lawrence

"I do hereby Certify that Lawrence Everhart Sergeant in the 3 Regiment of Light Dragoons has served three years the term of his enlistment as a brave faithful & attentive soldier and is discharged from the said regiment. He has received several wounds which have disabled him from being a soldier." George Baylor, Col., Petersburg, March 21, 1782. (Virginia Governor's Office. Bounty Warrants, 1779-1860. Accession 41429, The Library of Virginia, Richmond, Va.)

Lawrence Everhart, S25068 and W9431. In Washington D.C, in April 1834, Lawrence Everhart, about age 79 declared he enlisted first in August 1776 in Maryland with Captain Good in the Flying Camp. After being discharged, he returned home to Frederick County, Maryland in the spring of 1777. After the harvest in 1778, he next enlisted under Captain John Swan in the 3rd Regiment of Light Dragoons under William Washington, and marched to Petersburg, Virginia. He was wounded at Cowpens in January 1781, was captured by the British, and spent several months recovering, but was never fit for duty. He was discharged at Petersburg, Virginia in the fall of 1782. Lawrence Everhart was born May 6, 1755, in Frederick County, Maryland.

Mary Anne Everheart, nee Bechenbaugh, age 84 in 1840, of Frederick County, Maryland said she was married to Lawrence Everheart about 1781 in Frederick County, and he died August 2, 1840. Included in the application is a listing of their nine children. (Revolutionary War Pension and Bounty-Land Warrant Application Files. National Archives Microfilm Publication M804, roll 944.)

Fauntleroy, Griffin

John Biswell of Jessamine County, Kentucky, claimed that in 1778 he enlisted at Hillsborough in the 1st Virginia Regiment, under Captain Griffin Fauntleroy, and served until the end of the war. During this enlistment, he was annexed to Colonel William Washington's regiment of light dragoons, where he served about three and a half years. (Revolutionary War Pension and Bounty-Land Warrant Application Files. National Archives Microfilm Publication M804, roll 249; also Dorman, John Frederick. 1958. Virginia Revolutionary Pension Applications, 7:22-23.)

Thomas Gibson enlisted with Captain Fauntleroy under Colonel William Washington, and was in the battles of Cowpens, Guilford, and Eutaw Springs. (Revolutionary War Pension and Bounty-Land Warrant Application Files. National Archives Microfilm Publication M804, roll 1067; also Dorman, John Frederick. 1958. Virginia Revolutionary Pension Applications, 43:54-55.)

George Tennell stated that he enlisted in 1776 for 18 months with Captain Fauntleroy in the 3rd Regiment under Colonel Baylor. (Revolutionary War Pension and Bounty-Land Warrant Application Files. National Archives Microfilm Publication M804, roll 2357.)

Jonathan White, of Cecil County, Maryland in 1818, stated that he enlisted in the spring of 1776 under Captain Fauntleroy of the 1st Regiment under William Washington. (Revolutionary War Pension and Bounty-Land Warrant Application Files. National Archives Microfilm Publication M804, roll 2556.)

Griffin Fauntleroy was killed at the battle of Guilford in March 1781. (Gwathmey, John Hastings. 1938. Historical Register of Virginians in the Revolution: Soldiers, sailors, marines, 1775-1783. Dietz Press, Richmond, Va.)

Bounty land of 300 acres was granted August 29, 1810 to Jesse McKay, assignee of the heirs of Griffin Fauntleroy of Virginia. (Revolutionary War Pension and Bounty-Land Warrant Application Files. National Archives Microfilm Publication M804, roll 959.)

"Your petitioner Thomas Fauntleroy of the County of Fauquier and State of Virginia most respectfully represent that his brothers and sisters together with himself are the surviving heirs of their mother Eliza F Fauntleroy who was the only surviving heir of their uncle Griffin Fauntleroy who was killed as an officer in the war of the revolution in the battle which took place at Guilford Court house in North Carolina on the 15th of March 1781... [Griffin Fauntleroy] was a Captain for a long time in Colonel Geo. Baylor's Regiment of Cavalry & was finally killed at the above mentioned engagement as a Major of Cavalry to which he had been promoted but a short time before...." Thomas Fauntleroy, Henrico County, Virginia, April 16, 1835. (Virginia Governor's Office. Revolutionary War Rejected Claims, 1779-1860. Accession 41986, State government records collection, The Library of Virginia, Richmond, Va.)

Ferrill, Zephaniah

Zephaniah Ferrell, S35928. Zephaniah Ferrell enlisted in Alexandria, Virginia, in Captain Cadwallader Jones' company of the 3rd Regiment of light dragoons, and served to the end of the war. He was in the battles of Tarleton's defeat, Guilford, Camden, and Eutaw Springs. He received a furlough at Winchester, Virginia, and peace was shortly afterwards proclaimed. In 1818, Zephaniah Ferrell was living in Washington, D.C., age 57 years. (Revolutionary War Pension and Bounty-Land Warrant Application Files. National Archives Microfilm Publication M804, roll 967; also Dorman, John Frederick. 1958. Virginia Revolutionary Pension Applications, 36:69-70.)

Finney, Reuben

"It appears from the Size Roll of the 3d Troop that Reuben Finny was enlisted for the war in Baylor's Dragoons Sept 1781 & served the full term of his enlistment." William Barret, Captain, Baylor's Dragoons, December 3, 1785. (Virginia Governor's Office. Bounty Warrants, 1779-1860. Accession 41429, The Library of Virginia, Richmond, Va.)

Reuben Finney, W10024. In 1838, Elizabeth, the widow of Reuben Finney of Jessamine County, Kentucky, declared that Reuben was from Orange County, Virginia, and first enlisted for not less than two years, and then enlisted for the war. She said he was at the taking of Stony Point and in the battles of Brandywine and Monmouth. She stated that she and Reuben Finney were married at the house of her father in Orange County, in the fall of 1784, and that he died in Jessamine County, Kentucky, in 1813 or 1814. One of the records in the file is the Orange County marriage bond, dated 13 December 1784, between Reuben Finney and Elizabeth Bourn.

William Barrett, Captain in Baylor's Dragoons, affirmed Reuben Finny enlisted 1 September 1781 and served the full term of his enlistment. In 1843 Elizabeth Finney, widow, was living in Shelby County, Missouri. (Revolutionary War Pension and Bounty-Land Warrant Application Files. National Archives Microfilm Publication M804, roll 977; also Dorman, John Frederick. 1958. Virginia Revolutionary Pension Applications, 37:23-24.)

Fitzgerald, Bartlett Hawkins

Bartolet Hawkins, private, 5th troop. He was quartered with his troop in a barn near Tappan when the British attacked. He asked for quarters but a British officer standing nearby told the soldiers to stab him, whereupon he was stabbed three times and left for dead. This deposition was taken by William Livingston, Governor of New Jersey, and sent to Henry Laurens; see the letter dated Morris Town, 22 October 1778, in Papers of the Continental Congress. (David Griffith. Letter, 20 October 1778. Accession 22789. Personal papers collection. The Library of Virginia, Richmond, Va.)

"I do hereby certify that Bartlett Hawkins a Dragoon in the 3d Regiment of Light Dragoons was discharged the 18 Apl '82 & that his wages remain due to him since the 1st Dec. 1779." Ambrose Gordon, Lieutenant and Paymaster, 3d Regiment Light Dragoons. (Virginia Governor's Office. Bounty Warrants, 1779-1860. Accession 41429, The Library of Virginia, Richmond, Va.)

In a voucher written by Nathaniel Greene, near Bacon's Bridge, South Carolina, April 18, 1782, he stated that Major Richard Call certified that Bartlett Hawkins, private in the 3rd Regiment was incapable of discharging his duty from the wounds he had received, and was to be discharged. (Virginia Governor's Office. Bounty Warrants, 1779-1860. Accession 41429, The Library of Virginia, Richmond, Va.)

Bartlett H. Fitzgerald, S9562. Bartlett Hawkins, alias Fitzgerald, enlisted in the summer of 1777 in Fredericksburg, Virginia, under Captain William Barret, and served until 1780, when he was put under Captain Swan, and served under him until 1 May 1782, when he was discharged at Camp Bacon's Bridge near Dorchester, South Carolina. He was wounded in the attack at Tappan, and after a lengthy recovery, was in the battles of Cowpens, Eutaw Springs, and others. Bartlett H. Fitzgerald was born about 1759, in Orange County, Virginia. At the time of his enlistment, he was living in Orange County, and after the war lived first in

Albemarle County, and in 1833 stated that he had lived in Nelson County, Virginia, for the past twenty-six years. (Revolutionary War Pension and Bounty-Land Warrant Application Files. National Archives Microfilm Publication M804, roll 984; also Dorman, John Frederick. 1958. Virginia Revolutionary Pension Applications, 37:52-54.)

Fitzgerald, Benjamin Hawkins

"I do Certify Ben: Hawkins enlisted for the war in Colonel Baylor's Dragoons 1780 & has faithfully served the term of his enlistment." William Barret, August 27, 1784. (Virginia Governor's Office. Bounty Warrants, 1779-1860. Accession 41429, The Library of Virginia, Richmond, Va.)

Benjamin Hawkins Fitzgerald, S13308. Benjamin Hawkins Fitzgerald claimed that he is the Benjamin Hawkins who enlisted in 1777 in the 7th Virginia Regiment under Captain Garland Burnly and served two years. He was then at the battles of Monmouth and Stoney Point as a volunteer under General Wayne, and in 1780 he joined Colonel Washington's regiment of cavalry and fought at the battles of Cowpens, Camden, Guilford Court House, and Eutaw Springs. He was discharged at Lenud's Ferry on the Santee River in South Carolina. Bartlet Hawkins, also of Nelson County of 1818, affirmed Benjamin Hawkins' service. Benjamin Hawkins was born about 1761. He and his wife and family were living in Nelson County, Virginia, when he made statements in 1810, 1811, 1818, and 1820. (Revolutionary War Pension and Bounty-Land Warrant Application Files. National Archives Microfilm Publication M804, roll 984; also Dorman, John Frederick. 1958. Virginia Revolutionary Pension Applications, 37:54-55.)

Fitzhugh, Peregrine

Peregrine Fitzhugh, Cornet, Date of Commission June 16, 1778. Arrangement of Light Dragoons, 3^d Regiment, undated. (Revolutionary War Rolls, 1775-1783. National Archives Microfilm Publication M246. Roll 115, folder 13, 3^d Regiment Light Dragoons, 1779, item 3.)

Perry Fitzhugh, Cornet, June 16, 1778. A Return of Officers in the 3rd Regiment of Light Dragoons with the Dates of their Commissions, Sept. 18, 1777. (Revolutionary War Rolls, 1775-1783. National Archives Microfilm Publication M246. Roll 115, folder 13, 3^d Regiment Light Dragoons, 1779, item 6.)

Perrygrin Fitzhugh, Prisoner. Muster Roll of the 2nd Troop in the 3^d Regiment Light Dragoons in the Service of the United States commanded by Lieutenant Colonel William Washington for the Months of May, June, July August, September, October 1779. (Revolutionary War Rolls, 1775-1783. National Archives Microfilm Publication M246. Roll 115, folder 13, 3^d Regiment Light Dragoons, 1779, item 1.)

Perry Fitzhugh, mentioned on a roster of officers of 3rd Regiment. (University of Virginia. Alderman Library Special Collections. Accession 2257, Papers of the Baylor Family of Newmarket, Caroline County, Va, in part transcripts: [manuscript], 1653-1915. Box 4: the folder is labeled "1756, 1777-1781; Military Papers," item 21:, "ca. 1780 Continental Troops, roster of Officers, 1st & 3rd Regiments.")

Peregrine Fitzhugh, Cornet, cash paid to him by Colonel Palfrey, 4 August 1780; also cash paid to him by Mr. Pierce, 26 May 1780. (Miscellaneous Numbered Records [The Manuscript File] in the War Department Collection of Revolutionary War Records, 1775-1790's. National Archives Microfilm Publication M859. Manuscript 17584, "George Baylor's Regiment of Horse," undated.)

Peregrine Fitzhugh, W16989. In April 1837, Elizabeth C. Fitzhugh of Sodus, Wayne County, New York, the widow of Peregrine Fitzhugh, stated that he was a captain in the 3rd Regiment of Dragoons of the Virginia Continental Line commanded by Colonel George Baylor. He joined the army as a Lieutenant in 1778, was promoted to captain, and served to the end of the war. The Third Auditor's Office reports that Peregrine Fitzhugh was a Lieutenant of Dragoons from 1 June 1778 to 16 November 1781, and Captain from 16 November 1781 to 31 December 1782. Major General Weedon certified that Captain Peregrine Fitzhugh received a commission 5 May 1778 in Baylor's Light Dragoons and served to the end of the war.

William Fitzhugh, brother of Peregrine, stated that Peregrine was a captain in the 3rd Regiment of Light Dragoons. Peregrine Fitzhugh was the son of Colonel William Fitzhugh, and married Elizabeth C. Chew in the fall of 1781, in Maryland, while he was still in service. He was captured at the massacre in Tappan, and was held at Flatbush on Long Island. He died in November 1811, in Sodus, Wayne County, New York. (Revolutionary War Pension and Bounty-Land Warrant Application Files. National

Archives Microfilm Publication M804, roll 985; also Dorman, John Frederick. 1958. Virginia Revolutionary Pension Applications, 37:59-61.)

Fitzhugh, William

"Lieutenant Fitzburgh" for goods issued to him, 27 November 1779. (Miscellaneous Numbered Records [The Manuscript File] in the War Department Collection of Revolutionary War Records, 1775-1790's. National Archives Microfilm Publication M859. Manuscript 17584, "George Baylor's Regiment of Horse," undated.)

William Fitzhugh, mentioned on a roster of officers of the 3rd Regiment. (University of Virginia. Alderman Library Special Collections. Accession 2257, Papers of the Baylor Family of Newmarket, Caroline County, Va, in part transcripts: [manuscript], 1653-1915. Box 4: the folder is labeled "1756, 1777-1781; Military Papers," item 21: "ca. 1780 Continental Troops, roster of Officers, 1st & 3rd Regiments.")

William Fitzhugh, Lieutenant. On 27 September 1783, G. Weedon certified that William Fitzhugh was appointed an officer in Baylor's Light Dragoons in 1781, and was still in service. (Miscellaneous Numbered Records [The Manuscript File] in the War Department Collection of Revolutionary War Records, 1775-1790's. National Archives Microfilm Publication M859. Manuscript 18006, dated 27 September 1783.)

William Fitzhugh. On 18 April 1783, Colonel George Baylor certified that William Fitzhugh was appointed a Cornet in October 1781 in the 3rd Regiment of Light Dragoons, with the recommendation of Governor Nelson of Virginia. (Miscellaneous Numbered Records [The Manuscript File] in the War Department Collection of Revolutionary War Records, 1775-1790's. National Archives Microfilm Publication M859. Manuscript 18052, dated 18 April 1783.)

William Fitzhugh, Lieutenant, 1st Light Dragoons. (Miscellaneous Numbered Records [The Manuscript File] in the War Department Collection of Revolutionary War Records, 1775-1790's. National Archives Microfilm Publication M859. Manuscript 17513, "The United States in Account with Lieut^t Wm Fitzhugh of the 1st Reg Light Dragoons, Southern Army, for subsistence from the 1st of Jany to the 20th Feby 1783," undated. Also manuscripts 17514, dated 7 September 1782, and 17516, dated 7 September 1784.)

"I certify that William Fitzhugh Esq was appointed a Cornet in Baylor's Regiment L Dragoons in the year 1781, and continued a subaltern therein to the end of the war." Lt. Col. Ed Carrington, February 5, 1784. (Virginia Governor's Office. Bounty Warrants, 1779-1860. Accession 41429, The Library of Virginia, Richmond, Va.)

William Fitzhugh, S17948. William Fitzhugh was a Cornet of the 3rd Virginia Regiment commanded by Colonel Washington, from 1 January 1782 to 1 March 1782, and a Lieutenant from 1 March 1782 to 13 November 1783. In May 1829 he was living in Groveland, Livingston County, New York, and he died there in December 1839. (Revolutionary War Pension and Bounty-Land Warrant Application Files. National Archives Microfilm Publication M804, roll 985; also Dorman, John Frederick. 1958. Virginia Revolutionary Pension Applications, 37:61-62.)

Fitzpatrick, John

John Fitzpatrick signed a return of supplies as Quarter Master for the 3rd Regiment Light Dragoons, February 6, 1778. (University of Virginia. Alderman Library Special Collections. Accession 2257, Papers of the Baylor Family of Newmarket, Caroline County, Va, in part transcripts: [manuscript], 1653-1915. Box 4: the folder is labeled "1756, 1777-1781; Military Papers," item 10: "1778 Feb 6 Continental Troops, Return of Arms etc. in store; [3rd] Regiment Light Dragoons.")

William Madison of Madison County, Virginia, stated in 1836 that John Fitzpatrick acted as a recruitment officer for Baylor's Regiment in 1780, and that John Fitpatrick died in Philadelphia, leaving three sons. Humphrey Major, also of Madison County, saw John Fitzpatrick in 1781 in Yorktown, at which time he was an officer in Col. Baylor's Regiment, and that he was highly spoken of as an officer. William Troyman claimed that John Fitzpatrick lived in Culpeper County, he saw him recruiting in Orange County during the war. (Virginia Governor's Office. Bounty Warrants, 1779-1860. Accession 41429, The Library of Virginia, Richmond, Va.)

Fletcher, James

"I do certify that I enlisted James Fletcher as a private in the third Regiment of Light Dragoons commanded by Colonel George

Baylor in the year 1777 and that the enlistment was for three years or during the war and from circumstances I have no hesitation in saying that he served during the war." Walker Baylor, formerly a Captain in the 3rd Regiment of Light Dragoons, September 16, 1819. (Virginia Governor's Office. Bounty Warrants, 1779-1860. Accession 41429, The Library of Virginia, Richmond, Va.)

James Fletcher, S35941. James Fletcher enlisted in Caroline County, Virginia, in 1777 in the 3rd Regiment commanded by George Baylor. He served until 1782, when he was discharged in Richmond, Virginia, and was in the battles of Cowpens, Guilford, and Eutaw Springs. In September of 1819 he claimed to have enlisted in Captain Parsons' company, but in June of 1820, he stated that it was Captain Walker Baylor's company. He was born about 1763, and was living in Fayette County, Kentucky when he made his statements. (Revolutionary War Pension and Bounty-Land Warrant Application Files. National Archives Microfilm Publication M804, roll 989; also Dorman, John Frederick. 1958. Virginia Revolutionary Pension Applications, 38:18.)

Fortune, John

John Fortune, W7309. John Fortune enlisted in Amherst County, Virginia, in Captain Chiswell Barrett's company in Colonel Baylor's Regiment and served until discharged in Maryland. William Lockhart stated that John Fortune was a private in the 4th troop of William Washington's cavalry. John Fortune was born about 1763, and married Nancy Henderson in Albemarle County, Virginia, on 1 November 1785. In January 1834 they were living in Rockbridge County, Virginia, and in 1839 his widow was living in Kanawha County, West Virginia. John Fortune died 16 March 1834. (Revolutionary War Pension and Bounty-Land Warrant Application Files. National Archives Microfilm Publication M804, roll 1005; also Dorman, John Frederick. 1958. Virginia Revolutionary Pension Applications, 39:26-27.)

Foster, Cosbey

Cosbey Foster, Private. Muster Roll of the 2nd Troop in the 3^{d} Regiment Light Dragoons in the Service of the United States commanded by Lieutenant Colonel William Washington for the Months of May, June, July August, September, October 1779. (Revolutionary War Rolls, 1775-1783. National Archives

Microfilm Publication M246. Roll 115, folder 13, 3^d Regiment Light Dragoons, 1779, item 1.)

Cosby Foster was issued a cap at Petersburg, Virginia on April 3, 1782. (University of Virginia. Alderman Library Special Collections. Accession 2257, Papers of the Baylor Family of Newmarket, Caroline County, Va, in part transcripts: [manuscript], 1653-1915. Box 4: the folder is labeled "Military Papers, 1782, 1814, & n.d.," item 6: "1782 April 3, Continental Troops Clothing & Accoutrement Issue Slip of 3rd Regiment Lt. Dragoons by Lydnor [Sydnor] Cosby.")

"I do Certify that Cosby Foster enlisted himself July 1776 to serve during the War and has continued to Serve until he was disabled by a wound." William Barret, Captain, Baylor's Light Dragoons, July 15, 1783. (Virginia Governor's Office. Bounty Warrants, 1779-1860. Accession 41429, The Library of Virginia, Richmond, Va.)

Cosby Foster, W3010. In December 1840, Susan Foster of Madison County, Kentucky, the widow of Cosby Foster, stated that he was a private in Colonel Washington's regiment, under an officer named Merryweather, and served five years. Cosby Foster and Susan Duke were married in September 1791 in Louisa County, Virginia, where they resided for several years after the war. They next lived in Tennessee for three years, and then moved to Madison County, Kentucky, where they lived until his death on 17 January 1793.

Anderson Foster, the son of Cosby Foster, claimed his father was wounded in South Carolina and lay confined almost a year before he could return to Virginia. A certificate for £65.0.0, dated 28 March 1783, from the state of Virginia, granted Cosby Foster the balance of his full pay and was delivered to John Conner. On 17 March 1784, warrant 2767, for 200 acres, was issued by Virginia to Cosby Foster, private in the Continental Line. (Revolutionary War Pension and Bounty-Land Warrant Application Files. National Archives Microfilm Publication M804, roll 1006; also Dorman, John Frederick. 1958. Virginia Revolutionary Pension Applications, 39:34-35.)

Franklin, John (of Virginia)

John Franklin, S39541. John Franklin enlisted in South Carolina, in Captain Churchill Jones' company in Colonel George Baylor's regiment and served until he was discharged at Aquia,

Virginia. He was in the battles of Camden, Ninety-Six, Cowpens, and was wounded at Eutaw. On 1 May 1820, Churchill Jones verified that John Franklin was a soldier in the 3rd Regiment of Light Dragoons commanded by Colonel George Baylor, was appointed a corporal in June 1781, and served to the end of the war. John Franklin was born about 1748, and his wife's name was Elizabeth. In May of 1818 they were living in Stafford County, Virginia, and in 1820, they were in Fauquier County, Virginia. (Revolutionary War Pension and Bounty-Land Warrant Application Files. National Archives Microfilm Publication M804, roll 1017; also Dorman, John Frederick. 1958. Virginia Revolutionary Pension Applications, 40:13-14.)

Franklin, John (of Warren County, Kentucky)
"It appears from the Size Roll of 2d Troop that Jno Franklin enlisted for the war Apl. 81 in 3 Regiment LD & Con^d until the Mutiny May 83." William Barret, Baylor's Dragoons, April 28, 1785. (Virginia Governor's Office. Bounty Warrants, 1779-1860. Accession 41429, The Library of Virginia, Richmond, Va.)

Jno. Franklin. On 30 April 1785, a certificate was issued by Virginia to John Franklin, soldier of cavalry, Continental Line, for £22.10 and was delivered to William Reynolds. On 21 June 1785, warrant 3901 for 200 acres, due John Franklin, private on the Continental Line, was issued by Virginia to William Reynolds. On 5 December 1785, John Franklin assigned full balance of his pay and bounty land to Edward Valentine. (Dorman, John Frederick. 1958. Virginia Revolutionary Pension Applications, 38:10.)

John Franklin, S35952. John Franklin enlisted 10 August 1776 in Colonel William Washington's Regiment, in the 2nd troop commanded by Captain William Barret. He served until 25 June 1782, was discharged by Captain Robert Morrow at Winchester, Virginia, and gave his discharge to Edward Valentine of Richmond. He was in the battles of Cowpens, Guilford, Camden and Eutaw Springs, where he was wounded in both legs. John Franklin was born in December 1748. In 1818 and 1821 he was living with his wife and several children in Warren County, Kentucky. (Revolutionary War Pension and Bounty-Land Warrant Application Files. National Archives Microfilm Publication M804, roll 1017; also Dorman, John Frederick. 1958. Virginia Revolutionary Pension Applications, 40:13.)

Frey or Fry, John

John Frey, R3819. On 11 September 1843, Benjamin Fry of Stokes County, North Carolina, declared that his father, John Fry, was born in Albemarle County, Virginia, and first enlisted in that county for eighteen months under Captain Lewis. When he was discharged, he returned home and enlisted, this time for three years in Colonel Washington's light horse. John Frey remained in Stokes County after the war, married, and was about 83 years old when he died in March 1825. (Revolutionary War Pension and Bounty-Land Warrant Application Files. National Archives Microfilm Publication M804, roll 1028; also Dorman, John Frederick. 1958. Virginia Revolutionary Pension Applications, 40:70-71.)

Fugler, William

William Fugler first enlisted March 15, 1777 for three years under Captain Abraham Crump, and was discharged December 22, 1779 at Philadelphia. (Virginia Governor's Office. Bounty Warrants, 1779-1860. Accession 41429, The Library of Virginia, Richmond, Va.)

"I do Certify that William Fugler enlisted as Soldier in the 3rd Regiment Dragoons 23rd of December 1779 for the war and is now on furlough." Robert Morrow, undated. (Virginia Governor's Office. Bounty Warrants, 1779-1860. Accession 41429, The Library of Virginia, Richmond, Va.)

William Fugler was issued a shirt and a cap at Petersburg, Virginia on April 3, 1782. (University of Virginia. Alderman Library Special Collections. Accession 2257, Papers of the Baylor Family of Newmarket, Caroline County, Va, in part transcripts: [manuscript], 1653-1915. Box 4: the folder is labeled "Military Papers, 1782, 1814, & n.d.," item 6: "1782 April 3, Continental Troops Clothing & Accoutrement Issue Slip of 3rd Regiment Lt. Dragoons by Lydnor [Sydnor] Cosby.")

Gale, John

John Gale, Captain, goods issued to him, 27 November 1779. (Miscellaneous Numbered Records [The Manuscript File] in the War Department Collection of Revolutionary War Records, 1775-1790's. National Archives Microfilm Publication M859. Manuscript 17584, "George Baylor's Regiment of Horse," undated.)

Garnett, Benjamin

Ben Garnett, Lt. Officer of the Day signed a Morning Report, April 23, 1782. (University of Virginia. Alderman Library Special Collections. Accession 2257, Papers of the Baylor Family of Newmarket, Caroline County, Va, in part transcripts: [manuscript], 1653-1915. Box 4: the folder is labeled "Military Papers, 1782, 1814, & n.d.," item 9: "1782 April 23, Continental Troops, morning reports, 3rd Regiment Light Dragoons signed by Ben Ganett [Garnett] Lt. Officer of the Day.")

Benjamin Garnett, Lieutenant; pay due him as Cornet from 20 March 1781 to 1 November 1781; pay due him as Lieutenant from 1 November 1781 to 1 January 1782; subsistence due him from 20 March 1781 to 1 January 1782; pay due him as Quartermaster from 15 October 1781 to 1 January 1782; pay due him as Lieutenant from 1 January 1782 to 1 Jan 1783, at which time he was discharged. (Miscellaneous Numbered Records [The Manuscript File] in the War Department Collection of Revolutionary War Records, 1775-1790's. National Archives Microfilm Publication M859. Manuscript 17649, "The United States in Account with Lieut. Benjamin Garnett of Colonel Baylor's Dragoons," dated 30 September 1785. Also Manuscript 17666, dated 30 September 1785)

Benjamin Garnett, BLWt 328-200. In March 1806, James A. Bayard wrote to the Virginia Senate asking "Will you have the goodness to inform me whether Benjamin Garnett who served during the war as a Lieutenant in the 3rd Regiment Light Dragoons had any land rights under the provision made by Congress in favor of the officers of the revolutionary army. Garnett is dead and the inquiry is made in behalf of a daughter he left...." In February 1807, Elizabeth Bassett stated that Captain Benjamin Garnett died some years prior in Queen Anne's County, Maryland, leaving only a daughter, Ann Garnett, who was currently living with her. (Revolutionary War Pension and Bounty-Land Warrant Application Files. National Archives Microfilm Publication M804, roll 1050.)

Garrett, John

"I do Certify that John Garrett enlisted for three years in Baylor's Dragoons Dec. 26th 1777 & Serv'd the full Term of his Enlistment." William Barret, Captain, undated. (Virginia Governor's Office. Bounty Warrants, 1779-1860. Accession 41429, The Library of Virginia, Richmond, Va.)

Gatewood, Grafton

Settlement of account with Grafton Gatewood for pay due him from 1 May 1780 to 28 August 1782; also received clothing from Lieutenant Ambrose Gordon of the 3rd Regiment. (Miscellaneous Numbered Records [The Manuscript File] in the War Department Collection of Revolutionary War Records, 1775-1790's. National Archives Microfilm Publication M859. Manuscript 17544.)

Gerard, John

John Gerard, S42740. John Gerard entered service at Pittsburgh, Pennsylvania in 1775 as private under Captain John Nevil, for six months. He reenlisted under Captain Andrew Wagoner and was attached to the 12th Virginia Regiment, and was in the battles of Brandywine and Germantown, and in December 1777, while at Valley Forge, he reenlisted under Cornet Presley Thornton, in the 5th troop in the 3rd Virginia Regiment commanded by Colonel Baylor. He was with the regiment during the massacre at Tappan, was taken prisoner and kept at the Sugar House prison. When exchanged, he rejoined the light dragoons and continued until discharged in South Carolina on 26 December 1780. In both 1819 and 1821, John Gerard claimed to be age 63. In 1819 he was living in Miami County, Ohio, and in 1821 he was in Hamilton County, Ohio. (Revolutionary War Pension and Bounty-Land Warrant Application Files. National Archives Microfilm Publication M804, roll 1063; also Dorman, John Frederick. 1958. Virginia Revolutionary Pension Applications, 43:8-10.)

Gibson, Thomas

Thomas Gibson, S39573. Thomas Gibson enlisted as a private in June or July of 1776, with Cornet John Watts, for two years in Colonel Theodorick Bland's regiment. He served until December 1778 when they were marched to Winchester, Virginia, and discharged. He next enlisted with Captain Fauntleroy under Colonel William Washington, and was in the battles of Cowpens, Guilford, where he broke one of his legs, and Eutaw Springs, where he was wounded in the head. In 1822, Thomas Gibson stated he was age 72, and was living in Pittsylvania County, Virginia. (Revolutionary War Pension and Bounty-Land Warrant Application Files. National Archives Microfilm Publication M804, roll 1067;

also Dorman, John Frederick. 1958. Virginia Revolutionary Pension Applications, 43:54-55.)

Glason or Glayson or Gleason, Patrick

"I do Certify that Patrick Glayson enlisted himself in 3 Regiment L Dragoons May 1780 to serve the war." William Barret, Captain, November 15, 1783. (Virginia Governor's Office. Bounty Warrants, 1779-1860. Accession 41429, The Library of Virginia, Richmond, Va.)

Patrick Glason or Gleason, S39590. Patrick Glason belonged to Captain Thomas Hamilton's company of infantry of the 1st Virginia Regiment, starting in 1777, and served for three years. In 1780 he enlisted in the 5th troop of cavalry of the 3rd Regiment of Light Dragoons, and served to the end of the war. He was wounded in his right hand during the battle at Cowpens. Patrick Gleason was born about 1752, and lived in Caroline County, Virginia after the war, until about 1784, when he moved to King and Queen County. In September 1820, he was still living in King and Queen County, Virginia, with his wife, a granddaughter, and a poor child. (Revolutionary War Pension and Bounty-Land Warrant Application Files. National Archives Microfilm Publication M804, roll 1080; also Dorman, John Frederick. 1958. Virginia Revolutionary Pension Applications, 44:41-42.)

Goatley, John

John Goatly was issued a cap at Petersburg, Virginia on April 3, 1782. (University of Virginia. Alderman Library Special Collections. Accession 2257, Papers of the Baylor Family of Newmarket, Caroline County, Va, in part transcripts: [manuscript], 1653-1915. Box 4: the folder is labeled "Military Papers, 1782, 1814, & n.d.," item 6: "1782 April 3, Continental Troops Clothing & Accoutrement Issue Slip of 3rd Regiment Lt. Dragoons by Lydnor [Sydnor] Cosby.")

"John Goatley a Soldier in the 3d Regiment Light Dragoons presenting a Certificate from a Continental Doctor June 17th 1782 that he was unfit for Service has Permission to remain in Virginia until fit for Service then to Join the Regiment as soon as Possible." Robert Morrow, Captain 3rd Regiment, Richmond, June 17, 1782. "I do Certify that I enlisted John Goatley December 24 1779 for the war." William Barrett, July 30, 1784. (Virginia Governor's Office.

Bounty Warrants, 1779-1860. Accession 41429, The Library of Virginia, Richmond, Va.)

John Goatley, S35972. John Goatley enlisted under Captain John Alison in the 3rd Virginia Regiment of Colonel Gibson, at Alexandria, Virginia, in 1776. He served for almost three years, and when his time had almost expired, he enlisted under Captain Morrow under Colonel William Washington until the end of the war. In Hanover County, Virginia, he was taken prisoner by the British, and was sent to Richmond, Virginia, where he continued until the war ended.

John Goatley was born about 1752, and was living in Breckenridge County, Kentucky, in 1818 and 1828. (Revolutionary War Pension and Bounty-Land Warrant Application Files. National Archives Microfilm Publication M804, roll 1084; also Dorman, John Frederick. 1958. Virginia Revolutionary Pension Applications, 44:64-65.)

Gordon, Ambrose

Ambrose Gordon, mentioned on a roster of officers of 3rd Regiment. (University of Virginia. Alderman Library Special Collections. Accession 2257, Papers of the Baylor Family of Newmarket, Caroline County, Va, in part transcripts: [manuscript], 1653-1915. Box 4: the folder is labeled "1756, 1777-1781; Military Papers," item 21: "ca. 1780 Continental Troops, roster of Officers, 1st & 3rd Regiments.")

Ambrose Gordon, Lieutenant, Paymaster 3rd regiment; cash paid by Mr. Clay, 14 April 1781. (Miscellaneous Numbered Records [The Manuscript File] in the War Department Collection of Revolutionary War Records, 1775-1790's. National Archives Microfilm Publication M859. Manuscript 17584, "George Baylor's Regiment of Horse," undated.)

Lieutenant Gordon was "recruiting." (University of Virginia. Alderman Library Special Collections. Accession 2257, Papers of the Baylor Family of Newmarket, Caroline County, Va, in part transcripts: [manuscript], 1653-1915. Box 4: the folder is labeled "Military Papers, 1782, 1814, & n.d.," item 16: "1782 July 8, Continental Troops, Weekly return, 3 & 4th Regiments, Lt. Dragoons, commanded by Col. George Baylor.")

"I do Certify that Lieut. Ambrose Gordon was appointed an officer in 3 Regiment L Dragoons by Lt. Colonel Washington & has serv'd to the end of the War." William Barret, Captain, January 21,

1784. (Virginia Governor's Office. Bounty Warrants, 1779-1860. Accession 41429, The Library of Virginia, Richmond, Va.)

Ambrose Gordon, pay as Lieutenant and Paymaster from 1 January to 10 November 1782; pay as Lieutenant and Adjutant from 11 November to 31 December 1782; pay as Lieutenant and Adjutant from 1 January to 15 November 1783. (Miscellaneous Numbered Records [The Manuscript File] in the War Department Collection of Revolutionary War Records, 1775-1790's. National Archives Microfilm Publication M859. Manuscript 17523, "The United States in Account with Lieut^t Ambrose Gordon," dated 26 August 1785, and Manuscript 17525, dated 2 June 1784.)

Ambrose or Ambrus Gordon, BLWt 539-200. Colonel George Mathews of the 3rd Virginia Regiment certified that Ambrus Gordon entered service in January 1777 as a lieutenant of cavalry, and served for the war. (Revolutionary War Pension and Bounty-Land Warrant Application Files. National Archives Microfilm Publication M804, roll 1096; also Dorman, John Frederick. 1958. Virginia Revolutionary Pension Applications, 45:79.)

Grady, John

John Grady was issued a cloak and two curry combs at Petersburg, Virginia on April 3, 1782. (University of Virginia. Alderman Library Special Collections. Accession 2257, Papers of the Baylor Family of Newmarket, Caroline County, Va, in part transcripts: [manuscript], 1653-1915. Box 4: the folder is labeled "Military Papers, 1782, 1814, & n.d.," item 6: "1782 April 3, Continental Troops Clothing & Accoutrement Issue Slip of 3rd Regiment Lt. Dragoons by Lydnor [Sydnor] Cosby.")

Gray, Daniel

Daniel Gray, Private. Muster Roll of the 2nd Troop in the 3^d Regiment Light Dragoons in the Service of the United States commanded by Lieutenant Colonel William Washington for the Months of May, June, July August, September, October 1779. (Revolutionary War Rolls, 1775-1783. National Archives Microfilm Publication M246. Roll 115, folder 13, 3^d Regiment Light Dragoons, 1779, item 1.)

Green, Charles

Charles Green had sword, belt, cartridge box; "Pistol Broke in Store." Return, dated 1 March 1778, of arms and accouterments in the Third Troop belonging to Colonel George Baylor's Regiment of Light Dragoons. (Virginia Office of the Quartermaster General, Fredericksburg. Returns of Colonel George Baylor's Regiment, 1778-1779. Accession 22547, The Library of Virginia, Richmond, Va.)

Walker Baylor, Captain in the third Virginia Continental Regiment of Light Dragoons, certified that Charles Green was a soldier in the Regiment, was enlisted in the year 1777, and was honorably discharged. Voucher dated June 11, 1814. (Virginia Governor's Office. Bounty Warrants, 1779-1860. Accession 41429, The Library of Virginia, Richmond, Va.)

"I Charles Green of the County of Scott & State of Kentucky do on oath declare that I in the year 1777 enlisted as a soldier in Capt. Churchill Jones' company of Light Dragoons in the third Virginia Regiment of Light Dragoons upon Continental establishment in the Revolutionary war to serve for three years. In a few months after I enlisted I was appointed a Sergeant in the same company. I continued to serve as a Sergeant until the expiration of the said three years when I was honorably discharged but which discharge I have now lost & can not find it, and that I have never received my bounty land Warrant... ." Charles Green, July 15, 1818. (Virginia Governor's Office. Bounty Warrants, 1779-1860. Accession 41429, The Library of Virginia, Richmond, Va.)

Charles Green, S35991. Charles Green enlisted on 4 February 1777 in Captain Churchill Jones' company in the 3rd Regiment commanded by Colonel George Baylor. He served three years and was discharged by Colonel William Washington at Cross Creek, North Carolina. (Revolutionary War Pension and Bounty-Land Warrant Application Files. National Archives Microfilm Publication M804, roll 1118; also Dorman, John Frederick. 1958. Virginia Revolutionary Pension Applications, 46:83.)

Green, Jesse

Jessey Green, Private, enlisted June 2, 1777, on command. Muster Roll of the 2nd Troop in the 3d Regiment Light Dragoons in the Service of the United States commanded by Lieutenant Colonel William Washington for the Months of May, June, July August, September, October 1779. (Revolutionary War Rolls, 1775-1783. National Archives Microfilm Publication M246. Roll 115, folder 13, 3d Regiment Light Dragoons, 1779, item 1.)

"Jesse Green soldier in the 3d Regiment of Light Dragoons having served faithfully three years is honorably Discharg'd." "I do hereby Certify that the above is a true Copy of Jesse Green's Discharge given him by Colonel Washington." Lieutenant L. Cannon, Richmond, May 31, 1783. (Virginia Governor's Office. Bounty Warrants, 1779-1860. Accession 41429, The Library of Virginia, Richmond, Va.)

Green, John

John Green was "sick absent." (University of Virginia. Alderman Library Special Collections. Accession 2257, Papers of the Baylor Family of Newmarket, Caroline County, Va, in part transcripts: [manuscript], 1653-1915. Box 4: the folder is labeled "1756, 1777-1781; Military Papers," item 14: "A list of the men's names absent belonging to Colonel Baylor's Regiment, Fredericksburg, June 27, 1778.")

Gresham, Lieutenant

John Bryant stated that he enlisted 10 March 1777 as a private under Lieutenant Gresham of the light dragoons commanded by Colonel George Baylor for three years. (Revolutionary War Pension and Bounty-Land Warrant Application Files. National Archives Microfilm Publication M804, roll 391; also Dorman, John Frederick. 1958. Virginia Revolutionary Pension Applications, 12:29.)

Griffin, Reuben

Reuben Griffin, Private. Muster Roll of the 2nd Troop in the 3^d Regiment Light Dragoons in the Service of the United States commanded by Lieutenant Colonel William Washington for the Months of May, June, July August, September, October 1779. (Revolutionary War Rolls, 1775-1783. National Archives Microfilm Publication M246. Roll 115, folder 13, 3^d Regiment Light Dragoons, 1779, item 1.)

"I do hereby Certify that Reuben Griffin served three years in the 3 Regiment of Light Dragoons & was Discharged in October 1781." George Baylor, Col. 1st Regiment Light Dragoons, June 26, 1783. (Virginia Governor's Office. Bounty Warrants, 1779-1860. Accession 41429, The Library of Virginia, Richmond, Va.)

Reuben Griffin, S35993. Reuben Griffin, at the age of 17 or 18, enlisted at Fredericksburg, Virginia, about February 1777, in the 3rd Virginia Regiment of Light Dragoons, commanded by Colonel George Baylor, and afterward by Colonel William Washington. He was with the regiment at the attack in Tappan, and was at the battles of Monmouth, Guilford, Cowpens, and Eutaw Springs.

In both 1819 and 1821 he stated that he was about 60 years old. In 1819, he was of Louisville, Kentucky, and in 1821, was in Jefferson County, Kentucky. (Revolutionary War Pension and Bounty-Land Warrant Application Files. National Archives Microfilm Publication M804, roll 1132; also Dorman, John Frederick. 1958. Virginia Revolutionary Pension Applications, 47:82.)

In September 1820, Reuben Griffin was of Franklin County, Kentucky. (under William Woolfolk. Virginia Governor's Office. Bounty Warrants, 1779-1860. Accession 41429, The Library of Virginia, Richmond, Va.)

Griffin, Sherrod

Sherrod Griffin, S13219. Sherrod Griffin started his Revolutionary service under Major Dunn, by guarding the prisoners who had been taken at Cowpens, taking them from Amherst County, Virginia to Winchester, Virginia. Around February 1781 he was in the militia raised in Amherst County. He enlisted in June 1781 in the 3rd Regiment of light horse, and was under Captains John Stith, Robert Morrow, Henry Bell and Lieutenant Charles Yarborough. While the regiment was in Culpeper County, Virginia, he was appointed a sergeant, and continued in service almost two years, receiving his discharge in November 1782, at Button Hall, about 30 miles from Charleston, South Carolina. Sherrod Griffin was born in Amherst County, Virginia, 29 November 1759, and was living in Amherst County when he enlisted. In 1832, he was living in Green County, Kentucky. (Revolutionary War Pension and Bounty-Land Warrant Application Files. National Archives Microfilm Publication M804, roll 1132; also Dorman, John Frederick. 1958. Virginia Revolutionary Pension Applications, 47:82-83.)

Griffith, David

"I do Certify that the Rev'd David Griffith did actually server as Surgeon to the 3d Virginia Regiment of Continental Troops from the 28th day of February 1776 to the 18th day of

March 1779." G. Weedon, Brigadier-General, 25 September 1780. (Virginia Governor's Office. Bounty Warrants, 1779-1860. Accession 41429, The Library of Virginia, Richmond, Va.)

Guillams or Gwelliams, William

"This is to Certify that William Gwelliams enlisted in the 3d Regiment Light Dragoons to Serve during the war." William Barret, undated. (Virginia Governor's Office. Bounty Warrants, 1779-1860. Accession 41429, The Library of Virginia, Richmond, Va.)

William Guillams, Private; pay due him for 1782 and 1783. (Miscellaneous Numbered Records [The Manuscript File] in the War Department Collection of Revolutionary War Records, 1775-1790's. National Archives Microfilm Publication M859. Manuscript 17646, "The United States in Acc^t with William Guillams priv^t 3rd & 1st Regiment light Dragoons," dated 5 February 1794.)

Gulley, Richard

"I do Certify that Richard Gulley enlisted for three years in Colonel Baylor's Regiment Dragoons March 1778 & served the full term of his enlistment." William Barret, August 3, 1786. (Virginia Governor's Office. Bounty Warrants, 1779-1860. Accession 41429, The Library of Virginia, Richmond, Va.)

Richard Gulley, S38781. Richard Gulley enlisted in March 1778 under Captain William Barret in the 3rd Regiment of Dragoons, and served two years. He was at the massacre at Tappan, and was at the battle of Stony Point, and in several other skirmishes, and was taken prisoner near Georgetown, South Carolina. He was a prisoner in Charleston about one year before escaping. Richard Gulley was born 29 October 1756. He was in Elbert County, Georgia, in 1819, and in Pendleton District, South Carolina in March 1821. He then moved back to Elbert County, and was there in March 1828. (Revolutionary War Pension and Bounty-Land Warrant Application Files. National Archives Microfilm Publication M804, roll 1145; also Dorman, John Frederick. 1958. Virginia Revolutionary Pension Applications, 48:53-54.)

Gunnell, John

"I do Certify that Jno Gunnell of 3 Troop Enlisted for the war May 20th, 80 in Baylor's Dragoons & is entitled to the Bounty

Land." William Barret, Baylor's Dragoons, December 16, 1784. (Virginia Governor's Office. Bounty Warrants, 1779-1860. Accession 41429, The Library of Virginia, Richmond, Va.)

John Gunnell, S40062. John Gunnell enlisted in Petersburg, Virginia, in 1780, with Captain John Linton, in a regiment commanded by Lt. Colonel Washington. He was at the battles of Eutaw Springs, and Cowpens, where he was wounded in the sword arm, and he served to the end of the war. John Gunnell was born about 1758, and was living with his family in Bedford County, Pennsylvania in 1818, and 1821, when he made his statements. He declared in March 1827 that he had moved to Westmoreland County, Pennsylvania. (Revolutionary War Pension and Bounty-Land Warrant Application Files. National Archives Microfilm Publication M804, roll 1146; also Dorman, John Frederick. 1958. Virginia Revolutionary Pension Applications, 48:62-63.)

Hale, Samuel

Samuel Hale, Trumpet or Farrier, enlisted March 2, 1777. Muster Roll of the 2nd Troop in the 3^{d} Regiment Light Dragoons in the Service of the United States commanded by Lieutenant Colonel William Washington for the Months of May, June, July August, September, October 1779. (Revolutionary War Rolls, 1775-1783. National Archives Microfilm Publication M246. Roll 115, folder 13, 3^{d} Regiment Light Dragoons, 1779, item 1.)

Haley, George (see George Sway)

Hambrick or Hamrick, David

"David Hambrick, Corporal having served with Fidelity Three years in the 3d Regiment of Light Dragoons Is Hereby Discharged." William Washington, Lt. Col., July 7, 1780. (Virginia Governor's Office. Bounty Warrants, 1779-1860. Accession 41429, The Library of Virginia, Richmond, Va.)

David Hamrick, W5292. David Hamrick was living in Clinton County, Ohio in November 1832, a resident of Clark Township, aged 72 years. He was born 22 May 1760 in Fauquier County, Virginia. In 1777 while living in Fauquier County, he enlisted with Edward Connor, and served in 3rd Regiment of Light Dragoons for three years. Major Call was the field officer. The regiment went from Fredericksburg through Maryland, Pennsylvania, then through New Jersey. He was at battle of

Monmouth Court House then followed the British to Sandy Hook. The regiment then moved to West Point, to Philadelphia, then to Charleston, South Carolina, to Camden, then through North Carolina to Halifax where he was discharged in the summer of 1780, his discharge given by Col. Wm. Washington. He was married in February 1788 in Halifax County, Virginia, to Lettice (no last name given), and then moved to Pittsylvania County until 1816, when they moved to Ohio. David Hamrick died 12 July 1839. (Revolutionary War Pension and Bounty-Land Warrant Application Files. National Archives Microfilm Publication M804, roll 1177.)

Hambright, Frederick

Frederick Hambright had pistol and belt, and is "on command." Return, dated 1 March 1778, of arms and accouterments in the Third Troop belonging to Colonel George Baylor's Regiment of Light Dragoons. (Virginia Office of the Quartermaster General, Fredericksburg. Returns of Colonel George Baylor's Regiment, 1778-1779. Accession 22547, The Library of Virginia, Richmond, Va.)

Frederick Hambright, a Sergeant in Baylor's Dragoons, was discharged by Colonel Parker in Augusta, Georgia. The discharge is dated 18 January 1780 at Fort Farley, with notes regarding Frederick Hambright's pay while a prisoner. (Miscellaneous Numbered Records [The Manuscript File] in the War Department Collection of Revolutionary War Records, 1775-1790's. National Archives Microfilm Publication M859. Manuscript 20293, dated 14 December 1792.)

Hamilton, William

William Hamilton had "Belt; sword Broke in the Store Pistol given to John Finney in C Bland's Regiment." Return, dated 1 March 1778, of arms and accouterments in the Third Troop belonging to Colonel George Baylor's Regiment of Light Dragoons. (Virginia Office of the Quartermaster General, Fredericksburg. Returns of Colonel George Baylor's Regiment, 1778-1779. Accession 22547, The Library of Virginia, Richmond, Va.)

William Hamilton. On 11 March 1786, Captain William Parsons certified that William Hamilton enlisted in the Continental Cavalry 21 May 1777 and served to the end of the war. (Miscellaneous Numbered Records [The Manuscript File] in the War Department Collection of Revolutionary War Records, 1775-

1790's. National Archives Microfilm Publication M859. Manuscript 17990, dated 11 March 1786.)

Hampton, John

"It appears from the Size Roll of 1st Troop that Jno Hampton Enlisted for the war in Colonel Baylor's Dragoons April 1781 & Served until the mutiny 10th May 83." William Barret, Baylor's Dragoons, December 10, 1784. (Virginia Governor's Office. Bounty Warrants, 1779-1860. Accession 41429, The Library of Virginia, Richmond, Va.)

Harris, Henry

Henry Harris, of Frederick County, Virginia, age 58 in May 1818, stated that he enlisted April 1776 in Virginia, in Captain Robert Smith's company of the 3rd Regiment of Light Dragoons, commanded by Col. George Baylor and finally by William Washington. He served until the fall of 1781, when he was discharged in Fredericksburg, Virginia, having served in the battles of Brandywine, Monmouth, Cowpens and various skirmishes. (Virginia Governor's Office. Bounty Warrants, 1779-1860. Accession 41429, The Library of Virginia, Richmond, Va.)

Captain William Ball verified Henry Harris' service in the 3rd Regiment of Light Dragoons, commanded by Colonel George Baylor, May 22, 1818. (Virginia Governor's Office. Bounty Warrants, 1779-1860. Accession 41429, The Library of Virginia, Richmond, Va.)

Henry Harris, S37986. He enlisted in April 1778 in Virginia, with Captain Robert Smith, of the state of Maryland, in the 3rd Regiment of Dragoons commanded by Col. George Baylor, and finally by Col. William Washington. He served until the fall 1781, and was discharged in Fredericksburg. He was in the battles of Brandywine, Monmouth and Cowpens. At the time of his affidavit, made 22 May 1818, he was age 58, and a resident of Frederick County, Virginia and said he was born in April 1759. In 1820, he referred to a wife of the same age, and a daughter who was 24 years old, but gave no names. In 1824, he was living in Madison County, Georgia. (Revolutionary War Pension and Bounty-Land Warrant Application Files. National Archives Microfilm Publication M804, roll 1199.)

Hart, Benjamin

Benjamin Hart, Cornet, Date of Commission July 26, 1778. Arrangement of Light Dragoons, 3^d Regiment, undated. (Revolutionary War Rolls, 1775-1783. National Archives Microfilm Publication M246. Roll 115, folder 13, 3^d Regiment Light Dragoons, 1779, item 3.)

Benjamin Hart, Q.M., July 26, 1778. A Return of Officers in the 3rd Regiment of Light Dragoons with the Dates of their Commissions, Sept. 18, 1777. (Revolutionary War Rolls, 1775-1783. National Archives Microfilm Publication M246. Roll 115, folder 13, 3^d Regiment Light Dragoons, 1779, item 6.)

Hawkins, Bartlett (see Bartlett Hawkins Fitzgerald)

Hawkins, Benjamin (see Benjamin Hawkins Fitzgerald)

Healy or Haley, Daniel

David Healy of Fauquier County, Virginia, in July 1832 made oath that his brother, Daniel Healy, enlisted at Guilford Court House and served as a trumpeter in the 3rd Regiment of Dragoons under Colonel William Washington, and that he served until his death in the battle at Eutaw Springs. Rush Hudson of Fauquier County, Virginia, claimed that Daniel Haley enlisted at Guilford Court House in the 3rd Regiment commanded by George Baylor, and afterwards served under Col. William Washington until he was killed at Eutaw Springs. (Virginia Governor's Office. Bounty Warrants, 1779-1860. Accession 41429, The Library of Virginia, Richmond, Va.)

Hebb, William

William Hebb, 61, of Preston County, Virginia, declared on September 6, 1819 that he enlisted in 1777 in Westmoreland County in the Regiment commanded by Colonel Baylor, being the 3d Regiment of Light Dragoons, the life guard of General George Washington. He served until his discharge at Bacon's Bridge in South Carolina, March 19, 1780, having been in the battles of Germantown and Brandywine. Henry Harris of Frederick County, Virginia affirmed that William Hebb served with him in the 3rd Regiment under Colonel George Baylor. (Virginia Governor's Office. Bounty Warrants, 1779-1860. Accession 41429, The Library of Virginia, Richmond, Va.)

William Hebb, S38022. In September 1819, William Hebb of Preston County, Virginia, stated that he enlisted for three years March 17, 1777 in the company of Captain John Thorn of the regiment commanded by Col. Baylor, the 3rd Regiment of Light Dragoons. He was in the battles of Germantown and Brandywine, and was discharged near Bacon's Bridge in South Carolina by Lt. Col. William Washington. Henry Harris of Frederick County, Virginia, and Charles Swan of Fauquier County, in 1820 affirmed William Hebb's service. (Revolutionary War Pension and Bounty-Land Warrant Application Files. National Archives Microfilm Publication M804, roll 1245.)

Hendren, William

"I do hereby Certify that Sergeant Wm Hendren was enlisted into the third Regiment of light Dragoons the 7 June 1781 to serve during the war & that he was a Sergeant in the first Regiment of Lt Dragoons at the time when it was disbanded, he was appointed a Sergeant the 10 July 1781." George Baylor, Caroline County, February 20, 1784. (Virginia Governor's Office. Bounty Warrants, 1779-1860. Accession 41429, The Library of Virginia, Richmond, Va.)

Hert, F

F. Hert, listed as a prisoner on a report of the Quarter Guard, May 2, 1782, confined for two days and nights for "Loseing Currycomb." (University of Virginia. Alderman Library Special Collections. Accession 2257, Papers of the Baylor Family of Newmarket, Caroline County, Va, in part transcripts: [manuscript], 1653-1915. Box 4: the folder is labeled "Military Papers, 1782, 1814, & n.d.," item 13: "1782 May 2, Continental Troops, report of Quarter Guard, 3rd Regiment Light Dragoons, Report signed by James Meriwether, Lt. Officer of the Day.")

Higg, John

"John Higg Deserted with them all." Return, dated 1 March 1778, of arms and accouterments in the Third Troop belonging to Colonel George Baylor's Regiment of Light Dragoons. (Virginia Office of the Quartermaster General, Fredericksburg. Returns of Colonel George Baylor's Regiment, 1778-1779. Accession 22547, The Library of Virginia, Richmond, Va.)

Hill, George

"I do Certify that George Hill served as a soldier in the Cavalry of Virginia in service during the Revolutionary War that I was personally acquainted with him at that time and he received a wound that fractured his leg in the Action at the Eutaw Springs." William McGuire, Lieutenant 1st Regiment of Artillery. (Virginia Governor's Office. Bounty Warrants, 1779-1860. Accession 41429, The Library of Virginia, Richmond, Va.)

George Hill, W4987. While a resident of Culpeper County, he enlisted in August 1780 as a private in Lt. McGuire's company in Col. Green's Virginia Regiment, and fought in the battle of Guilford Court House. In March 1781, he enlisted as a private in Captain Parsons' company in Col. William Washington's 3rd Regiment, and fought at Camden and Eutaw Springs. While in this last battle, he was wounded by a musket ball in his leg. He was discharged in June or July 1783. He married 17 October 1785, in Culpeper County, Hannah Hickman. While receiving his pension in February 1813, he was a resident of Hampshire County, Virginia, and moved afterwards to Ross County, Ohio. In 1829 he lived in Monroe Township, Pickaway County, Ohio, and in 1833, at the age of 79, he was in Muhlenburg Township, Pickaway County, and died there April 25, 1838. (Revolutionary War Pension and Bounty-Land Warrant Application Files. National Archives Microfilm Publication M804, roll 1275.)

Hill, John

John Hill, W3814. While a resident of Northumberland County, Virginia, John Hill enlisted in the spring of 1776 as a private in Captain Thomas Gaskin's company of Col. Parker's 5th Virginia Regiment. When his enlistment expired, he joined Captain Alexander Spotswood Dandridge's company, under Col. Theodorick Bland. He was transferred to an infantry unit, and was captured at the siege and surrender of Charleston. He escaped after three weeks and joined the cavalry under Col. William Washington, and was discharged by him in 1780. He was wounded in the breast at the battle of Brandywine, in the wrist at the siege of Savannah, and also wounded in his leg during the war. He lived in Maryland after the war, then moved to Hancock County, Georgia, where he made his statement, in 1833, at the age of 82 or 83. He married in 1779 or 1780, in Northumberland County, Virginia, Nancy Kesterson, and he died 12 November 1842, in Hancock County,

Georgia. (Revolutionary War Pension and Bounty-Land Warrant Application Files. National Archives Microfilm Publication M804, roll 1276.)

Hite, George

George Hite, mentioned on a roster of officers of 3rd Regiment. (University of Virginia. Alderman Library Special Collections. Accession 2257, Papers of the Baylor Family of Newmarket, Caroline County, Va, in part transcripts: [manuscript], 1653-1915. Box 4: the folder is labeled "1756, 1777-1781; Military Papers," item 21: "ca. 1780 Continental Troops, roster of Officers, 1st & 3rd Regiments.")

"This will Certify that George Hight a private in the third Virginia Regiment of L.D. enlisted into my troop the 14th day of Augt 1777... ." Henry Bell, Captain 3rd Regiment, January 10, 1784. (Virginia Governor's Office. Bounty Warrants, 1779-1860. Accession 41429, The Library of Virginia, Richmond, Va.)

"George Hight private in 3d Regiment LD... is hereby discharged from the said regiment." Richard Call, August 12, 1781. (Virginia Governor's Office. Bounty Warrants, 1779-1860. Accession 41429, The Library of Virginia, Richmond, Va.)

"I do hereby Certify that M. George Hite has Served as a Lieutenant of Dragoons ... three Years. Given under my hand this 11th Day of September 1783." Colonel James Wood. (Virginia Governor's Office. Bounty Warrants, 1779-1860. Accession 41429, The Library of Virginia, Richmond, Va.)

George Hite, Lieutenant; pay due him for 1782 and 1783. (Miscellaneous Numbered Records [The Manuscript File] in the War Department Collection of Revolutionary War Records, 1775-1790's. National Archives Microfilm Publication M859. Manuscript 17650, "The United States to George Hite Lieut. 1st Regiment L.D.," dated 8 October 1784.)

George Hite, W5105. He was born 25 October 1761. He enlisted about 1779 in Lee's Corps of Dragoons, then served as Ensign in the 8th Virginia Regiment from 10 September 1780 to 22 June 1781. He then served as Cornet in the 3rd Regiment of Light Dragoons from 22 June 1781 to 16 November 1781, and as Lieutenant from then until 15 November 1783. He was wounded in his sword arm at the Siege of Ninety-Six. He married 4 February 1783, Deborah Rutherford, and died 16 December 1816, in Jefferson County, Virginia. (Revolutionary War Pension and

Bounty-Land Warrant Application Files. National Archives Microfilm Publication M804, roll 1291.)

Hood, George

George Hood, W8939. In December 1828, while living in Philadelphia, George Hood stated that he enlisted in October 1776 in the 2nd Virginia Regiment of General Muhlenberg's brigade. In the fall of 1777, he was at Valley Forge, and in 1778 was in the battle of Monmouth. In July 1779, he helped build the garrison at West Point under General Putnam. After his term expired, he went to Philadelphia, where he met Lieutenant David Ballieu, of Col. Washington's cavalry, whom he knew from Virginia, and enlisted with him. He got his gear and headed south to South Carolina, where he was in the 1st troop under Captain Lewis.

Catherine Hood stated that while George Hood was a resident of Philadelphia, he enlisted as a private in the Virginia State Regiment under General Gibson. He marched to Valley Forge, Pennsylvania, and joined General P. Muhlenberg's Regiment, built the garrison at West Point under General Putnam, and was at the storming of the garrison at Stony Point in July 1779. When his term expired, he again enlisted in July or August 1779 in Col. William Washington's Dragoons. He went to South Carolina, joined the regiment under General Green, and was in the battle of Cowpens, and with General Morgan was at the battle of Guilford Court House, the Siege of Ninety-six, and the battle of Eutaw Springs. He was discharged at the end of the war in South Carolina.

He was born in Charles City County, Virginia in 1761, married on 30 January 1794 in Philadelphia, and died 16 March 1835. (Revolutionary War Pension and Bounty-Land Warrant Application Files. National Archives Microfilm Publication M804, roll 1320.)

George Hood stated that he was born in Virginia in 1751 in Charles City County between the James and Chickahominy Rivers, to Charles and Mary (nee Hood) Hood. In October 1776 he enlisted in the 2nd Virginia state regiment for three years, marched to Williamsburg, where he was taught as a musician. In November 1777 he was marched to Pennsylvania where they joined General Washington at Valley Forge, and there he met his brother William, who was in the 1st Virginia.

After the battle at Stony Point, George was asked to assist the wounded, and at the end of his enlistment in October 1779, was in Philadelphia. Being with no friends or money, he came across David Ballew, a friend of his father's and an officer of William Washington's regiment, who was recruiting there. George re-enlisted, based on the bounty of 700 Continental dollars, and 300 acres of land. He was marched to Kent County, Virginia, given a furlough for a few days to see his mother, but found only his brother James. He arrived in South Carolina in early 1780, and was in battles at Moncks Corner, Cowpens, Lenud's Ferry, and Eutaw Springs.

George Hood received his discharge in December 1782, and went home to Charles City, but having resolved to see more of the world he served on several sailing vessels for the next few years, survived the sinking of one ship, and ending up in Philadelphia in 1788, where he remained. (Virginia Governor's Office. Bounty Warrants, 1779-1860. Accession 41429, The Library of Virginia, Richmond, Va.)

Hood, John

"John Hood Soldier in the 3rd Virginia Regiment of light Dragoons having Served faithfully three years is hereby Discharged." William Washington, Lt. Col., December 24, 1780. (Virginia Governor's Office. Bounty Warrants, 1779-1860. Accession 41429, The Library of Virginia, Richmond, Va.)

Horn, Christopher

In Fayette County, Kentucky, in April 1823, Christopher Horn declared that he served in the 3rd Troop of Horse with Dennis Dailey. (under the name Dennis Dailey. Virginia Governor's Office. Revolutionary War Rejected Claims, 1779-1860. Accession 41986, State government records collection, The Library of Virginia, Richmond, Va.)

Christopher Horn, W664. Christopher Horn of Knox County, Kentucky, age 71, said he enlisted for two years in Captain John Hays company in the 9th Virginia, and then enlisted at Valley forge in the 1st Regiment of Light Dragoons, and served therein until he was discharged at Halifax, North Carolina in 1780. Elizabeth Horn, age 72 in 1853, stated that she married Christopher Horn in Knox County in December 1817, and her husband died in there March 9, 1837. (Revolutionary War Pension and Bounty-Land Warrant Application Files. National Archives Microfilm Publication M804, roll 1327.)

Hubbard, James

"I Do Certify that James Hubbard enlisted in 3d Regiment Dragoons for the War Decr 1st 1780 & that he has not drawn any pay & has served the war." William Barret, Captain, February 3, 1784. (Virginia Governor's Office. Bounty Warrants, 1779-1860. Accession 41429, The Library of Virginia, Richmond, Va.)

Hudgins, Samuel

"Saml Hudgins having served faithfully three years in the third regiment of Light Dragoons is hereby discharged." Lt. Col. William Washington, December 23, 1784. (Virginia Governor's Office. Bounty Warrants, 1779-1860. Accession 41429, The Library of Virginia, Richmond, Va.)

"This is to Certify that the within mentioned Saml. Hudgins Enlisted into my Company of Infantry the 11th March 1776 and served faithfully until about the 23rd of January 1778 when he was permitted to remove for three years into Colonel Baylor's regiment of Light Dragoons." James Lucas, Captain 4th Virginia Regiment, undated. (Virginia Governor's Office. Bounty Warrants, 1779-1860. Accession 41429, The Library of Virginia, Richmond, Va.)

Samuel Hudgins or Hudgeons, S1957. Samuel Hudgins, age 76 and a resident of Robertson County, Tennessee in 1832, stated that he first enlisted under Captain James Lucas in Brunswick County, Virginia, where he was born, in the 4th regiment for two years. When he was a Valley Forge, he reenlisted under Captain Churchill Jones in the light horse commanded by Col. Baylor for three years. (Revolutionary War Pension and Bounty-Land Warrant Application Files. National Archives Microfilm Publication M804, roll 1355.)

Hudson, Rush

"This may certify that Rush Hudson enlisted in the third Regiment of Light Dragoons in Decr 1777, the said Corpl Hudson Served in the Third Regiment until it was Consolidated with the first in which he continued until the Regiment was furloughed at Nelson's Ferry 13 June 1783." Ch. Jones, Captain, undated

"I do certify that Rush Hudson enlisted for the war." Chiswell Barret, former Captain, undated (Virginia Governor's Office. Bounty Warrants, 1779-1860. Accession 41429, The Library of Virginia, Richmond, Va.)

Rush Hudson, S38064. Rush Hudson enlisted in 1775 for two years with Ensign Thomas Catlett under Captain Samuel Hawes in Caroline County, Virginia, in the 3rd Virginia Regiment of Col. William Spotswood. At the end of his term, he was in Valley Forge, and enlisted for the rest of the war, under Cornet Presley Thornton in the 3rd Virginia Regiment of Cavalry under Col. George Baylor, commanded afterwards by Col. William Washington. He served as a corporal in Captain Churchill Jones' Company and was discharged at Nelson's Ferry in South Carolina in 1783 by General Greene. He was in the battles of Brandywine, Germantown, Cowpens, Guilford Court House, Camden, and Eutaw Springs.

On 30 August 1820, at the age of 67, he was living in Fauquier County, Virginia; his wife's name was Anne, age 65, and he had a daughter Elizabeth, age 32. He was born January 1753, moved to Fauquier County by 1818, was still living there on 3 May 1821, but had died by 19 February 1828. (Revolutionary War Pension and Bounty-Land Warrant Application Files. National Archives Microfilm Publication M804, roll 1357.)

Hughes, George

"I do Certify that Sergeant Geo. Hughes Enlisted for the war in Colonel Baylor's Dragoons Decr 22d 1779 & Contd to Serve as a true & faithful Soldier the full term of his Enlistment." William Barret, Captain, December 8, 1784. "For value received I do assign the within Discharge to Charles Lewis and Desire a Certificate may be granted to him for my bounty in Land." George Hughes, December 9, 1784. (Virginia Governor's Office. Bounty Warrants, 1779-1860. Accession 41429, The Library of Virginia, Richmond, Va.)

Hull, Beecham

"It appears from the size roll of the first troop of Baylor's dragoons that Beecham Hull enlisted January 1778 for the war, and served faithfully the term of his enlistment." William Barret, Captain, December 28, 1785. (Virginia Governor's Office. Bounty Warrants, 1779-1860. Accession 41429, The Library of Virginia, Richmond, Va.)

Hulse, William

"Sergeant Hulse having serv'd faithfully three years in the 3d Regiment of Light Dragons is hereby discharged. The Said Hulse is a man of Honesty and Integrity." William Washington, Lt. Col., Halifax, September 1, 1780. (Virginia Governor's Office. Bounty Warrants, 1779-1860. Accession 41429, The Library of Virginia, Richmond, Va.)

Hutchinson, Thomas

Thomas Hutchinson, Sergeant, 3rd troop, managed to escape from the British at Tappan, but heard them cry out "Skiver him" as he ran off. (David Griffith. Letter, 20 October 1778. Accession 22789. Personal papers collection. The Library of Virginia, Richmond, Va.)

Thomas Hutchinson, pay due him as Corporal from 10 September 1777 to 3 March 1778; pay due him as Quartermaster Sergeant from 3 March 1778 to 31 December 1780; pay due him for 1781, and the first three months of 1782. (Miscellaneous Numbered Records [The Manuscript File] in the War Department Collection of Revolutionary War Records, 1775-1790's. National Archives Microfilm Publication M859. Manuscript 17649, "The United States in Account with Thomas Hutchinson Corp^l & Q^{r}Mr Serg^t 3rd Regiment L.D.," dated 30 September 1785; also Manuscript 17669, dated 28 February 1799.)

"I do certify that Thos. Hutcheson enlisted as Sergeant in the 3d Regiment L. Dragoons for three years. After which he was appointed Quarter Master...." George Baylor, Richmond, October 22, 1783. (Virginia Governor's Office. Bounty Warrants, 1779-1860. Accession 41429, The Library of Virginia, Richmond, Va.)

Jacobs, John

In May 1839, John Jacobs, of Scott County, Kentucky declared that he enlisted under Lieutenant Francis Dade in the Third Regiment, served to the close of the war, and was discharged at Winchester, Virginia by Captain Robert Morrow. Peter Brumback of Boone County, Kentucky affirmed John Jacobs' service in the 3rd Regiment. Charles Neal and William Cardwell also signed affidavits confirming John Jacobs' service. (Virginia Governor's Office. Revolutionary War Rejected Claims, 1779-1860. Accession 41986, State government records collection, The Library of Virginia, Richmond, Va.)

John Jacobs, W9071. On 4 February 1833, stating that he was almost 70 years old, John Jacobs said he enlisted in Fredericksburg, in 1779 or 1780 in the 3rd Regiment of Light

Dragoons commanded by Col. William Washington, with Lieutenant F. Dade, and he served some time under Captain Barret, and was in the 3rd troop under Captain Henry Bowyer at the time of his discharge. He was in the battles of Cowpens, Guilford Court House, Ninety-six, Camden, and Eutaw Springs, and was wounded four times. He was born 26 March 1763. On 31 July 1855, his widow Ann was living in Owen County, Kentucky, and stated that he enlisted in 1779 for three years, under Captain Baylor in Baylor's Regiment of Virginia, and was discharged 3 November 1783. They were married in Stafford County, Virginia, on 12 February 1784, and he died in Scott County, Kentucky, on 1 November 1847. (Revolutionary War Pension and Bounty-Land Warrant Application Files. National Archives Microfilm Publication M804, roll 1402.)

Jarman, William

William Jarman, W4003. On 16 October 1828, William Jarman stated that he enlisted for the war and continued in service until the end, and at the time of his discharge was serving in Captain William Barret's company. William Jarman married Mary Hamer, in Anson County, North Carolina, in October 1783. He died 16 May 1845, in Anson County. (Revolutionary War Pension and Bounty-Land Warrant Application Files. National Archives Microfilm Publication M804, roll 1407.)

Javes or Jeves, Thomas

"Thomas Javes corporal in the third Regiment of Light Dragoons having faithfully served three years in the 3d Regiment of Light Dragoons is hereby Discharged, the said Javes is a discrete young fellow & of Great Integrity." William Washington, Lt. Col., October 14, 1780. Thomas Jeves assigned his land warrant to David A. Gray. (Virginia Governor's Office. Bounty Warrants, 1779-1860. Accession 41429, The Library of Virginia, Richmond, Va.)

Jenkins, John

"It Appears from the size roll of 5th Troop that John Jenkins enlisted for the war in 3d Regiment L.D. July 12th 1781 & served until the Mutiny May 83." William Barret, Captain, April 28, 1785. (Virginia Governor's Office. Bounty Warrants, 1779-1860. Accession 41429, The Library of Virginia, Richmond, Va.)

John Jenkins, rejected pension application, no number. In Fayette County, Ohio, in October 1831, John Jenkins, age 70 declared that he first enlisted in the 8th Virginia regiment, transferred to a troop of horse commanded by Col. William Washington in about 1780, and then served in Lee's Legion until the close of the war. (Revolutionary War Pension and Bounty-Land Warrant Application Files. National Archives Microfilm Publication M804, roll 1410.)

Jesse, William

William Jesse, with Lieutenant Barret. (University of Virginia. Alderman Library Special Collections. Accession 2257, Papers of the Baylor Family of Newmarket, Caroline County, Va, in part transcripts: [manuscript], 1653-1915. Box 4: the folder is labeled "1756, 1777-1781; Military Papers," item 14: "A list of the men's names absent belonging to Colonel Baylor's Regiment, Fredericksburg, June 27, 1778.")

Johnson, James

"It appears from the size roll of 2d Troop that James Johnson enlisted for the war in 3d Regiment of Light Dragoons July 1781 and served till the 10 May when he joined the Mutineers." William Barret, Captain, undated. (Virginia Governor's Office. Bounty Warrants, 1779-1860. Accession 41429, The Library of Virginia, Richmond, Va.)

James Johnson, S36664. In May 1818, James Johnson, age 58 and a resident of Shelby County, Kentucky, stated that he enlisted with Lieutenant John Harris under General Steuben. He then enlisted in the 1st Regiment of Light Dragoons after which he was transferred to the regiment commanded by Col. William Washington, and continued until the end of the war.

His deposition stated that at the end of the war he "together with about one hundred more of said Light Dragoon service came away from the State of Georgia with out permission not designing to desert but knowing their times to have Expired according to the terms of their Enlistment and proceeded to Prince Edward County in Virginia at which place they surrendered to General Morgan and was marched to Winchester where he received a furlow from Capt. Morrow...." (Revolutionary War Pension and Bounty-Land Warrant Application Files. National Archives Microfilm Publication M804, roll 1423.)

Johnson, John

John Johnson, R5635. John Johnson claimed that he enlisted in 1781 or 1782 for six months, and while he didn't remember his captain's name, he was in a company commanded by Colonel William Washington. For the first three months, he was at Rugeley's Mill in South Carolina, and then transferred to General Marion's Brigade. He was then employed in ranging and scouting after the British in South Carolina. At the time of his enlistment, he was living in Bladen County, North Carolina. After the war he moved to Tennessee, then to Kentucky, and then to Illinois. In November 1834 he was living in Hamilton County, Illinois, and he died 9 July 1853 at the age of 110. (Revolutionary War Pension and Bounty-Land Warrant Application Files. National Archives Microfilm Publication M804, roll 1424.)

Jones, Cadwallader

Cadwallader Jones, Captain, February 6, 1777, commission granted March 4, 1778. (Revolutionary War Rolls, 1775-1783. National Archives Microfilm Publication M246. Roll 115, folder 13, 3^d Regiment Light Dragoons, 1779, item 2.)

Cadwallader Jones, Date of Commission 6 February 1777. Arrangement of Light Dragoons, 3^d Regiment, undated. (Revolutionary War Rolls, 1775-1783. National Archives Microfilm Publication M246. Roll 115, folder 13, 3^d Regiment Light Dragoons, 1779, item 3.)

Cadwallader Jones, Captain, February 6, 1777. A Return of Officers in the 3rd Regiment of Light Dragoons with the Dates of their Commissions, Sept. 18, 1777. (Revolutionary War Rolls, 1775-1783. National Archives Microfilm Publication M246. Roll 115, folder 13, 3^d Regiment Light Dragoons, 1779, item 6.)

Captain Cadwallader Jones mentioned on a weekly return of the 3rd Regiment of Light Dragoons. Captain Cadwallader Jones had one captain, one lieutenant, two sergeants, one farrier, 13 privates present, and 29 privates "Sick Absent." 22 of the sick privates were "Under Inoculation" [probably inoculation for smallpox], three were sick in Frederickstown, Virginia, and two were sick in Lancaster, Pennsylvania. (University of Virginia. Alderman Library Special Collections. Accession 2257, Papers of the Baylor Family of Newmarket, Caroline County, Va, in part transcripts: [manuscript], 1653-1915. Box 4: the folder is labeled "1756, 1777-1781; Military Papers," item 9: "A Weekly Return of the 3d Regiment of Light Dragoons Commanded by Col. Baylor, Feb 5th 1778.")

"...poor Jones, you certainly mean to break his heart, or you would never leave him behind you. With grief, he has already lost the greater part of his hair, and I apprehend before your return, he will be quite bald..." (University of Virginia. Alderman Library Special Collections. Accession 2257, Papers of the Baylor Family of Newmarket, Caroline County, Va, in part transcripts: [manuscript], 1653-1915. Box 4: the folder is labeled "1756, 1777-1781; Military Papers," item 8: "Letter from Alexander Clough to George Baylor, 4 Feb 1778 at Millsone.")

Cadwallader Jones, Captain; commutation of five years full pay in lieu of half pay for life. (Miscellaneous Numbered Records [The Manuscript File] in the War Department Collection of Revolutionary War Records, 1775-1790's. National Archives Microfilm Publication M859. Manuscript 17659, "The United States in Account with Cadwallader Jones Capt in the late 3^d Regiment L. Dragoons," dated 20 April 1792. Also manuscript 17661, "The United States in Acc^t curr^t with Cadwallader Jones Cap in the late 3^d Reg. L. Dragoons," dated 8 May 1792.)

Cadwallader Jones, BLWt 2308. In 1839, Cad. Jones of Hillsborough, North Carolina, the son of Cadwallader Jones, stated that his father was a Captain in Bland's or Baylor's Regiment, and his father received 3000 or 4000 acres in Ohio for his services, possibly from the state of Virginia. Heirs-at-law Frederick Price of Chester District, South Carolina, and Lucy P. Green of Columbia, South Carolina stated that Cadwallader Jones served to the end of the war, and during that time, served as aide-de-camp to General Lafayette, and was at the Siege of Yorktown. (Revolutionary War Pension and Bounty-Land Warrant Application Files. National Archives Microfilm Publication M804, roll 1437.)

"I do certify that I served Three years ... as a Captain in Baylor's Regiment L. Dragoons." Signed by Cadwallader Jones, undated.

Between 1835 and 1837, the heirs of Cadwallader Jones filed for additional land based on his rank as Major. In January 1837, Robert Bolling stated that in 1779, Cadwallader Jones of Prince George County, Virginia commanded a troop of horse in Colonel Baylor's Regiment, and that in 1780 or 1781 both Cadwallader Jones and Churchill Jones were appointed Majors, and that after Cadwallader Jones married and settled in Petersburg,

Virginia he was known as Major Jones. The heirs were named as Cadwallader Jones, Frederick Pride and Lucy Green. (Virginia Governor's Office. Bounty Warrants, 1779-1860. Accession 41429, The Library of Virginia, Richmond, Va.)

Jones, Churchill

Churchhill M. Jones, Captain, June 1, 1777, commission granted March 4, 1778. (Revolutionary War Rolls, 1775-1783. National Archives Microfilm Publication M246. Roll 115, folder 13, 3^d Regiment Light Dragoons, 1779, item 2.)

Churchill Jones, Captain, Date of Commission July 1, 1777. Arrangement of Light Dragoons, 3^d Regiment, undated. (Revolutionary War Rolls, 1775-1783. National Archives Microfilm Publication M246. Roll 115, folder 13, 3^d Regiment Light Dragoons, 1779, item 3.)

Captain Churchill Jones, appointed Brigade Major in Virginia. A Return of the 3^d Regiment of L. D. Commanded by Captain Stith, October 23, 1778. (Revolutionary War Rolls, 1775-1783. National Archives Microfilm Publication M246. Roll 115, folder 13, 3^d Regiment Light Dragoons, 1779, item 5.)

Churchill Jones, Captain, July 1, 1777. A Return of Officers in the 3rd Regiment of Light Dragoons with the Dates of their Commissions, Sept. 18, 1777. (Revolutionary War Rolls, 1775-1783. National Archives Microfilm Publication M246. Roll 115, folder 13, 3^d Regiment Light Dragoons, 1779, item 6.)

Captain Churchill Jones mentioned on a weekly return of the 3rd Regiment Light Dragoons. Captain Churchill Jones had one sergeant, one trumpet, one farrier, eight privates present, two sick, seventeen on command, and one prisoner, leaving him eight men short. Since the last return had been taken, one man from his troop had been killed. (University of Virginia. Alderman Library Special Collections. Accession 2257, Papers of the Baylor Family of Newmarket, Caroline County, Va, in part transcripts: [manuscript], 1653-1915. Box 4: the folder is labeled "1756, 1777-1781; Military Papers," item 9: "A Weekly Return of the 3d Regiment of Light Dragoons Commanded by Col. Baylor, Feb 5th 1778.")

Churchill Jones signed an oath of allegiance 18 August 1778 "in camp", as Captain of Light Dragoons. (Numbered Record Books Concerning Military Operations and Service, Pay and Settlement of Accounts, and Supplies in the War Department Collection of Revolutionary War Records. National Archives

Microfilm Publication M853. Roll 12: Oaths of allegiance and fidelity and oaths of office 1778-1781. Book 166, page 110.)

Churchill Jones, mentioned on a roster of officers, 3rd Regiment. (University of Virginia. Alderman Library Special Collections. Accession 2257, Papers of the Baylor Family of Newmarket, Caroline County, Va, in part transcripts: [manuscript], 1653-1915. Box 4: the folder is labeled "1756, 1777-1781; Military Papers," item 21: "ca. 1780 Continental Troops, roster of Officers, 1st & 3rd Regiments.")

"I do certify that Capt. Churchill Jones was appointed captain in my Regiment In January 1777, that on the consolidation of the 1st & 3d Regiments, he was arranged to the 1st Regiment, to which he at present belongs." George Baylor, October 21, 1783. (Virginia Governor's Office. Bounty Warrants, 1779-1860. Accession 41429, The Library of Virginia, Richmond, Va.)

Churchill Jones, Captain; pay due him for 1782 and 1783. (Miscellaneous Numbered Records [The Manuscript File] in the War Department Collection of Revolutionary War Records, 1775-1790's. National Archives Microfilm Publication M859. Manuscript 17634, "The United States in account with Churchill Jones," dated 29 October 1784.)

Churchill Jones, Captain, mentioned as being in Colonel Baylor's Regiment. (Miscellaneous Numbered Records [The Manuscript File] in the War Department Collection of Revolutionary War Records, 1775-1790's. National Archives Microfilm Publication M859. Manuscript 20379, "Particulars referred to Colonel Baylor's Regiment," undated.)

Churchill Jones, BLWt 304-300, issued 3 January 1803. In December 1806, Churchill Jones of "Chatham," Stratford County, Virginia, stated that he served from 1 January 1777 to the end of the war in the 3rd Regiment of Cavalry. G. H. S. King stated that Churchill Jones had been married three times, but had no children, and his only brother was William Jones of "Ellwood," Spotsylvania County, Virginia. (Revolutionary War Pension and Bounty-Land Warrant Application Files. National Archives Microfilm Publication M804, roll 1437.)

William Jones, age 93, of Wilderness, Orange County, Virginia, on August 3, 1843, said his brother Churchill was a major in the Continental army. (under Samuel K. Bradford, W4608. Revolutionary War Pension and Bounty-Land Warrant Application Files. National Archives Microfilm Publication M804, roll 315.)

Jones, George

"I do certify that George Jones Serv'd as a Soldier in Colonel Baylor's Regiment of L Dragoons from Febr 1780 to the end of the war." C. Jones, Captain, undated. (Virginia Governor's Office. Bounty Warrants, 1779-1860. Accession 41429, The Library of Virginia, Richmond, Va.)

Jones, Griffith

"Griffith Jones, Prisoner." Return, dated 1 March 1778, of arms and accouterments in the Third Troop belonging to Colonel George Baylor's Regiment of Light Dragoons. (Virginia Office of the Quartermaster General, Fredericksburg. Returns of Colonel George Baylor's Regiment, 1778-1779. Accession 22547, The Library of Virginia, Richmond, Va.)

Jones, James

In 1832 James Jones, aged 68, of King George County, Virginia, stated that he enlisted under Captain Churchill Jones in 1777 to serve three years in Col. George Baylor's Regiment, and that at the end of the three years, he re-enlisted in the same regiment to serve during the war. He was discharged near the Santee River in South Carolina. In 1818 Churchill Jones affirmed James Jones' enlistment and service in Baylor's Regiment. (Virginia Governor's Office. Bounty Warrants, 1779-1860. Accession 41429, The Library of Virginia, Richmond, Va.)

James Jones, S45890. In 1818, James Jones was a resident of Stafford County, Virginia, with his wife Molly, and he was 57 years old. In August 1820, he and his wife were living in King George County, Virginia. At that time, he stated that he enlisted in November 1777 at Fredericksburg, Virginia in Captain Churchill Jones' company of Colonel Baylor's Regiment for three years. During that time, he marched from Fredericksburg to Valley Forge, and was in the battles of Brandywine and other skirmishes and scouting parties. He reenlisted for the rest of the war during the march to the South, and was in the battles of Guilford Courthouse, the Siege of Ninety-Six, Eutaw Springs, and Cowpens.

James Jones was discharged on the Santee River in South Carolina in July 1783. He had been taught the art of a tailor, but was forced to quit that occupation due to partial loss of eyesight. Captain Churchill Jones made statements verifying James Jones' claim of service on 30 March 1818 and again on 26 June 1818, both times in Stafford County, Virginia. (Revolutionary War Pension and Bounty-Land Warrant Application Files. National Archives Microfilm Publication M804, roll 1440.)

Jones, Richard

"I do Certify that Richd Jones enlisted in the 3 Regiment L Dragoons for Three Years Dec. 7, 1777 & that he has faithfully served the time of enlistment & that he was born in Hanover County." William Barret, Captain, January 6, 1784. (Virginia Governor's Office. Bounty Warrants, 1779-1860. Accession 41429, The Library of Virginia, Richmond, Va.)

Jones, Samuel

Samuel Jones, W3826. In May 1844, in Chesterfield County, Virginia, Patsey Jones, widow of Samuel Jones, stated that her late husband enlisted in Petersburg, Virginia, where he had been bound as an apprentice. She said he served for four years in Colonel William Washington's troops of light horse as a corporal, and was in the battles of Eutaw Springs, Camden Court House, and the Cowpens. A pension certificate noted that he died 6 June 1816 in Chesterfield County, Virginia. (Revolutionary War Pension and Bounty-Land Warrant Application Files. National Archives Microfilm Publication M804, roll 1444.)

Jones, Solomon

Solomon Jones, Trumpet Major, 3rd Regiment Light Dragoons; pay from 1 January 1782 to 15 November 1783. (Miscellaneous Numbered Records [The Manuscript File] in the War Department Collection of Revolutionary War Records, 1775-1790's. National Archives Microfilm Publication M859. Manuscript 17529, "The United States in Account with Solomon Jones late Trumpet Maj^r 3rd Regiment Light Dragoons," dated 2 August 1792.)

"I do certify that Sollomon Jones Trumpeter in the 1st Regiment Light Dragoons has been in the continental Cavalry since March one thousand seven hundred and Eighty." William Parsons, November 4, 1783. (Virginia Governor's Office. Bounty Warrants, 1779-1860. Accession 41429, The Library of Virginia, Richmond, Va.)

Solomon Jones, S38083. In January 1827, Solomon Jones declared that he was enlisted in 1776 in Virginia by Andrew Geter, and served three years in the regiment commanded by Colonel Stuart. He was discharged in Charleston, South Carolina by an officer named McIntosh and returned to Virginia. He next enlisted in North Carolina in Weiland's company of militia. After serving his term, he then enlisted under Sergeant Lunsford in Charleston with Colonel William Washington for the remainder of the war. He was discharged at Santee in South Carolina. While serving as a trumpet under Colonel Washington, he was in the battles of Eutaw Springs, where he had a horse shot out from under him, and at Cowpens, where he was wounded in his right arm. (Revolutionary War Pension and Bounty-Land Warrant Application Files. National Archives Microfilm Publication M804, roll 1445.)

Jones, Stephen

Stephen Jones, W7916. In May 1833, Stephen Jones, of Bedford County, Virginia, age 70, stated that he was born in Dinwiddie County, Virginia, his wife's maiden name was Mary Gibbs, and that he enlisted in 1781 under Captain Moore, who was killed in the battle of Guilford Courthouse. He was then attached to Colonel Charles Lynch and Major Callaway. He next enlisted with Colonel Washington, in Captain Charles Yarborough's company of Baylor's Horse.

In August 1835, still age 70, he declared that after he enlisted in 1781, he served three months as a private under Captain Moon, Colonel Lynch and General Greene, then three months as a private under Captain Callaway. He served eight months as a Trooper under Colonel Washington and Colonel Baylor, and was in the battle of Guilford Courthouse. In January 1839, Mary, his widow, of Bedford County, Virginia, stated that Stephen Jones died 3 January 1834. She further said that they had married in Bedford County, Virginia, on 28 December 1782, and had resided there ever since. Payment voucher #3683, dated 31 July 1839, and signed by Captain Callaway of Colonel Baylor's Regiment records payment of $163.31 to the widow. (Revolutionary War Pension and Bounty-Land Warrant Application Files. National Archives Microfilm Publication M804, roll 1445.)

Jones, William (absent)

William Jones, absent without leave. (University of Virginia. Alderman Library Special Collections. Accession 2257, Papers of the Baylor Family of Newmarket, Caroline County, Va, in part transcripts: [manuscript], 1653-1915. Box 4: the folder is labeled "1756, 1777-1781; Military Papers," item 14: "A list of the men's names absent belonging to Colonel Baylor's Regiment, Fredericksburg, June 27, 1778.")

Jones, William (of Pittsylvania County, Virginia)

William Jones, R5727. In Pittsylvania County, Virginia in July 1827, William Jones, age 65, said he enlisted May or June 1779 in the 3rd Regiment of Colonel William Washington, served under Captain Churchill Jones, and was discharged at the end of the war at Winchester, Virginia. He said he was a bricklayer and carpenter by trade. In Wilson County, Tennessee in January 1839, Mary Jones, age 77 years, stated that William Jones entered service at the age of 17 or 18 at Petersburg, Virginia, under an officer named Barrett, and served for four years and six months, during which time he was promoted to sergeant. He served in seven engagements, of which two were Cowpens and Guilford Courthouse. They were in Amelia County, Virginia in October 1782. (Revolutionary War Pension and Bounty-Land Warrant Application Files. National Archives Microfilm Publication M804, roll 1447.)

Keen, John

In Fayette County, Kentucky, in April 1823, John Keen declared that he served in the 3rd Troop of Horse with Dennis Dailey. (under the name Dennis Dailey. Virginia Governor's Office. Revolutionary War Rejected Claims, 1779-1860. Accession 41986, State government records collection, The Library of Virginia, Richmond, Va.)

Kelly, James

James Kelly had sword, pistol, belt; "absent on command Cartridge Box top off." Return, dated 1 March 1778, of arms and accouterments in the Third Troop belonging to Colonel George Baylor's Regiment of Light Dragoons. (Virginia Office of the Quartermaster General, Fredericksburg. Returns of Colonel George Baylor's Regiment, 1778-1779. Accession 22547, The Library of Virginia, Richmond, Va.)

James Kelly, S1544. In September 1833, James Kelly, of Hickman County, Tennessee, who said he would be 74 next October 22, enlisted in 1777 as a drafted militia man in Kershaw County, South Carolina for three months under Captain Craton, and Colonel

Simmons. He was near Charleston when his term expired, and volunteered for six months under Captain Grimes. After being discharged, he next served as a light horseman under Colonel Washington for six months, and was in the battles of Eutaw Springs and Cowpens. James Kelly next trained under Captain Arbuckle and marched against the Indians, serving two years in this capacity. In 1835 James Kelly stated that he was born in Pittsylvania County, Virginia about 1760. His family moved to Greenbriar County, Virginia shortly before the war, then back to Pittsylvania County shortly after the war started. (Revolutionary War Pension and Bounty-Land Warrant Application Files. National Archives Microfilm Publication M804, roll 1466.)

Kelty or Kilty, John

John Kelty, Cadet, Date of Commission July 1, 1778. Arrangement of Light Dragoons, 3[d] Regiment, undated. (Revolutionary War Rolls, 1775-1783. National Archives Microfilm Publication M246. Roll 115, folder 13, 3[d] Regiment Light Dragoons, 1779, item 3.)

John Kelty, Cadet, July 1, 1778. A Return of Officers in the 3rd Regiment of Light Dragoons with the Dates of their Commissions, Sept. 18, 1777. (Revolutionary War Rolls, 1775-1783. National Archives Microfilm Publication M246. Roll 115, folder 13, 3[d] Regiment Light Dragoons, 1779, item 6.)

Kilty, volunteer. "There are, besides, Prisoners in New York, A Captain (Swan) two subalterns, (Randolph and Dade) a volunteer, (Kilty) and the Surgeons Mate...." (David Griffith. Letter, 20 October 1778. Accession 22789. Personal papers collection. The Library of Virginia, Richmond, Va.)

"M[r] Kilty Volunteer Taken Prisoner." A Return of the 3[d] Regiment of L. D. Commanded by Captain Stith, October 23, 1778. (Revolutionary War Rolls, 1775-1783. National Archives Microfilm Publication M246. Roll 115, folder 13, 3[d] Regiment Light Dragoons, 1779, item 5.)

John Kilty, Cornet, Dragoons. In an account dated 5 August 1782, in New Burgh, John Kilty owes a total of £79.3.6 to the inhabitants of Long Island for maintenance during his captivity. (Compiled Service Records of Soldiers who Served in the American Army During the Revolutionary War. National Archives Microfilm Publication M881, Continental Troops, Miscellaneous.)

John Kilty, Captain, Baylor's Dragoons; pay as Lieutenant in 4th Maryland Regiment from 1 January 1777 to 1 August. (Miscellaneous Numbered Records [The Manuscript File] in the War Department Collection of Revolutionary War Records, 1775-1790's. National Archives Microfilm Publication M859. Manuscript 17527, "Captain John Kilty Baylor's Dragoons formerly 4th Maryland Regiment," undated)

John Kilty; subsistence due him while a prisoner on Long Island from 28 September 1778 to 18 February 1781; allowance due him of one day's pay and rations for every twenty miles in traveling from New York to Petersburg to re-join his regiment; pay due as Lieutenant of Dragoons from 1 August 1780 to 1 February 1782; subsistence due from 18 February 1781 to 1 January 1782; pay due him as Captain from 1 February 1782 to 1 January 1783; five years full pay in lieu of half-pay for life. (Miscellaneous Numbered Records [The Manuscript File] in the War Department Collection of Revolutionary War Records, 1775-1790's. National Archives Microfilm Publication M859. Manuscript 17693, "The United States in Account with Cap^n John Kilty of Baylor's Dragoons," dated 6 May 1783.)

John Kilty, Captain, Baylor's Dragoons; subsistence due while a prisoner on Long Island from 28 September 1778 to 18 February 1781; pay due as Lieutenant of Dragoons from 1 August 1780 to 1 January 1783. (Miscellaneous Numbered Records [The Manuscript File] in the War Department Collection of Revolutionary War Records, 1775-1790's. National Archives Microfilm Publication M859. Manuscript 17528, "The United States in Account with Capt John Kilty of Baylor's Dragoons," dated 6 May 1785.)

"I hereby certify that John Kilty Esq of Annapolis was an officer in the Maryland line from early in the year 1776 to the year 1778 and from that time to the end of the war, was an officer and during the last campaign in Carolina, a Captain in the Virginia Cavalry commanded by Col. Baylor." John Davidson, Major of the Maryland line. Annapolis, March 25, 1793. (Virginia Governor's Office. Bounty Warrants, 1779-1860. Accession 41429, The Library of Virginia, Richmond, Va.)

John Kilty, W26183. In 1834, Catherine Kilty, nee Quynn, the widow of John Kilty, was living in Baltimore and was 64 years old. She stated that John Kilty died near Annapolis, Maryland, 27 May 1812, and that he served seven years in the Revolutionary War.

They were married in Annapolis in 1792. (Revolutionary War Pension and Bounty-Land Warrant Application Files. National Archives Microfilm Publication M804, roll 1482.)

King, Charles

Charles King appointed Thomas Beatty of Maryland to act for him in power of attorney to collect any monies due for his service in the 3rd Regiment Light Dragoons. (Virginia Governor's Office. Bounty Warrants, 1779-1860. Accession 41429, The Library of Virginia, Richmond, Va.)

King, Elisha

Lieutenant King "Recruiting." (University of Virginia. Alderman Library Special Collections. Accession 2257, Papers of the Baylor Family of Newmarket, Caroline County, Va, in part transcripts: [manuscript], 1653-1915. Box 4: the folder is labeled "Military Papers, 1782, 1814, & n.d.," item 16: "1782 July 8, Continental Troops, Weekly return, 3 & 4th Regiments, Lt. Dragoons, commanded by Col. George Baylor.")

"I do certify that Lt. Elisha King was appointed in my Regiment in Dec. 1780, in which he continued until the consolidation of the 1st & 3 Regiments which happened on the tenth day of Nov. 1782...." Col. George Baylor, October 21, 1783. (Virginia Governor's Office. Bounty Warrants, 1779-1860. Accession 41429, The Library of Virginia, Richmond, Va.)

Elisha King; pay as Lieutenant for 1782. (Miscellaneous Numbered Records [The Manuscript File] in the War Department Collection of Revolutionary War Records, 1775-1790's. National Archives Microfilm Publication M859. Manuscript 17565, "The United States in Account with Lieut. Elisha King," dated 17 November 1784.)

Elisha King, BLWt 324-200, issued 14 February 1807, delivered to L. Goodwyn. (Revolutionary War Pension and Bounty-Land Warrant Application Files. National Archives Microfilm Publication M804, roll 1487.)

In Dinwiddie County, Virginia, in December 1817, Elisha King stated that he enlisted first in the 14th Virginia Regiment commanded by Col. Charles Lewis, and was promoted to Ensign in July 1779. In 1780 he was promoted to Lieutenant, and served until the battle of Cowpens, when he transferred to Colonel Baylor's Regiment, commanded by Lt. Col. William Washington, and served in this regiment until the end of the war. (Virginia Governor's Office. Bounty Warrants, 1779-1860. Accession 41429, The Library of Virginia, Richmond, Va.)

King, George

"G° King" had sword, pistol, belt, cartridge box; "on command." Return, dated 1 March 1778, of arms and accouterments in the Third Troop belonging to Colonel George Baylor's Regiment of Light Dragoons. (Virginia Office of the Quartermaster General, Fredericksburg. Returns of Colonel George Baylor's Regiment, 1778-1779. Accession 22547, The Library of Virginia, Richmond, Va.)

King, James

James King, "armes and Acutrements left at Redon by Capt Jones orders." Return, dated 1 March 1778, of arms and accouterments in the Third Troop belonging to Colonel George Baylor's Regiment of Light Dragoons. (Virginia Office of the Quartermaster General, Fredericksburg. Returns of Colonel George Baylor's Regiment, 1778-1779. Accession 22547, The Library of Virginia, Richmond, Va.)

"Sergeant James King having Served three years faithfully in the third Regiment of Light Dragoons is hereby Discharged. The Said King is an Intelligent and Brave officer." Lt. Col. William Washington, August 8, 1780.

"I do hereby Certify that the within copy of a Certificate relating to Sergeant James King a just one." George Baylor, Sweet Springs, August 29, 1783. (Virginia Governor's Office. Bounty Warrants, 1779-1860. Accession 41429, The Library of Virginia, Richmond, Va.)

James King, in August 1819, of Jefferson County, Tennessee, stated that he knew George Emmert in service in the Colonel Washington's dragoons, until August 1781, at which time James King was acting as quartermaster sergeant to the regiment. (under George Emmert, S38680. Revolutionary War Pension and Bounty-Land Warrant Application Files. National Archives Microfilm Publication M804, roll 927; also Dorman, John Frederick. 1958. Virginia Revolutionary Pension Applications, 34:9.)

King, Julian or Julius

Julian King, Corporal, enlisted May 7, 1777. Muster Roll of the 2nd Troop in the 3^d Regiment Light Dragoons in the Service of the United States commanded by Lieutenant Colonel William Washington for the Months of May, June, July August, September, October 1779. (Revolutionary War Rolls, 1775-1783. National Archives Microfilm Publication M246. Roll 115, folder 13, 3^d Regiment Light Dragoons, 1779, item 1.)

Julian King, 2nd troop. Received sixteen wounds in the attack at Tappan before making his escape. He asked for quarter, but was told that the British officers had ordered them all killed. (David Griffith. Letter, 20 October 1778. Accession 22789. Personal papers collection. The Library of Virginia, Richmond, Va.)

Julian or Julius King, S38120. Julian King, of Orange County, Virginia, stated on 20 August 1820 that he enlisted in 1777 in the 3rd Regiment of Colonel Baylor for three years, and was discharged in South Carolina. In 1820 he was by trade a weaver, age 74, had a wife Margaret, age 70, and a grandson who would be age 13 the next February. (Revolutionary War Pension and Bounty-Land Warrant Application Files. National Archives Microfilm Publication M804, roll 1489)

King, Snelling

Snelling King, deceased, had pistol, belt, and cartridge box, which were given to John Aplin. Return, dated 1 March 1778, of arms and accouterments in the Third Troop belonging to Colonel George Baylor's Regiment of Light Dragoons. (Virginia Office of the Quartermaster General, Fredericksburg. Returns of Colonel George Baylor's Regiment, 1778-1779. Accession 22547, The Library of Virginia, Richmond, Va.)

Land, Benjamin

Ben Land, Col. Washington's Light Horse, received as a deserter July 24, 1782. (M859, Miscellaneous Numbered Records [The Manuscript file] of the War Department Collection of Revolutionary War Records, 1775-1790's. Manuscript number 034159)

Benjamin Land "appears on a return of Delinquents, Deserters, &c." Dated 13 August 1781, Benjamin Land is listed as a deserter from the Continental Army, Colonel Washington's Cavalry. (Compiled Service Records of Soldiers who Served in the American

Army During the Revolutionary War. National Archives Microfilm Publication M881, Continental Troops, Miscellaneous.)

Langford, Joseph

Joseph Langford, Private, 3 Reg. Light Dragoons. (General Index to Compiled Military Service Records of Revolutionary War Soldiers. National Archives Microfilm Publication M860, Card 55.)

Langford, Peter

Peter Langford, Private, 3 Reg. Light Dragoons. (General Index to Compiled Military Service Records of Revolutionary War Soldiers. National Archives Microfilm Publication M860, Card 57.)

"It appears from the Size Roll of the 1st Troop that Peter Langford enlisted for the war in Baylor's Dragoons Febry 1780 & served faithfully the full term of his enlistment." William Barret, December 12, 1785. (Virginia Governor's Office. Bounty Warrants, 1779-1860. Accession 41429, The Library of Virginia, Richmond, Va.)

Langley, William

William Langley, Private, 3 Virginia Regiment. (General Index to Compiled Military Service Records of Revolutionary War Soldiers. National Archives Microfilm Publication M860, Card 108.)

In an affidavit sent to the Governor of Virginia on 18 October 1811, William Langley stated that on the first day of May 1777 he enlisted in Petersburg, Virginia in the 3rd Virginia Regiment of Light Dragoons, commanded by Col. George Baylor for the term of three years, and faithfully served until the fifteenth day of May 1780, at which time he was discharged by Lieut. Col. William Washington, at that time commanding the Regiment in South Carolina. He further stated that in the spring of 1791 he obtained certificates of his enlistment from Major Cadwallader Jones, of Petersburg, Virginia, who enlisted him, and of his discharge from Major John Stith and Capt. William Barret, of Richmond, Virginia. (Virginia Governor's Office. Bounty Warrants, 1779-1860. Accession 41429, The Library of Virginia, Richmond, Va.)

William Langley was to be paid from 15 May 1777 to 15 May 1780, three years at $100 each year. Actually paid $23.80 for 1777, $20.34 for 1778, $4.56 for 1779, and $.68 for 1780. Balance due him $250.62, and account settled April 24, 1792. (M859

Miscellaneous Numbered Records [The Manuscript File] in the War Department Collection of Revolutionary War Records, 1775-1790's. Manuscript 17675, "The United States in Account with William Langley Dragoon in ye late 3rd Regiment L.D., Colonel Baylor.")

William Langley, R6147. Colonel Samuel Hammond, in December 1839, said that William Langley had been a member of Colonel Washington's cavalry. He had often heard of William Langley having his horse shot out from under him in one of the battles, and heard fellow officers speak of William Langley escaping from the Tories through a chimney; he further stated that he had often heard soldiers singing a song about the escape.

Lucy Langley, nee Howze, widow of William Langley, in a deposition in 1841 stated that William Langley enlisted in Col. Washington's Cavalry in Petersburg, Virginia, and that she married William Langley September 18, 1783, and he died July 24, 1815. (Revolutionary War Pension and Bounty-Land Warrant Application Files. National Archives Microfilm Publication M804, roll 1523.)

Langsdon, Charles

"It appears from the Size Roll 2d troop that Charles Langsdon enlisted for the war July 1781 in Baylor's Dragoons and served the full term of his enlistment." William Barrett, 4 January 1785. (Virginia Governor's Office. Bounty Warrants, 1779-1860. Accession 41429, The Library of Virginia, Richmond, Va.)

Charles Langsdon. W441. In September 1819, in Bullitt County, Kentucky, Charles Langsdon stated that in about 1780 he enlisted under Captain John Watts, in a regiment commanded by Col. White. After some time, he was marched to South Carolina and transferred to Col. William Washington's Regiment of Dragoons, and served to the end of the war, but he never applied for his discharge. In 1837, Eda or Edith Langsdon stated that she was the widow of Charles Langsdon, who died in Jefferson County, Kentucky, October 11, 1831. (Revolutionary War Pension and Bounty-Land Warrant Application Files. National Archives Microfilm Publication M804, roll 1523.)

Langsdon, Samuel

"It appears from the Size Roll of the first Troop that Samuel Langsdon Enlisted for the war in Baylor's Dragoons 2d Sepr 1781 and Served the full term of his enlistment." William Barret, May

1783. (Virginia Governor's Office. Bounty Warrants, 1779-1860. Accession 41429, The Library of Virginia, Richmond, Va.)

Lawes, William

William Lawes, private, 3rd troop; pay due him for 1782 and 1783. (Miscellaneous Numbered Records [The Manuscript File] in the War Department Collection of Revolutionary War Records, 1775-1790's. National Archives Microfilm Publication M859. Manuscript 17657, "The United States in a/c with Wm Lawes p^t 3^d Regiment light Dragoons," dated 5 May 1794.)

Legear, Henry

Henry Legear, 3 Reg. Light Dragoons. (General Index to Compiled Military Service Records of Revolutionary War Soldiers. National Archives Microfilm Publication M860, Card 5999; also card 1587, 2 reg LD.)

Leonard or Leaner, George

George Leonard, W3834. In October 1842, Susanna, nee Minerich, age 79, widow of George Leonard, said he died 17 February 1818. She said that he enlisted under Captain Belfield as a Dragoon, and also served as a wagoner, and that John Hughes was the Quarter Master and Colonel Washington was commander. George Leonard was in battles at or near Savannah. He and Susanna were married in Berkshire County, Hudlebury Township, Pennsylvania, and moved to Augusta County in 1797 or thereabouts. The page from the family Bible showed eleven children with surname Leaner. Certificate dated 10 January 1781 and signed by J. Belfield, Captain L. Dragoons, verified that George Leonard served in the 1st Regiment. (Revolutionary War Pension and Bounty-Land Warrant Application Files. National Archives Microfilm Publication M804, roll 1549.)

Level, Henry

"I do hereby Certify that Henry Level enlisted in 3d Regiment L Dragoons in April 81 for the war...." William Barret, Baylor's Dragoons, Richmond, November 11, 1784. (Virginia Governor's Office. Bounty Warrants, 1779-1860. Accession 41429, The Library of Virginia, Richmond, Va.)

Lewis, Fielding

Fielding Lewis, Captain. Adam Andrews enlisted in August 1777 with Captain Fielding Lewis in the 3rd Regiment of Light Dragoons. (Revolutionary War Pension and Bounty-Land Warrant Application Files. National Archives Microfilm Publication M804, roll 60; also Dorman, John Frederick. 1958. Virginia Revolutionary Pension Applications, 2:48-49.)

John Thorp, of Fauquier County, Virginia, stated in November 1833 that he personally knew Captain Fielding Lewis, deceased, who was an officer in Colonel George Baylor's Regiment, and that he served until the end of the war. James Jones, age 70, of King George County, Virginia, in June 1834 said that Fielding Lewis was a recruiting officer in Baylor's Regiment.

George Baylor wrote to Captain Lewis from Fredericksburg, April 23, 1777: "Dear Sir you will observe in our next Virginia Paper, an advertisement of mine directing all the officers of the Regiment, immediately to bring to this place, all the men they have enlisted... I am with much esteem your Friend, George Baylor."

In an account sent to George Baylor in 1778, Fielding Lewis asks for twelve months pay due him, reimbursement for bounties paid to new recruits, and expenses for corn, horses, and travel expenses for the men of the regiment.

In September 1834, Gilson Foote, widower of Lucinda Foote, nee Lewis, and Eleanor Lewis, widow of Robert Lewis, both of the state of Virginia, claimed to be heirs-at-law of Fielding Lewis, and that the other heirs were residents of Tennessee and other states. (Virginia Governor's Office. Revolutionary War Rejected Claims, 1779-1860. Accession 41986, State government records collection, The Library of Virginia, Richmond, Va.)

Lewis, George

George Lewis, Captain, January 1, 1777. Arrangement of Light Dragoons, 3^d Regiment, undated. (Revolutionary War Rolls, 1775-1783. National Archives Microfilm Publication M246. Roll 115, folder 13, 3^d Regiment Light Dragoons, 1779, item 3.)

Captain Lewis's Commission, 12 Dec 1776. Arrangement of part of Colonel Baylor's Regiment, showing the date of Lieutenant Colonel Byrd's, Captain Smith's, Lieutenant Page's, Lieutenant Randolph's, and Lieutenant Baylor's commissions, undated. (Revolutionary War Rolls, 1775-1783. National Archives

Microfilm Publication M246. Roll 115, folder 13, 3^d Regiment Light Dragoons, 1779, item 4.)

George Lewis, Captain, Dec. A Return of Officers in the 3rd Regiment of Light Dragoons with the Dates of their Commissions, Sept. 18, 1777. (Revolutionary War Rolls, 1775-1783. National Archives Microfilm Publication M246. Roll 115, folder 13, 3^d Regiment Light Dragoons, 1779, item 6.)

George Lewis, Captain, 3 Reg. Light Dragoons. (General Index to Compiled Military Service Records of Revolutionary War Soldiers. National Archives Microfilm Publication M860, Card 5524.)

Lewis, James

"I do certify that James Lewis a Soldier in 1st Regt Light Dragoons enlisted in the Continental Cavalry April 1780 for the war continued to the end of the war." William Parsons, December 4, 1784. (Virginia Governor's Office. Bounty Warrants, 1779-1860. Accession 41429, The Library of Virginia, Richmond, Va.)

James Lewis, S35520. In 1818, James Lewis stated that he first enlisted in Amelia County, Virginia in August 1780 as a private in the company of Captain Bentley, in Colonel Hawes' regiment. When discharged, he then enlisted as a Light Dragoon under Captain Parsons and Colonel William Washington for 27 months. He was in the battle of Guilford Court House, and received a head wound from a broadsword in the battle of Camden, and further stated that he never recovered from this wound.

In August 1820, James Lewis of Washington County, Kentucky, age 60, said he enlisted about 1780 for 18 months in Virginia in Captain Parsons' company commanded by Colonel William Washington. (Revolutionary War Pension and Bounty-Land Warrant Application Files. National Archives Microfilm Publication M804, roll 1556.)

Lewis, Joseph

Joseph Lewis, Farrier, 3 Reg. Dragoons. (General Index to Compiled Military Service Records of Revolutionary War Soldiers. National Archives Microfilm Publication M860, Card 5708.)

Linnard, John

John Linnard had pistol, cartridge box; "Sword and Belt left at Minton." Return, dated 1 March 1778, of arms and accouterments in the Third Troop belonging to Colonel George Baylor's Regiment of Light Dragoons. (Virginia Office of the Quartermaster General, Fredericksburg. Returns of Colonel George Baylor's Regiment, 1778-1779. Accession 22547, The Library of Virginia, Richmond, Va.)

Linton, John

John Linton, Lieutenant, 3 Reg. Light Dragoons. (General Index to Compiled Military Service Records of Revolutionary War Soldiers. National Archives Microfilm Publication M860, Card 799.)

John Linton, mentioned on a roster of officers of 3rd Regiment. (University of Virginia. Alderman Library Special Collections. Accession 2257, Papers of the Baylor Family of Newmarket, Caroline County, Va, in part transcripts: [manuscript], 1653-1915. Box 4: the folder is labeled "1756, 1777-1781; Military Papers," item 21: "ca. 1780 Continental Troops, roster of Officers, 1st & 3rd Regiments.")

Lt. Col. Ed Carrington stated in February 1784 that John Linton first enlisted in the 2nd Virginia regiment in September 1775, re-enlisted in the same regiment in 1776, and at the end of that term, was appointed a Lieutenant in Baylor's Regiment, in which capacity he continued until the end of the war. (Virginia Governor's Office. Bounty Warrants, 1779-1860. Accession 41429, The Library of Virginia, Richmond, Va.)

"I do Certify that Lieut. Jno Linton was appointed an officer in 3 Regiment L Dragoons 1779 & has continued to serve to end of the war." William Barret, Baylor's Dragoons, January 27, 1784. (Virginia Governor's Office. Bounty Warrants, 1779-1860. Accession 41429, The Library of Virginia, Richmond, Va.)

Locket, Benjamin

"I do Certify that Ben. Locket enlisted for the war June 80 in Colonel Baylor's Regiment L Dragoons and has faithfully served the end of the war." William Barret, Captain, November 11, 1784. (Virginia Governor's Office. Bounty Warrants, 1779-1860. Accession 41429, The Library of Virginia, Richmond, Va.)

In September 1822, Benjamin Lockett of Fayette County, Kentucky, declared that he enlisted in 1779 under Captain Barret in the 3rd Regiment of Light Dragoons, commanded by William Washington, and served until July 4, 1783, when he was discharged in Charleston, South Carolina. (Virginia Governor's Office. Bounty Warrants, 1779-1860. Accession 41429, The Library of Virginia, Richmond, Va.)

In September 1822, Benjamin Lockett of Scott County, Kentucky stated that he served with Charles Neale in the 3rd Regiment of Light Dragoons until he was discharged in May 1780 at Nelson's Ferry in South Carolina by Captain Will Parsons. (under Charles Neale. Virginia Governor's Office. Bounty Warrants, 1779-1860. Accession 41429, The Library of Virginia, Richmond, Va.)

Benjamin Lockett, S41780. Benjamin Lockett of Clarke County, Kentucky stated in June 1818 that he was born in Virginia, and was age 56. He enlisted in 1779 in Captain Churchill Jones' troop of dragoons, and was discharged in July 1783 in Charleston, South Carolina. (Revolutionary War Pension and Bounty-Land Warrant Application Files. National Archives Microfilm Publication M804, roll 1576.)

Lockhert, William

"It appears from the Size Roll 3 Troop that Wm Lockhert Enlisted for the war in Baylor's Regiment July 1st 1781 & serv'd faithfully the full term of his Enlistment." William Barret, Baylor's Dragoons. (Virginia Governor's Office. Bounty Warrants, 1779-1860. Accession 41429, The Library of Virginia, Richmond, Va.)

Logen, Hugh

Hugh Logen had sword, pistol, belt, cartridge box; "Present." Return, dated 1 March 1778, of arms and accouterments in the Third Troop belonging to Colonel George Baylor's Regiment of Light Dragoons. (Virginia Office of the Quartermaster General, Fredericksburg. Returns of Colonel George Baylor's Regiment, 1778-1779. Accession 22547, The Library of Virginia, Richmond, Va.)

Long, John

"John Long a Soldier in the 3d Regiment of L. Dragoons having Serv'd faithfully three years is hereby discharged." William Washington, Lt. Col., December 4, 1780. (Virginia Governor's Office. Bounty Warrants, 1779-1860. Accession 41429, The Library of Virginia, Richmond, Va.)

John Long, W5029. John Long of Edgecombe County, North Carolina in November 1824, age 70 or 75, stated that he enlisted for two years in January or February 1776 in Virginia, under Captain Nathaniel Mason, in the regiment commanded by Colonel Lawson. In 1778 he enlisted under Captain William Barret in the Regiment commanded by Col. George Baylor, and was discharged in January or February of 1781. John Long married about 1783 in Sussex County, Virginia, Mary or Polly Armstrong, and lived in Sussex for ten years before moving to Edgecombe County, North Carolina with Mary's father and family. According to William Norfleet of Tarboro, North Carolina, John Long died 11 October 1826 in Edgecombe County. (Revolutionary War Pension and Bounty-Land Warrant Application Files. National Archives Microfilm Publication M804, roll 1580.)

Long, Levi

"It appears from the Size Roll 4th Troop that Levy Long enlisted for the war in Baylor's Dragoons the 30th of April 1781 & serv'd until the Mutiny May 1783." William Barret, Captain, April 19, 1785. (Virginia Governor's Office. Bounty Warrants, 1779-1860. Accession 41429, The Library of Virginia, Richmond, Va.)

Levi Long, BLWt 924-100. In April 1819, in Sussex, Virginia, Levi Long stated that he joined Captain Parson's company in Colonel Washington's Regiment of Cavalry shortly after the battle of Guilford Court House, and before Eutaw Springs. He further stated that he was sick and on furlough when the troops were discharged and so did not receive a discharge certificate. (Revolutionary War Pension and Bounty-Land Warrant Application Files. National Archives Microfilm Publication M804, roll 1581.)

Lovell, James

James Lovell, Lieutenant, 3 Reg. Light Dragoons. (General Index to Compiled Military Service Records of Revolutionary War Soldiers. National Archives Microfilm Publication M860, Card 4050.)

"This is to certify that James Lovell received at this office on the Eighteenth day of May last a Warrant for Two Hundred Acres of Continental Bounty Lands, as a Lieutenant of dragoons during the late war...." Lieutenant John Stagg, June 1785. (Virginia Governor's Office. Bounty Warrants, 1779-1860. Accession 41429, The Library of Virginia, Richmond, Va.)

Loyd, William

Willliam Loyd, S38145. William Loyd enlisted at Chesterfield Court House, Virginia, in Captain David Min's company in Colonel Campbell's Regiment of Infantry for 18 months starting in September 1780. After that term of service, he enlisted in Captain Bell's company in Colonel Washington's Corp, and was in the battles of Camden and Ninety-Six. After the battle of Eutaw Springs, William Loyd served in Colonel Lee's Corps, and was discharged at Winchester, Virginia at the close of the war. In September 1819, William Loyd stated that he was 58 years old, and in 1820, he was living in Halifax County, Virginia, and referred to his wife, age 50 years, and seven children. His widow, Mary Loyd, later stated that he died 10 June 1835. (Revolutionary War Pension and Bounty-Land Warrant Application Files. National Archives Microfilm Publication M804, roll 1596.)

Luallen, Daniel

Daniel Luallen, Private, 3 Reg. Light Dragoons. (General Index to Compiled Military Service Records of Revolutionary War Soldiers. National Archives Microfilm Publication M860, Card 4921.)

Daniel Luallen, Private, enlisted March 9, 1777, "on furlow." Muster Roll of the 2nd Troop in the 3^d Regiment Light Dragoons in the Service of the United States commanded by Lieutenant Colonel William Washington for the Months of May, June, July August, September, October 1779. (Revolutionary War Rolls, 1775-1783. National Archives Microfilm Publication M246. Roll 115, folder 13, 3^d Regiment Light Dragoons, 1779, item 1.)

Lunsford, William

"I do certify that Wm. Lunsford enlisted in the 3d regiment light dragoons Jany 1st 1778 for 3 years and was apptd. Corpl. May 1st 1778 and to the rank of Sergt 1st Nov 1778 and was payed agreeable to my former certificates to the Soldr of the 3d Regiment of L.D. He continued in the Regiment Until he was promoted to the rank of Cornet in Colonel Lee's Legion as Witness my hand." William Barret, June 2, 1784.

"I certify that Mr. William Lunsford was promoted from Baylor's Regiment of dragoons to a commission in the partisan Legion." Henry Lee, February 1792. (Virginia Governor's Office.

Bounty Warrants, 1779-1860. Accession 41429, The Library of Virginia, Richmond, Va.)

Macklin, James

"December 23d 1780 James Macklin Having Served faithfully three years in the 3rd Regiment of Light Dragoons is Hereby discharged." William Washington, Lt. Col. (Virginia Governor's Office. Bounty Warrants, 1779-1860. Accession 41429, The Library of Virginia, Richmond, Va.)

Mann, Claiborne

"I do Certify that Claiborne Mann Enlisted for the war in Colonel Baylor's Dragoons July 15 1780 and Cont'd to serve as a good faithful soldier until his death August 1782." William Barret, Baylor's Dragoons. Olive Mann is heir-at-law of Claiborne Mann, December 13, 1784. (Virginia Governor's Office. Bounty Warrants, 1779-1860. Accession 41429, The Library of Virginia, Richmond, Va.)

Marshall, Richard

Richard Marshall, W7391. Richard Marshall stated that he enlisted as a private about May 1, 1776 for three years in Captain Merryweather's 1st Regiment under Colonel George Gibson. After serving two years and nine months, he enlisted 1 February 1779 for four years in Captain Jones' company of the 3rd Regiment of Light Dragoons, under Colonel Washington. He was discharged at Winchester, Virginia, and his discharge was written by Captain Robert Morrow.

In May of 1818, he was living in Muskingum County, Ohio; in 1820 Richard Marshall stated that he was aged 63, his wife Keziah (nee Sherer) was 71, and they had living with them two grandchildren. In October 1847, his widow was a resident of Jonathan Township, Guernsey County, Ohio, age about 90, and residing in the house of Samuel Steel, with her granddaughter's family. She stated that Richard Marshall died in Meigs Township, Washington County, Ohio, 4 November 1841. She also said that she thought they had married about 1784 in Spotsylvania County, Virginia. She was still alive in 1856, stating her age as 94. (Revolutionary War Pension and Bounty-Land Warrant Application Files. National Archives Microfilm Publication M804, roll 1635.)

Martin, Boling

Boling Martin was listed as a prisoner on a report of the Quarter Guards of the 3rd Regiment Light Dragoons, April 26, 1782 at Halifax, Virginia, for "Leaving his guard in the night & Suppos'd with an Intent to Desert." (University of Virginia. Alderman Library Special Collections. Accession 2257, Papers of the Baylor Family of Newmarket, Caroline County, Va, in part transcripts: [manuscript], 1653-1915. Box 4: the folder is labeled "Military Papers, 1782, 1814, & n.d.," item 11: "1782 Apr 26 Continental Troops, Report 3rd Regiment Light Dragoons detachments stationed at Halifax, Va.")

Massey, John

"Massey, John, Cornet and Paymaster 1st Continental Dragoons in 1781; trans. To Baylor's Reg. Of Dragoons Nov. 9, 1782; awarded 150 acres." (Gwathmey, John Hastings. 1938. Historical Register of Virginians in the Revolution: Soldiers, sailors, marines, 1775-1783. Dietz Press, Richmond, Va.)

In a letter to the Governor of Virginia in 1834, written by the heirs of the late John Massey, they were listed as Robert Massey, Susan Jack, and William Massey of Alexandria, Virginia, and John Henry Massey of Charleston, South Carolina. "I certify that Land Warrant No. 2076 for 150 acres issued at this office, this day, to Robert Massey, & Susan Jack, grand children, William & John H. Massey, great grand children, and the only heirs at law of John Massey, deceased who was a Cornet in the Virginia Continental Line." William Gordon of the Bounty Land Office, December 1, 1834. (Virginia Governor's Office. Bounty Warrants, 1779-1860. Accession 41429, The Library of Virginia, Richmond, Va.)

John Massey, BLWt 2076-150. In 1834, Robert Massey and Susan Jack, heirs-at-law of John Massey, late of King George County, Virginia, stated that he served as a cornet of Dragoons, and died intestate in King George County in 1795. (Revolutionary War Pension and Bounty-Land Warrant Application Files. National Archives Microfilm Publication M804, roll 1648.)

May, Thomas

"I do Certify that Thomas May enlisted for the war Dec. 20th 1779 in 3d Regiment Dragoons & was paid in paper dollars to 1st August 1780, was appointed Corporal August 1780. He served to 5th May 1783 when he left his officers in South Carolina, for which default Congress has Given them a full pardon, as witness my hand." William Barret, Captain, Baylor's Dragoons, May 25, 1784. (Virginia Governor's Office. Bounty Warrants, 1779-1860. Accession 41429, The Library of Virginia, Richmond, Va.)

On August 27, 1840, Polly May of Richmond stated that Thomas enlisted at a place called Cold Harbor in Hanover County, Virginia. Thomas received a pension until he died in 1830. (under William May. Virginia Governor's Office. Bounty Warrants, 1779-1860. Accession 41429, The Library of Virginia, Richmond, Va.)

Thomas May. S38175. In 1818, Thomas May, age 58 declared that he enlisted in the 3rd Regiment of Light Dragoons in December 1779 and served to the close of the war. Previous to this service, he served in the infantry under General William Woodford, and was bayoneted at the battle of Monmouth Court House.

"I do certify that Thomas May was enlisted a Soldier in the 3rd Regiment of Light Dragoons (commanded by Colonel George Baylor) in December 1779 for the war – he was appointed a Corporal in said Regiment which warrant he held at the close of the war. That he was wounded at the Battle of Eutaw (I believe). That he is now a cripple and merits the consideration of Congress. I served as an officer in said Regiment from January 1777 to the end of the war." Churchill Jones, March 13, 1818. (Revolutionary War Pension and Bounty-Land Warrant Application Files. National Archives Microfilm Publication M804, roll 1658.)

May, William

"I do Certify that Wm May deceased enlisted in 3 Regiment L Dragoons for the war Dec. 20 79 and served faithfully until the action at Eutaw when he was killed, was payed to the 1 Augt 1780." William Barret, May 20, 1784.

In August 1820, in Henrico County, Virginia, Thomas and Molly May stated that they were the heirs of their brother William May, who enlisted first in the Virginia Infantry under Captain William Campbell, then enlisted in the 3rd Regiment Light Dragoons and was killed at Eutaw Springs. Their father, Benjamin May, received a warrant for 200 acres of land for William's service. (Virginia Governor's Office. Bounty Warrants, 1779-1860. Accession 41429, The Library of Virginia, Richmond, Va.)

"I do certify that William May was enlisted in the 3d Regiment of Light Dragoons (Commanded by Colonel George

Baylor) on the 18th Dec. 1779 for the war. The said May was appointed a Sergeant in the Regiment. The date of his appointment I cannot appertain. He had first been discharged from the Infantry of Virginia, when he enlisted..." Churchill Jones, 9 July 1830.

On August 27, 1840, Polly May of Richmond stated that she was the only surviving heir of her brother William May, who enlisted under Captain William Barret in the Dragoons, and was killed at the battle of Cowpens. She also said that William enlisted at a place called Cold Harbor in Hanover County, Virginia. (Virginia Governor's Office. Bounty Warrants, 1779-1860. Accession 41429, The Library of Virginia, Richmond, Va.)

McByrde, James or James M Byrde

"Jams M'Byrde" his "Sword Belt and Cartridge Box given to Minton." Return, dated 1 March 1778, of arms and accouterments in the Third Troop belonging to Colonel George Baylor's Regiment of Light Dragoons. (Virginia Office of the Quartermaster General, Fredericksburg. Returns of Colonel George Baylor's Regiment, 1778-1779. Accession 22547, The Library of Virginia, Richmond, Va.)

McClanahan or McLanahan, Thomas

Thomas McClanahan, W1052. In September 1832, Thomas McClanahan stated that he was born in Westmoreland County, Virginia, and raised in Fauquier and Culpeper counties. In late summer of 1775 he enlisted for twelve months with Colonel Patrick Henry, Lt. Colonel Christy, in the company of Captain John Green. After nine months he transferred to the 2nd regiment commanded by Colonel Alexander Spotswood, under Captain Francis Taylor for two years, by trading places with Reuben McKinney.

Thomas McClanahan moved with the Regiment in the fall of 1776 to Fredericksburg, then Baltimore, and in the spring of 1777 to Philadelphia. He was at Valley Forge when his term of enlistment expired, and in January 1778 he enlisted in the Company of Horse commanded by Captain William Barret of Colonel Baylor's Regiment for three years. Thomas stated that one of the terms of his enlistment was a three-month furlough, so he was ordered to rendezvous on April 10, 1778 at Fredericksburg. He stated that during his furlough, he married the sister of John Green in Culpeper County, and got Captain Barret to write his discharge and enlist John Green in his place. His discharge was burned in a fire at his father's (William McClanahan's) house, in Culpeper. Thomas McClanahan also said he enlisted in Botetourt County, Virginia, where he was living, and did a short tour of militia duty in North Carolina under Captain James Wood and Colonel Preston.

Thomas McClanahan moved from Botetourt County to Montgomery County, Virginia, then to Bourbon County, Kentucky. In March 1833, Thomas McClanahan was a resident of Simpson County, Kentucky, and stated that he was born 1753 in Westmoreland County, Virginia. He referred to seven children living with him, out of a total of 20. In Simpson County, in June 1855, Tabitha McClanahan stated that Thomas McClanahan died in Simpson County September 1, 1845, and a certificate from the Logan County, Kentucky, clerk's office stated that Thomas McClanahan and Tabitha Williams were married 28 February 1817. (Revolutionary War Pension and Bounty-Land Warrant Application Files. National Archives Microfilm Publication M804, roll 1667.)

McCraw, Francis

"It appears from the size roll of the 4th Troop that Francis McCraw enlisted for the war in Baylor's Dragoons March 15, 1781." William Barret, January 12, 1786. (Virginia Governor's Office. Bounty Warrants, 1779-1860. Accession 41429, The Library of Virginia, Richmond, Va.)

Francis McCraw, W7410. In Surrey County, North Carolina, in January 1819, Francis McCraw stated that he enlisted in Henry County, Virginia in 1780, with Captain Elijah King and served to the end of the war. He was in the battles of Ninety-Six and Eutaw Springs, and served under the command of Col. William Washington. He was discharged in Virginia. In January 1803, Samuel McCraw (no relationship given) declared that Francis McCraw enlisted in 1781 for three years or the duration. In September 1820, Francis was age 62, and said that he served three years and two months, and got a furlough from Major Swan to go to Henry County, Virginia. He mentioned his sons, George, age 8, and Francis, age 10, and mentioned a tract of land belonging to the heirs of Jacob McCraw, in Surrey County. In March 1829, he stated that he served under Captain Gordon.

His widow stated that he died 2 June 1839, and she mentioned three children. Sally McCraw died 27 September 1843, in Carroll County, Virginia. In a summary letter written by Winfield Scott of the War Department, it stated that Francis

McCraw married in Surrey County, North Carolina, in 1786, Sally Burruss, and that he was living in Grayson County, Virginia in September 1818, age 58, and that his widow was in Grayson County in Jan 1842, age over 80. (Revolutionary War Pension and Bounty-Land Warrant Application Files. National Archives Microfilm Publication M804, roll 1673.)

McDonnaugh, Jonathan

Jno. McDonnaugh, Private, enlisted March 4, 1777, on command. Muster Roll of the 2nd Troop in the 3d Regiment Light Dragoons in the Service of the United States commanded by Lieutenant Colonel William Washington for the Months of May, June, July August, September, October 1779. (Revolutionary War Rolls, 1775-1783. National Archives Microfilm Publication M246. Roll 115, folder 13, 3d Regiment Light Dragoons, 1779, item 1.)

McElroy or Mackelroy, James

James Mackelroy, Private, enlisted October 17, 1779. Muster Roll of the 2nd Troop in the 3d Regiment Light Dragoons in the Service of the United States commanded by Lieutenant Colonel William Washington for the Months of May, June, July August, September, October 1779. (Revolutionary War Rolls, 1775-1783. National Archives Microfilm Publication M246. Roll 115, folder 13, 3d Regiment Light Dragoons, 1779, item 1.)

James McElroy, pay due him as Dragoon from 17 October 1779 to 18 October 1782. (Miscellaneous Numbered Records [The Manuscript File] in the War Department Collection of Revolutionary War Records, 1775-1790's. National Archives Microfilm Publication M859. Manuscript 17665, "The United States in a/c with James McElroy late Dragoons 3d Reg Virginia," dated 30 November 1792.)

McLaughter, Thomas

Thomas McLaughter, Sergeant, March 1, 1777. Muster Roll of the 2nd Troop in the 3d Regiment Light Dragoons in the Service of the United States commanded by Lieutenant Colonel William Washington for the Months of May, June, July August, September, October 1779. (Revolutionary War Rolls, 1775-1783. National Archives Microfilm Publication M246. Roll 115, folder 13, 3d Regiment Light Dragoons, 1779, item 1.)

McMahan, Andrew

"I do Certify that Andrew McMahan was enlisted for the war in Colonel Geo. Baylor's Regiment L. Dragoons Feby 7th 1780 & was appointed Sergeant July 1780 & Continued to serve as a good & faithful soldier the full term of his enlistment." William Barret, Captain. December 6, 1784. (Virginia Governor's Office. Bounty Warrants, 1779-1860. Accession 41429, The Library of Virginia, Richmond, Va.)

Andrew McMahan, S38931. In August 1819, Andrew McMahan claimed that he enlisted in King and Queen County, Virginia, under Captain William Campbell of the 1st Virginia Regiment, commanded by Col. Gibson in the winter of 1776, and served for three years. He was discharged in Alexandria, Virginia, by Major Ellison, and there enlisted in the 3rd Regiment commanded by Col. Baylor and William Washington, serving to the end of the war. He was discharged on the Santee River in South Carolina, but didn't receive a written discharge. Andrew McMahan was in the battles of Monmouth, Guilford Court House, Camden, and Eutaw Springs, and was not wounded during the war.

In 1819 he was age 58, had been nearly blind for ten years, and was living with two unmarried daughters on his son's land, in Wilson County, Tennessee. Also in 1819, his son William, who was also known as William McHaney, stated that Andrew McMahan lived in Pittsylvania County, Virginia right after the war. In 1820, Andrew, age 59, was still living in Wilson County, and stated that his daughter Polly was age 22 or 23. The summary letter from the War Department stated that Andrew McMahan enlisted in March 1777 and served as a fifer for three years, until April 1780, under Captain Thomas Hamilton in the 1st Virginia Regiment commanded by Col. George Gibson. He then served as a sergeant in the 4th troop under Captain William Parsons in the 1st Regiment of Light Dragoons, under William Washington. (Revolutionary War Pension and Bounty-Land Warrant Application Files. National Archives Microfilm Publication M804, roll 1695.)

Meredith, Jesse

Jesse Meredith, Sergeant, sick. Muster Roll of the 2nd Troop in the 3^{d} Regiment Light Dragoons in the Service of the United States commanded by Lieutenant Colonel William Washington for the Months of May, June, July August, September, October 1779. (Revolutionary War Rolls, 1775-1783. National Archives

Microfilm Publication M246. Roll 115, folder 13, 3^d Regiment Light Dragoons, 1779, item 1.)

Jesse Meredith, S38205. In September 1819, Jesse Meredith, a resident of Smith County, Tennessee, stated that he enlisted in March 1776 for two years under Captain James Lucas of the 4th Virginia Regiment, and served until December 1777. He then enlisted in Col. Baylor's Regiment for three years under Captain Cadwallader Jones, and served two years and three months, at which time he fell from his horse and hired a man to complete his service, receiving a certificate from his captain and being discharged. He fought in the battles of Trenton, Princeton, Brandywine and Germantown.

In February of 1822, Jesse Meredith was a resident of Dallas County, Alabama, age 67, and stated that he enlisted in Brunswick Court House, Virginia in the late winter 1776 in the 4th Regiment of the Virginia line under Col. Lawson and Captain James Lucas. He served two years, then enlisted at Valley Forge under Captain Jones and Col. Baylor. He served two years and nine months, and obtained a substitute at Petersburg, Virginia. In June 1860, his son Jesse, of Claiborne County, Louisiana, said that Jesse Meredith died in Dallas County, Alabama, 22 February 1834, and that he had lived there for eight years prior to his death. In February 1791, Cadwallader Jones affirmed Jesse Meredith's service. (Revolutionary War Pension and Bounty-Land Warrant Application Files. National Archives Microfilm Publication M804, roll 1711.)

Meriwether, James

James Meriwether signed a report of the Quarter Guard of the 3rd Regiment Light Dragoons, May 2, 1782. (University of Virginia. Alderman Library Special Collections. Accession 2257, Papers of the Baylor Family of Newmarket, Caroline County, Va, in part transcripts: [manuscript], 1653-1915. Box 4: the folder is labeled "Military Papers, 1782, 1814, & n.d.," item 13: "1782 May 2, Continental Troops, report of Quarter Guard, 3rd Regiment Light Dragoons, Report signed by James Meriwether, Lt. Officer of the Day.")

Metheany, Luke

Luke Metheany, R7149. In Overton County, Tennessee, in 1818, Luke Metheany, age 65, stated that he enlisted 27 March 1777 in Berkeley county, Virginia, under Captain Francis Willis, in the

16th Virginia Regiment, commanded by Col. Grayson for three years. On 1 September 1777, he was taken prisoner at Brandywine, and was exchanged 14 June 1778. He was in the battle at Monmouth, and then attached to the regiment under Col. Gist. In 1779 he was one of the troops volunteered under General Wayne to storm Stony Point. After the battle of Trenton, he enlisted for the duration of the war. On 13 April 1780, he was replaced by a substitute, and at the time of this discharge, was attached to the cavalry of Col. William Washington. In October 1820, he was living in Overton county, Tennessee, age 67, and stated that he had been held prisoner on board the prison ship on the Delaware River, and that he had been exchanged at a place named Rising Sun, near Philadelphia. He wintered in 1779 at Trenton Barracks in Col. Washington's service, and was discharged April 1780 in Petersburg, due to bad health.

In 1820, Luke Methaney had three children with him, and his wife was 63. In June of 1826 he was living in Monroe County, Kentucky, because his children moved there and he was too old to live alone. In January 1840, according to his son William, Luke's wife, Eleander, was age 80, and living in Fredericksburg, Virginia. They had been married 25 December 1781, and he had a total of ten children. His son Joshua Metheany said Eleander died 15 May 1842 and his father died about 4 August 1839. (Revolutionary War Pension and Bounty-Land Warrant Application Files. National Archives Microfilm Publication M804, roll 1719.)

Minton, Abnezor or Ebenezer

"Abnezor Minton" had sword, belt; "Sword Broke in Store." Return, dated 1 March 1778, of arms and accouterments in the Third Troop belonging to Colonel George Baylor's Regiment of Light Dragoons. (Virginia Office of the Quartermaster General, Fredericksburg. Returns of Colonel George Baylor's Regiment, 1778-1779. Accession 22547, The Library of Virginia, Richmond, Va.)

"I do Certify that Ebenezer Minton enlisted with the first Regiment of Light Dragoons for the war and served until the end thereof." Captain John Watts, August 17, 1807. (Virginia Governor's Office. Bounty Warrants, 1779-1860. Accession 41429, The Library of Virginia, Richmond, Va.)

Ebenezer Minton, S38949. In September, 1819, in Lee County, Virginia, Ebenezer Minton stated that he enlisted 11 August

1777 at Petersburg, in the 3rd Regiment commanded by Col. George Baylor, in the troop under Capt. Churchill Jones for three years. He re-enlisted in 1780 in the same regiment, which was then under the command of Col. William Washington, and served to the end of the war. He was in the battles of Cowpens, Guilford Courthouse, Camden, and Eutaw Springs.

In September 1820, still in Lee County, Ebenezer Minton said he enlisted under an officer named Fitzpatrick of the Dragoons, marched to Fredericksburg, and placed in the 3rd troop commanded by Capt. Churchill Jones. He wintered in Fredericksburg in 1777-1778, and in the spring marched north. He was at the surprise at Tappan, where Col. Baylor was badly wounded, and served to the end of the war. He was at the defeat of Bluford at Moncks Corner, and re-enlisted at Hillsborough in North Carolina under Capt. William Barret or Capt. Churchill Jones, and was discharged on the Santee by Major John Watts. In 1820, his wife, Elizabeth, was age about 55, and he had seven children and two orphaned grandchildren living with him. In 1826, Ebenezer Minton was living with his son Ebenezer, in Blount County, Tennessee. (Revolutionary War Pension and Bounty-Land Warrant Application Files. National Archives Microfilm Publication M804, roll 1740.)

Moore, David

David Moore, R7349. In September 1819, in Jessamine County, Kentucky, David Moore stated that he first enlisted in Dinwiddie County, Virginia, under Capt. Nathan Fox, of the 5th Virginia Regiment for two years. After that service, and while under Capt. Churchill Jones in the 3rd Regiment, he was taken prisoner at Wilmington, but escaped with two others after two days and rejoined his regiment at Chatham, New Jersey. He says that others who are acquainted with his service are Reuben Plunkett, William Bryant, and William Carter. David Moore in January 1821, at age 60, said he enlisted in the horse service under Capt. C. Jones, in the 3rd Virginia Regiment under Col. Baylor. He was at Valley Forge, in the battles of Monmouth, Santee, Moncks Corner, served three years, and was discharged at Guilford Court House.

His wife, Nancy, was over 70 years old and he spoke of one granddaughter, age about 28, who had two children. In 1853, David Moore's widow claimed he died in Jessamine County, Kentucky, in August 1838 in "Roasting ear" time, and she had a granddaughter living with her who would be 14 in November 1853. His widow stated that she was born Nancy Garner, and married David Moore in Virginia, two miles east of Fredericksburg, in Spotsylvania County, about 1815. Their oldest child now living was born about two years afterwards. In 1861, Nancy Moore was living in Mercer County, Kentucky, age 65-70. (Revolutionary War Pension and Bounty-Land Warrant Application Files. National Archives Microfilm Publication M804, roll 1753.)

Morrow, Robert

Robert Morrow, Lieutenant, Present. Muster Roll of the 2nd Troop in the 3^d Regiment Light Dragoons in the Service of the United States commanded by Lieutenant Colonel William Washington for the Months of May, June, July August, September, October 1779. (Revolutionary War Rolls, 1775-1783. National Archives Microfilm Publication M246. Roll 115, folder 13, 3^d Regiment Light Dragoons, 1779, item 1.)

Robert Morrow, Cornet, February 20, 1777, commission granted March 4, 1778. (Revolutionary War Rolls, 1775-1783. National Archives Microfilm Publication M246. Roll 115, folder 13, 3^d Regiment Light Dragoons, 1779, item 2.)

Robert Morrow, Lieutenant, Date of Commission January 3, 1779. Arrangement of Light Dragoons, 3^d Regiment, undated. (Revolutionary War Rolls, 1775-1783. National Archives Microfilm Publication M246. Roll 115, folder 13, 3^d Regiment Light Dragoons, 1779, item 3.)

Robert Morrow, Cornet, February 20, 1777. Robert Morrow, Adjutant, June 1, 1778. A Return of Officers in the 3rd Regiment of Light Dragoons with the Dates of their Commissions, Sept. 18, 1777. (Revolutionary War Rolls, 1775-1783. National Archives Microfilm Publication M246. Roll 115, folder 13, 3^d Regiment Light Dragoons, 1779, item 6.)

"I am glad to hear Mr Morrow has been so successful in getting accouterments for the Regiment..." (University of Virginia. Alderman Library Special Collections. Accession 2257, Papers of the Baylor Family of Newmarket, Caroline County, Va, in part transcripts: [manuscript], 1653-1915. Box 4: the folder is labeled "1756, 1777-1781; Military Papers," item 8: "Letter from Alexander Clough to George Baylor, 4 February 1778.")

Lieutenant Morrow, Adjutant in Baylor's Regiment, gave deposition that upon finding himself surrounded by the British troops, he offered to surrender, upon which the British stabbed him seven times and stripped him of all his clothes. (David Griffith. Letter, 20 October 1778. Accession 22789. Personal papers collection. The Library of Virginia, Richmond, Va.)

Lieutenant Morrow. "...and besides Major Clough who died of his wounds, there were wounded of the Officers, Colonel Baylor, Lieutenant Morrow and Mr. Evans the Surgeon." (David Griffith. Letter, 20 October 1778. Accession 22789. Personal papers collection. The Library of Virginia, Richmond, Va.)

Robert Morrow, BLWt 1508-300-Capt issued September 5 1799 to James Taylor, assignee of David Morrow, only surviving brother and heir of Robert Morrow. (Revolutionary War Pension and Bounty-Land Warrant Application Files. National Archives Microfilm Publication M804, roll 1774.)

"I do certify that Capt. Robert Morrow Served as Adjutant to the 3rd Reg. Dragoons From the 25 of July 1778 until the 25 of Feby. 1780." John Belfield, Major Light Dragoons. Virginia Governor's Office. Bounty Warrants, 1779-1860. Accession 41429, The Library of Virginia, Richmond, Va.)

Moxley, George

"I do Certify that Capt. Geo. Moxley enlisted for the war the 12th Decr. 1776 to serve in 3 Reg. LD. He drew pay from his Enlistment to 1st Augt. 1780 & no more as witness my hand." William Barret, 15 April 1784. (Virginia Governor's Office. Bounty Warrants, 1779-1860. Accession 41429, The Library of Virginia, Richmond, Va.)

Mullen or Mullens, Anthony

"I Certify that Antoney Mulens enlisted for the war Febry 79 and has been in actual Service ever since." John Perry, Cornet 1st Regiment Light Dragoons, August 21, 1783. (Virginia Governor's Office. Bounty Warrants, 1779-1860. Accession 41429, The Library of Virginia, Richmond, Va.)

Anthony Mullen, W8280. In January 1829 in Lincoln County, Tennessee, Anthony Mullen, age 78, claimed that he enlisted in February 1777 in Fredericksburg, Virginia for three years under Capt. William Barret and Col. William Washington. They marched to Fredericktown, Maryland, and then to Philadelphia. He was in the battles at Guilford Court House, and Hillsborough. He re-enlisted at Camp Creek, North Carolina for the duration of the war, marched to Charleston, and was discharged at Richmond. His last captain was Churchill Jones.

At the time of his statement, he had eighteen children, and that there were currently ten in his family. In 1854, also in Lincoln County, his wife declared that Anthony Mullen died 3 November 1836, and that they had married in November 1808, and that she was 74. William Mullen of Lincoln County, age 65, and Andrew Mullen, age 55, stated that they were from Anthony's first marriage; his second wife was Sarah Rambles, who married Anthony in Albemarle County, Virginia. In November 1801, Churchill Jones affirmed that Anthony Mullen enlisted in February 1779, and served until the end of the war. John Perry, Cornet in the 1st Light Dragoons also affirmed his service in August 1783. (Revolutionary War Pension and Bounty-Land Warrant Application Files. National Archives Microfilm Publication M804, roll 1786.)

Mullen, George

George Mullen, Private, enlisted in 1777, sick. Muster Roll of the 2nd Troop in the 3d Regiment Light Dragoons in the Service of the United States commanded by Lieutenant Colonel William Washington for the Months of May, June, July August, September, October 1779. (Revolutionary War Rolls, 1775-1783. National Archives Microfilm Publication M246. Roll 115, folder 13, 3d Regiment Light Dragoons, 1779, item 1.)

Muse, George

"I do hereby Certify that Mr. George Muse served three years in the 3rd Regiment of Light Dragoons. He was enlisted in December 1777 & was discharged 14 January 1781, the last two years that he was in the Regiment he was appointed Sergeant." George Baylor, Colonel of the 1st Regiment of Cavalry, Caroline County, Virginia, June 26, 1783.

"Sir, please to deliver my Land warrant to Mr. Lawrence Muse as it is inconvenient for me to come to Richmond...." Signed by George Muse, June 26, 1783, with witnesses Caroline Muse and Francis Muse. (Virginia Governor's Office. Bounty Warrants, 1779-1860. Accession 41429, The Library of Virginia, Richmond, Va.)

Neal or Neale, Charles

Charles Neal, belonging to the third troop of the first regiment of dragoons commanded by Colonel George Baylor, given leave of absence until summoned by notice printed in the Virginia newspapers. (Miscellaneous Numbered Records [The Manuscript File] in the War Department Collection of Revolutionary War Records, 1775-1790's. National Archives Microfilm Publication M859. Manuscript 17664, "Charles Neal, Discharge," dated 12 June 1783, at Nelson's Ferry.)

Charles Neal. On 29 December 1784, William Barret of Baylor's Dragoons certified that according to the size roll of the 3rd troop, Charles Neal enlisted 6 October 1780 and served to the end of his enlistment. (Miscellaneous Numbered Records [The Manuscript File] in the War Department Collection of Revolutionary War Records, 1775-1790's. National Archives Microfilm Publication M859. Manuscript 20326, dated 29 December 1784.)

Charles Neal, pay as Dragoon for 1782 and 1783, dated 31 July 1786. (Miscellaneous Numbered Records [The Manuscript File] in the War Department Collection of Revolutionary War Records, 1775-1790's. National Archives Microfilm Publication M859. Manuscript 17627, "Pay to Charles Neal drag^n," dated 31 July 1786.)

Charles Neal, W9587. In April 1818, at Great Crossings, Scott County, Kentucky, Charles Neal declared that he served as a regular soldier for two years, enlisting in 1779 or 1780 in Colonel William Washington's Regiment of Light Dragoons. He was at the Battle of Cowpens, Camden, Guilford Court House, and Eutaw Springs. He received an honorable discharge at Nelson's Ferry on the Santee River in June 1782 or 1783. At the time of this statement, Charles Neal was 55, infirm and poor.

According to his widow, Ann, nee Miller, who was living in Switzerland County, Indiana, in October 1838, Charles Neal died 27 August 1831. In 1784 or 1785, the family had lived in Orange County, Virginia, but then moved to Madison County, Kentucky; from there they moved to Scott County, Kentucky and then to Switzerland County, Indiana. Charles Neal married Ann Miller; the marriage bond was dated 22 August 1785. They had seven children. The widow was living in Pleasant Township in Switzerland County in 1844, and she died 30 July 1854. (Revolutionary War Pension and Bounty-Land Warrant Application Files. National Archives Microfilm Publication M804, roll 1803.)

Charles Neal, of Scott County, Kentucky, in October 1818, declared he was a soldier in Colonel William Washington's regiment in the Virginia Line. On 5 September 1823, Charles Neal of Scott County, Kentucky, aged 61, declared he and John Casey enlisted on the same day in 1779 at Hillsborough, North Carolina, in Colonel Washington's Light Dragoons, and served together until the close of the war, fighting at Cowpens, Guilford, Camden and Eutaw Springs. (under John Casey. Revolutionary War Pension and Bounty-Land Warrant Application Files. National Archives Microfilm Publication M804, roll 493; also Dorman, John Frederick. 1958. Virginia Revolutionary Pension Applications, 16:73.)

In June 1819, Charles Neal of Scott County, Kentucky, stated that he was raised in Culpeper County, Virginia, and in 1780 enlisted in the militia, and traveled to Hillsborough, North Carolina. After his release from the militia, he enlisted under Captain William Barret in the 3rd Light Dragoons, and fought at Cowpens, Camden, Guilford Court House, and Eutaw Springs. He was discharged at Nelson's Ferry on the Santee River in South Carolina.

In July 1819, William Cardwell of Bullett County, Kentucky stated that he was a Quartermaster Sergeant in the 3rd Light Dragoons and that he was acquainted with Charles Neal, who enlisted in 1780 and served to the close of the war. Also John Story, of Franklin County Kentucky, stated that he enlisted in the fall of 1780, at Hillsborough, North Carolina, and that Charles Neal enlisted at the same time as he did, in the 3rd Regiment. He further stated that Charles Neal was a good and faithful soldier. (Virginia Governor's Office. Bounty Warrants, 1779-1860. Accession 41429, The Library of Virginia, Richmond, Va.)

"I find by the papers in my possession that Charles Neal was enlisted as a soldier in the 3d Regiment L Dragoons for 3 years in the month of October 1780 that he joined the Regiment in the same month. I further find him on the Muster Roll in the month of August 1782 therefore have no doubt but he served to the end of the war." Churchill Jones, Orange County, undated. (Virginia Governor's Office. Bounty Warrants, 1779-1860. Accession 41429, The Library of Virginia, Richmond, Va.)

Neilson, John

John Neilson, mentioned on a roster of officers of 3rd Regiment. (University of Virginia. Alderman Library Special Collections. Accession 2257, Papers of the Baylor Family of Newmarket, Caroline County, Va, in part transcripts: [manuscript], 1653-1915. Box 4: the folder is labeled "1756, 1777-1781; Military

Papers," item 21: "ca. 1780 Continental Troops, roster of Officers, 1st & 3rd Regiments.")

Nelson, George

"I do Certify that Sergeant Geo. Nelson enlisted as a Soldier in Colonel Baylor's Dragoons for three years 1st Feby 1777 & served as a Good & faithful Soldier the full time of his enlistment." William Barret, Captain, undated.

"Geo. Nelson to receive pay as private from the time of his enlistment to first September 1778. He acted as Sergeant." Churchill Jones, December 11, 1784. (Virginia Governor's Office. Bounty Warrants, 1779-1860. Accession 41429, The Library of Virginia, Richmond, Va.)

Nelson, Roger

"I do hereby Certify that Lieut. Roger Nelson was an arranged officer in the consolidated 1st & 3d Regiment of Cavalry." George Baylor, Caroline County, March 28, 1785. (Virginia Governor's Office. Bounty Warrants, 1779-1860. Accession 41429, The Library of Virginia, Richmond, Va.)

Roger Nelson, Lieutenant of Col. Baylor's Dragoons; pay as Lieutenant from 1 January 1782 to 1 January 1783. (M859 Miscellaneous Numbered Records (Miscellaneous Numbered Records [The Manuscript File] in the War Department Collection of Revolutionary War Records, 1775-1790's. National Archives Microfilm Publication M859. Manuscript 17518, "The United States in Account with Lt. Roger Nelson of Colonel Baylor's Dragoons," dated 30 September 1785.)

Nevil, Zachariah

Zachariah Nevil, Private, pay due him from 20 May 1781 to 15 November 1783. (Miscellaneous Numbered Records [The Manuscript File] in the War Department Collection of Revolutionary War Records, 1775-1790's. National Archives Microfilm Publication M859. Manuscript 17660, "The United States in Account Zachariah Nevil priv^e late 3rd Regiment Light Dragoons," dated 27 January 1794.)

Newlin or Newland, Mathew

"It appears from the size roll of 5th Troop that Mathew Newlin enlisted for the war in 3d Regiment L. D. Jany 1780 &

Served until the Mutiny May 83." William Barrett, Captain, undated. (Virginia Governor's Office. Bounty Warrants, 1779-1860. Accession 41429, The Library of Virginia, Richmond, Va.)

Matthew Newland, S46396. In September 1828, Mathias Newland of Finley Township, Washington, Pennsylvania, said he enlisted as a private in Captain John Hughes' company under Col. William Washington's Regiment of cavalry. In another statement, he claimed to have enlisted on February 3, 1780 in Captain Griffin Fauntleroy's company, and served in that company until the end of the war, when he was discharged at Winchester, Virginia. (Revolutionary War Pension and Bounty-Land Warrant Application Files. National Archives Microfilm Publication M804, roll 1812.)

Newton, George

George Newton "Deserted with his arms." Return, dated 1 March 1778, of arms and accouterments in the Third Troop belonging to Colonel George Baylor's Regiment of Light Dragoons. (Virginia Office of the Quartermaster General, Fredericksburg. Returns of Colonel George Baylor's Regiment, 1778-1779. Accession 22547, The Library of Virginia, Richmond, Va.)

Nixon, Andrew

Andrew Nixon signed an oath of allegiance 18 August 1778, as Adjutant. (Numbered Record Books Concerning Military Operations and Service, Pay and Settlement of Accounts, and Supplies in the War Department Collection of Revolutionary War Records. National Archives Microfilm Publication M853. Roll 12: Oaths of allegiance and fidelity and oaths of office 1778-1781. Book 166, page 106.)

Andrew Nixon, Lieutenant, cash paid to him by Colonel Palfrey, 2 October 1780. Also cash paid him by Mr. Pierce for his pay, 30 April 1781. (Miscellaneous Numbered Records [The Manuscript File] in the War Department Collection of Revolutionary War Records, 1775-1790's. National Archives Microfilm Publication M859. Manuscript 17584, "George Baylor's Regiment of Horse," undated.)

"This may Certify that Captain Andrew Nixon of the Virginia light Dragoons on Continental establishment has served in the Army from 1776 to date & is still in Service." George Weedon, April 14, 1783. (Virginia Governor's Office. Bounty Warrants,

1779-1860. Accession 41429, The Library of Virginia, Richmond, Va.)

Nixon, John

"I do Certify that John Nixon enlisted in Baylor's Dragoons for three years July 1778 & served until his Death August 1779...." William Barret, Captain, December 21, 1785. (under Andrew Nixon. Virginia Governor's Office. Bounty Warrants, 1779-1860. Accession 41429, The Library of Virginia, Richmond, Va.)

Norris, Bezeled

"I do certify that Bezeled Norris enlisted in the Continental Cavalry the first Feby 1781 for during the war and until the month of May 1783 at which time he left the Regiment with Sergt. Dangerfield who revolted at that time." William Parsons, Captain 1st Regiment Light Dragoons, Petersburg, September 13, 1784. (Virginia Governor's Office. Bounty Warrants, 1779-1860. Accession 41429, The Library of Virginia, Richmond, Va.)

Norwood, Joseph

Joseph Norwood had sword, pistol, belt, cartridge box; "on command." Return, dated 1 March 1778, of arms and accouterments in the Third Troop belonging to Colonel George Baylor's Regiment of Light Dragoons. (Virginia Office of the Quartermaster General, Fredericksburg. Returns of Colonel George Baylor's Regiment, 1778-1779. Accession 22547, The Library of Virginia, Richmond, Va.)

"I do hereby Certify that Mr. Joseph Norwood served three years as a private in the 3d Regiment of Light Dragoons." George Baylor, Caroline County, June 17, 1783. (Virginia Governor's Office. Bounty Warrants, 1779-1860. Accession 41429, The Library of Virginia, Richmond, Va.)

Nowell, Richard

Richard Nowell had sword, pistol, belt, cartridge box; "Present." Return, dated 1 March 1778, of arms and accouterments in the Third Troop belonging to Colonel George Baylor's Regiment of Light Dragoons. (Virginia Office of the Quartermaster General, Fredericksburg. Returns of Colonel George Baylor's Regiment, 1778-1779. Accession 22547, The Library of Virginia, Richmond, Va.)

"I do hereby testify that the bearer Mr Richard Nowell Served three years as Corporal in the 3d Regiment of Light Dragoons." George Baylor, Caroline County, January 29, 1784. (Virginia Governor's Office. Bounty Warrants, 1779-1860. Accession 41429, The Library of Virginia, Richmond, Va.)

Oast, George

"This certifies that George Oast enlisted with me as a soldier in 3d Regiment L. Dragoons Decr 18 1779 to serve the war." William Barret, Richmond, July 20, 1783. (Virginia Governor's Office. Bounty Warrants, 1779-1860. Accession 41429, The Library of Virginia, Richmond, Va.)

Owens, Ephraim

"Ephraim Owens Corporal in the 3d Regiment of Light Dragoons having served three years is hereby discharged the said Owens has conducted himself with propriety." William Washington, March 6, 1781. (Virginia Governor's Office. Bounty Warrants, 1779-1860. Accession 41429, The Library of Virginia, Richmond, Va.)

Owens, Evan Owens

"I do Certify that I enlisted Evan Owens Owens ye 16th May 1778 to Serve three years in ye 3d Regiment of Light Dragoons & he was killed at the surprise of the said Redgmt at Tappan ye same year." Francis Dade, Captain. "The above mentioned Soldier was killed the 28 September 1778." Chiswell Barrett, Lieutenant. A request to settle the account for wages and land was made by Mason Owens, brother. (Virginia Governor's Office. Bounty Warrants, 1779-1860. Accession 41429, The Library of Virginia, Richmond, Va.)

Page, Carter

Carter Page, Captain, Date of Commission 30 April 1778. Arrangement of Light Dragoons, 3^d Regiment, undated. (Revolutionary War Rolls, 1775-1783. National Archives Microfilm Publication M246. Roll 115, folder 13, 3^d Regiment Light Dragoons, 1779, item 3.)

Carter Page, Captain, January 8, 1777. Arrangement of part of Colonel Baylor's Regiment, showing the date of Lieutenant Colonel Byrd's, Captain Smith's, Lieutenant Page's, Lieutenant

Randolph's, and Lieutenant Baylor's commissions, undated. (Revolutionary War Rolls, 1775-1783. National Archives Microfilm Publication M246. Roll 115, folder 13, 3^d Regiment Light Dragoons, 1779, item 4.)

Carter Page, Esq., of Baylor's Light Dragoons. (Miscellaneous Numbered Records [The Manuscript File] in the War Department Collection of Revolutionary War Records, 1775-1790's. National Archives Microfilm Publication M859. Manuscript 17681, undated.)

Carter Page, Captain. A Return of Officers in the 3rd Regiment of Light Dragoons with the Dates of their Commissions, Sept. 18, 1777. (Revolutionary War Rolls, 1775-1783. National Archives Microfilm Publication M246. Roll 115, folder 13, 3^d Regiment Light Dragoons, 1779, item 6.)

Carter Page was at Mansfield on 5 October 1778, when he wrote to Colonel George Baylor at Hackensack, New Jersey. In his letter he said he was taken ill at York, and after partial recovery, traveled to his brother Jack's house, where he was again taken ill. He traveled to Fredericksburg before he got ill again, but hoped to rejoin the regiment when he recovered. He also mentioned his brother Baylor Page, who knew Walker Baylor. (University of Virginia. Alderman Library Special Collections. Accession 2257, Papers of the Baylor Family of Newmarket, Caroline County, Va, in part transcripts: [manuscript], 1653-1915. Box 4: the folder is labeled "1756, 1777-1781; Military Papers," item 16: "1778 Oct 5, Carter Page to Col. George Baylor.")

Carter Page, W2161. A pay certificate listed Carter Page as Lieutenant of Dragoons, 6 February 1777 to 1 March 1778; Captain 1 March 1778 to June 1779. According a letter from the Pension Office, Carter Page resigned 4 June 1779. He served at Brandywine and Germantown, Guilford Court House, the Siege of Yorktown and was at the surrender of Lord Cornwallis. He also served as aide-de-camp to General Thomas Nelson in 1780 and 1781.

In June 1849, Lucy Page, age 72, widow of Carter Page, was living in Cumberland County, Virginia. According to a family register included with the pension application, Carter Page and Lucy were married at York, Virginia, 14 December 1799, and had seven children. Carter Page died Saturday, 9 April 1825, age 67, in Cumberland County. According to a son, John Page, who was a Justice of the Peace in Cumberland Court House, Carter Page had been married before, but the details were not known.

(Revolutionary War Pension and Bounty-Land Warrant Application Files. National Archives Microfilm Publication M804, roll 1876.)

Parsons, George

"...George Parsons enlisted in the Continental Army the 22d Dec. 1776 for the term of three years which time he faithfully served." Captain John Gillison, September 1783. (Virginia Governor's Office. Bounty Warrants, 1779-1860. Accession 41429, The Library of Virginia, Richmond, Va.)

George Parsons, S38991. In June 1818, George Parsons, of Queen County, Tennessee, age 57, stated that he enlisted in Culpeper County under Captain John Gillison in the 10th Virginia Regiment, commanded by Colonel Edward Stephens for three years. During that time, he was in the battles of Brandywine, Stony Point and Monmouth. He next enlisted in Colonel William Washington's horse regiment, and fought at Cowpens, Guilford Court House, and Camden. He was wounded in the arm, and was taken prisoner until the end of the war. In September 1820 he was living in Sevier County, Tennessee, and in 1849 was in Bradley County, Tennessee. (Revolutionary War Pension and Bounty-Land Warrant Application Files. National Archives Microfilm Publication M804, roll 1881)

In January 1823, in Sevier County, Tennessee, George Parsons stated that in 1779 Richard Porterfield joined Col. William Washington's Regiment of Light Dragoons, and that in or about the same time, he enlisted at Hillsboro, North Carolina. They were then marched to Salisbury, North Carolina, then to Charlotte, then to Providence where they stayed part of the winter. George Parsons then became associated with General Morgan's Rifles and marched to Pacolet, then to Cowpens, Guilford, and Camden, where he was taken prisoner. (under Richard Porterfield. Revolutionary War Pension and Bounty-Land Warrant Application Files. National Archives Microfilm Publication M804, roll 1956.)

Parsons, William

William Parsons, Cornet, February 6, 1777, commission granted March 4, 1778. (Revolutionary War Rolls, 1775-1783. National Archives Microfilm Publication M246. Roll 115, folder 13, 3^d Regiment Light dragoons, 1779, item 2.)

Will Parsons, Lieutenant, Date of Commission January 1, 1779. Arrangement of Light Dragoons, 3^d Regiment, undated. (Revolutionary War Rolls, 1775-1783. National Archives

Microfilm Publication M246. Roll 115, folder 13, 3ᵈ Regiment Light Dragoons, 1779, item 3.)

William Parsons, Cornet, February 6, 1777. William Parsons, P. Master November 1, 1777. A Return of Officers in the 3ʳᵈ Regiment of Light Dragoons with the Dates of their Commissions, Sept. 18, 1777. (Revolutionary War Rolls, 1775-1783. National Archives Microfilm Publication M246. Roll 115, folder 13, 3ᵈ Regiment Light Dragoons, 1779, item 6.)

Mr. Parsons. Alexander Clough mentions that since Mr. Parsons has been appointed paymaster, they need a new officer in the first troop. (University of Virginia. Alderman Library Special Collections. Accession 2257, Papers of the Baylor Family of Newmarket, Caroline County, Va, in part transcripts: [manuscript], 1653-1915. Box 4: the folder is labeled "1756, 1777-1781; Military Papers," item 8: "Letter from Alexander Clough to George Baylor, 4 Feb 1778 at Millsone.")

William Parsons, mentioned on a roster of officers of 3ʳᵈ Regiment. (University of Virginia. Alderman Library Special Collections. Accession 2257, Papers of the Baylor Family of Newmarket, Caroline County, Va, in part transcripts: [manuscript], 1653-1915. Box 4: the folder is labeled "1756, 1777-1781; Military Papers," item 21: "ca. 1780 Continental Troops, roster of Officers, 1ˢᵗ & 3ʳᵈ Regiments.")

William Parsons, R16965. BLWt 1752-300-Capt issued August 27 1795 to Smith and Ridgeway, assignees. In October 1839, James Parsons, Willoughby Parsons, Elizabeth Miller, Rebecca Carbell, and Abizah Parsons appointed John B. Ogg of Norfolk, Virginia, attorney to deal with land and to ask for half-pay for service of William Parsons; the claim was rejected. A letter from the war office stated that William Parsons died in 1797 in Norfolk, Virginia. (Revolutionary War Pension and Bounty-Land Warrant Application Files. National Archives Microfilm Publication M804, roll 1882.)

William Parsons was paid by the United States as a Captain from January 1782 through November 1783, as recorded by an account sheet from the Auditor's Office. Also in a petition made by his heirs, it is stated that William Parsons entered the Continental Line as a cadet on 6 September 1776, was a Cornet of Dragoons in February 1777, a Lieutenant in 1778 and Captain in 1779. (Virginia Governor's Office. Bounty Warrants, 1779-1860. Accession 41429, The Library of Virginia, Richmond, Va.)

Peek or Peak, Jesse

In Lincoln County, Kentucky in August 1822, Jesse Peek stated that he enlisted in Captain Churchill Jones' company of Light Dragoons in 1781, and served until honorably discharged at the end of the war in Winchester, Virginia. (Virginia Governor's Office. Bounty Warrants, 1779-1860. Accession 41429, The Library of Virginia, Richmond, Va.)

Jesse Peak, S35557. In August 1822, Jesse Peak of Lincoln County, Kentucky, age 58, stated that about six months before the battle of Guilford Court House, he enlisted under Col. Abraham Buford for eighteen months; two days after the battle, he enlisted for the war with Captain Churchill Jones under Col. William Washington. He had been living in Lincoln County for fifteen years, and had five children, but owned no property. (Revolutionary War Pension and Bounty-Land Warrant Application Files. National Archives Microfilm Publication M804, roll 1894.)

Perkinson, James

James Perkinson, S38296. In May 1819, in Petersburg, Virginia, James Perkinson stated that he first enlisted in Virginia, and was commanded by Col. White of the Virginia Line on Continental establishment, and last by Captain Watts of the Regiment of Light Dragoons. He was discharged at Lawrence's Ferry in South Carolina, and was in battle with the Indians near Savannah, Georgia. In March 1821, still in Petersburg, James Perkinson stated that he served for eighteen months under General Steuben, and was afterwards in the "Southern Tour" under General Green, commanded by Captain John Watts in Col. Washington's Regiment of Cavalry. He declared that he was currently about 62 years old, and was totally destitute with no family. (Revolutionary War Pension and Bounty-Land Warrant Application Files. National Archives Microfilm Publication M804, roll 1913.)

Perry, John

John Perry had pistol, belt, and cartridge box; "Sword Broke in Store." Return, dated 1 March 1778, of arms and accouterments in the Third Troop belonging to Colonel George Baylor's Regiment of Light Dragoons. (Virginia Office of the Quartermaster General, Fredericksburg. Returns of Colonel George Baylor's Regiment, 1778-1779. Accession 22547, The Library of Virginia, Richmond, Va.)

"I certify that John Perry is now a Cornet in Baylor's Regiment of Dragoons, & has served the United States three years in different Offices in the said Regiment of Dragoons." Jos. Eggleston, August 25, 1783. (Virginia Governor's Office. Bounty Warrants, 1779-1860. Accession 41429, The Library of Virginia, Richmond, Va.)

John Peery or Perry, R8127. In July 1845, Deborah Perry, of Tazewell County, Virginia, claimed that she was the widow of John Perry, Cornet for eighteen months in the Continental Line. She couldn't give details of his service, having never been informed on the subject, but said that they were married on 8 January 1787, and he died 5 March 1844. John Perry was born 28 September 1762, Deborah Kidd was born 11 February 1770, and they had thirteen children. (Revolutionary War Pension and Bounty-Land Warrant Application Files. National Archives Microfilm Publication M804, roll 1903.)

Plunket, James

"I do Certify that James Plunket enlisted under me some time in the spring of 1777 as a private in Colonel Baylor's Regiment of Light Dragoons for three years and died in the service." Presley Thornton, Captain, 19 June 1799. (Virginia Governor's Office. Bounty Warrants, 1779-1860. Accession 41429, The Library of Virginia, Richmond, Va.)

Plunkett, Reuben

Reuben Plunket "his armes and Acutrements destroid to the QMl at Riden By order of Ct. Jones." Return, dated 1 March 1778, of arms and accouterments in the Third Troop belonging to Colonel George Baylor's Regiment of Light Dragoons. (Virginia Office of the Quartermaster General, Fredericksburg. Returns of Colonel George Baylor's Regiment, 1778-1779. Accession 22547, The Library of Virginia, Richmond, Va.)

"I do certify that Ruben Plunket a native of the State of Virginia, served three years as Corporal in the 3d Regiment Dragoons & was Legally Discharged by the Commanding officer." Chiswell Barret, Lieutenant, Richmond, October 11, 1783. (Virginia Governor's Office. Bounty Warrants, 1779-1860. Accession 41429, The Library of Virginia, Richmond, Va.)

Reuben Plunkett, S25752. In March 1824, Reuben Plunkett stated that he had been a Sergeant in Capt. Churchill Jones'

Company of the 3rd Regiment of Dragoons under Colonel George Baylor. He was wounded on or about 28 September 1778 and was pensioned due to the disability. In 1811, according to a pension certificate on file, he was living in Caroline County, Virginia. (Revolutionary War Pension and Bounty-Land Warrant Application Files. National Archives Microfilm Publication M804, roll 1944.)

Porterfield, Richard

Richard Porterfield, W2341. In July 1820, Richard Porterfield, age about 50, a resident of Anderson County, Tennessee, stated that he enlisted in the spring of 1779 in the company of Captain Fauntleroy of the 1st and 3rd Regiments under Col. William Washington. He served until the battle of Camden, in which he was wounded, and obtained a certificate from Lieutenant Gunn, to recover from his wound until he was fit for service, but he was never called up, even though he was ready to obey after he got fit for duty. In 1820 he had no family living with him, no property, and no occupation except making "coarse shoes."

In 1824, Richard Porterfield of Greene County, Tennessee, age 60, stated that he enlisted in March 1779 in Albemarle County, Virginia, and served two years until the battle of Camden. He said that his wife had been dead about three years, and he had two sons and two daughters in the "Red River Country." James Dawson and George Parsons affirmed his claim of service.

Louisa Porterfield, nee Rose, a resident of Knox County, Tennessee in 1853, age 35, said that she married Richard Porterfield in Knox County on 12 July 1847, and that he died on 30 January 1852. (Revolutionary War Pension and Bounty-Land Warrant Application Files. National Archives Microfilm Publication M804, roll 1956.)

Pritchard or Pritchett, James

"Gentlemen Commissioners please to send me my pay by Captain John Whitby and my Land Warrant as I served to the end of the War faithfully. I was first in Capt. Dade's troop then in Capt. Parsons' and served to the end of the war in it...." Signed James Pritchard. "I do Certify that James Pritchet enlisted for the War in Baylor's Dragoons 27th April 81 & Continued the term of his enlistment." William Barret, February 18, 1785. (Virginia Governor's Office. Bounty Warrants, 1779-1860. Accession 41429, The Library of Virginia, Richmond, Va.)

James Pritchett or Pritchard, W8534. In July 1818, James Prichett, age 55, of Bourbon County, Kentucky, said he enlisted in Col. Davis' Regiment of Foot in 1779 for nine months, and when that term expired, he reenlisted under Francis Dade's troop under Col. William Washington. He served to the end of the war, and was discharged in 1783 at Nelson's Ferry on the Santee River, South Carolina. He fought at Cowpens, Guilford, Camden, and Eutaw, where he was wounded. His widow, Phebe Pritchard, age 75 in 1838, and said she married James Pritchard in Culpeper County, Virginia on December 28, 1788, and he died June 28, 1833. (Revolutionary War Pension and Bounty-Land Warrant Application Files. National Archives Microfilm Publication M804, roll 1979.)

Pritchard, Thomas

"It appears from the Size Roll 5 Troop that Thos. Pritchard Enlisted for the war in 3rd Regiment L. D. 18th March 1781 and served the full term of his Enlistment." William Barrett, 1785. (Virginia Governor's Office. Bounty Warrants, 1779-1860. Accession 41429, The Library of Virginia, Richmond, Va.)

Pucket, Josiah

"It appears from the Size roll 5th Troop that Josiah Puckett enlisted for the war in first Regiment Light Dragoons 25 March 1781 and served the full term of his enlistment." William Barrett, 1785. (Virginia Governor's Office. Bounty Warrants, 1779-1860. Accession 41429, The Library of Virginia, Richmond, Va.)

Josiah Puckett was of Humphreys County, Tennessee on 11 October 1826. Benjamin Clearwater stated that Josiah Puckett was a messmate of his in the 3rd Regiment of Light Dragoons. (under Benjamin Clearwater. Revolutionary War Pension and Bounty-Land Warrant Application Files. National Archives Microfilm Publication M804, roll 573; also Dorman, John Frederick. 1958. Virginia Revolutionary Pension Applications, 19:77-78.)

Josiah Puckett, R8510. Josiah Puckett, of Livingston County, Kentucky, in May 1818, stated that he enlisted in Col. Campbell's Regiment and after serving eighteen months, he entered into a regiment of continental light horse and served to the end of the war. He died about 1843 in Madison County, Kentucky, and left a widow Martha, and three heirs. (Revolutionary War Pension and Bounty-Land Warrant Application Files. National Archives Microfilm Publication M804, roll 1983.)

Pullen or Pulling, George

"G° Pulling" had sword, pistol, belt; "on Command Cartridge Box Lost." Return, dated 1 March 1778, of arms and accouterments in the Third Troop belonging to Colonel George Baylor's Regiment of Light Dragoons. (Virginia Office of the Quartermaster General, Fredericksburg. Returns of Colonel George Baylor's Regiment, 1778-1779. Accession 22547, The Library of Virginia, Richmond, Va.)

"George Pullen having served three years in the 3rd Regiment of Light Dragoons with Fidelity is hereby discharged." William Washington, Halifax, July 8, 1785. (Virginia Governor's Office. Bounty Warrants, 1779-1860. Accession 41429, The Library of Virginia, Richmond, Va.)

George Pullin or Pullen, W8539. In July 1818, George Pullin, a resident of Breckenridge County, Kentucky, stated that he enlisted in 1777 in Faquier County, Virginia under Cornet Edward Conner in Captain Baylor's company in the 3rd Regiment commanded by Col. Baylor. He served his full period of enlistment and was discharged by Col. Washington at Halifax, Virginia.

In August 1821, George Pullen claimed to be age 62, and was living with his wife, four sons and two daughters; the oldest son was 22. In January 1846, Nancy, the widow of George Pullen, said she was 77, her maiden name was Nancy Dotson, and that she married George Pullen in May 1785. She further stated that he died 16 June 1845. (Revolutionary War Pension and Bounty-Land Warrant Application Files. National Archives Microfilm Publication M804, roll 1984.)

Charles Randolph

Charles Randolph, Cornet 3rd Continental Dragoons in Feb 1777; Lieut. June 14, 1777; in service January 1780. (Gwathmey, John Hastings. 1938. Historical Register of Virginians in the Revolution: Soldiers, sailors, marines, 1775-1783. Dietz Press, Richmond, Va.) This may be the same person as Robert Randolph, below.

Randolph, Robert

Robert Randolph, Lieutenant, Date of Commission June 14, 1777. Arrangement of Light Dragoons, 3^{d} Regiment, undated. (Revolutionary War Rolls, 1775-1783. National Archives

Microfilm Publication M246. Roll 115, folder 13, 3^d Regiment Light Dragoons, 1779, item 3.)

Lieutenant Randolph, June 14, 1777. Arrangement of part of Colonel Baylor's Regiment, showing the date of Lieutenant Colonel Byrd's, Captain Smith's, Lieutenant Page's, Lieutenant Randolph's, and Lieutenant Baylor's commissions, undated. (Revolutionary War Rolls, 1775-1783. National Archives Microfilm Publication M246. Roll 115, folder 13, 3^d Regiment Light Dragoons, 1779, item 4.)

Robert Randolph, Lieutenant, June 14, 1777. A Return of Officers in the 3rd Regiment of Light Dragoons with the Dates of their Commissions, Sept. 18, 1777. (Revolutionary War Rolls, 1775-1783. National Archives Microfilm Publication M246. Roll 115, folder 13, 3^d Regiment Light Dragoons, 1779, item 6.)

Lieutenant Randolph, mentioned as receiving a set of officer's bridle bits on 8 April 1778, and a sword and accompanying equipment on 14 April 1778. (University of Virginia. Alderman Library Special Collections. Accession 2257, Papers of the Baylor Family of Newmarket, Caroline County, Va, in part transcripts: [manuscript], 1653-1915. Box 4: the folder is labeled "1756, 1777-1781; Military Papers," item 19: "Continental Troops, Itemized Account, September 1777 to June 1779.")

John Worain was with Lt. Randolph. (University of Virginia. Alderman Library Special Collections. Accession 2257, Papers of the Baylor Family of Newmarket, Caroline County, Va, in part transcripts: [manuscript], 1653-1915. Box 4: the folder is labeled "1756, 1777-1781; Military Papers," item 14: "A list of the men's names absent belonging to Colonel Baylor's Regiment, Fredericksburg, June 27, 1778.")

Randolph, subaltern. "There are, besides, Prisoners in New York, A Captain (Swan) two subalterns, (Randolph and Dade) a volunteer, (Kilty) and the Surgeons Mate...." (David Griffith. Letter, 20 October 1778. Accession 22789. Personal papers collection. The Library of Virginia, Richmond, Va.)

Robert Randolph, Lieutenant, prisoner, cash paid to him by Mr. Pierce, 4 April 1780. (Miscellaneous Numbered Records [The Manuscript File] in the War Department Collection of Revolutionary War Records, 1775-1790's. National Archives Microfilm Publication M859. Manuscript 17584, "George Baylor's Regiment of Horse," undated.)

Robert Randolph wrote from Hanover Court House to Col. Baylor at Newcastle, asking him to accept his resignation, which he offered due to his upcoming marriage. (University of Virginia. Alderman Library Special Collections. Accession 2257, Papers of the Baylor Family of Newmarket, Caroline County, Va, in part transcripts: [manuscript], 1653-1915. Box 4: the folder is labeled "1756, 1777-1781; Military Papers," item 23: "1781 Oct. 15, Robert Randolph to Col. George Baylor.")

Robert Randolph, Lieutenant, Dragoons. In an account dated 5 August 1782, New Burgh, Robert Randolph owes a total of £23.15.3 to the inhabitants of Long Island for maintenance during his captivity. (Compiled Service Records of Soldiers who Served in the American Army During the Revolutionary War. National Archives Microfilm Publication M881, Continental Troops, Miscellaneous.)

"This may Certify that Capt. Robert Randolph Served in the Continental Army from Jany 1776 to Sept. 1781." G. Weedon, February, 1784. (Virginia Governor's Office. Bounty Warrants, 1779-1860. Accession 41429, The Library of Virginia, Richmond, Va.)

Rankins, Benjamin

Benjamin Rankins, on furlough. (University of Virginia. Alderman Library Special Collections. Accession 2257, Papers of the Baylor Family of Newmarket, Caroline County, Va, in part transcripts: [manuscript], 1653-1915. Box 4: the folder is labeled "1756, 1777-1781; Military Papers," item 14: "A list of the men's names absent belonging to Colonel Baylor's Regiment, Fredericksburg, June 27, 1778.")

"Benjamin Rankins soldier in the 3d Regiment of Light Dragoons having served faithfully three years is hereby discharged." William Washington, May 17, 1781. (Virginia Governor's Office. Bounty Warrants, 1779-1860. Accession 41429, The Library of Virginia, Richmond, Va.)

Reason, Reuben

"I do Certify that Reuben Reason was enlisted as a soldier in Colonel Baylor's Dragoons for three years or the war & Cont'd in Service until his death sometime in March 1779." William Barret, March 26, 1787. (Virginia Governor's Office. Bounty Warrants,

1779-1860. Accession 41429, The Library of Virginia, Richmond, Va.)

Riding or Rider, Jesse

Jesse Rider had sword, belt, cartridge box; "Pistol from Capt Smiths servant got on command." Return, dated 1 March 1778, of arms and accouterments in the Third Troop belonging to Colonel George Baylor's Regiment of Light Dragoons. (Virginia Office of the Quartermaster General, Fredericksburg. Returns of Colonel George Baylor's Regiment, 1778-1779. Accession 22547, The Library of Virginia, Richmond, Va.)

Jesse Riding, 3rd troop. He was on guard duty over some forage when attacked by the British at Tappan, repeatedly asked for quarter, but was stabbed in the chest. (David Griffith. Letter, 20 October 1778. Accession 22789. Personal papers collection. The Library of Virginia, Richmond, Va.)

Roberts, Henry

In October 1830, Henry Roberts, of Frankfort, Kentucky stated that he entered the 3rd Regiment in September 1777 for three years, during which time he was in the 4th troop, commanded by Captain Cadwallader Jones. He obtained his discharge from Col. William Washington. (under James Southard. Virginia Governor's Office. Bounty Warrants, 1779-1860. Accession 41429, The Library of Virginia, Richmond, Va.)

Henry Roberts, W164. In July 1830, in Franklin County, Kentucky, Henry Roberts, age 72, said he enlisted September 1, 1777 in the 3rd Regiment under Col. George Baylor, for three years. He served in the fourth troop under Captain Cadwallader Jones, Lieutenant John Stith, and Cornet Chiswell Barrett. In 1853, Catherine Roberts, nee Austin, said she married Henry Roberts in Baltimore, Maryland June 20, 1810, and he died May 23, 1839. (Revolutionary War Pension and Bounty-Land Warrant Application Files. National Archives Microfilm Publication M804, roll 2057.)

Robertson, Benjamin

"I do Certify that Benjamin Robtson enlisted for three years in Baylor's Dragoons Decr 25th 1777 & was appointed Sergeant in April 1778 served faithfully the full time of his enlistment." William Barret, undated. (Virginia Governor's Office. Bounty Warrants,

1779-1860. Accession 41429, The Library of Virginia, Richmond, Va.)

Robertson, George

"I do Certify that Geo. Robtson enlisted Feby 79 for three years which time he has faithfully served & that he was born in this state." William Barret, January 6, 1784. (Virginia Governor's Office. Bounty Warrants, 1779-1860. Accession 41429, The Library of Virginia, Richmond, Va.)

George Robertson, W18834. George Robertson stated that he was in the Southern army under Col. Washington. Pages from the family Bible are included in the application of George Robertson, giving children and birth years. In 1838, in Essex County, Virginia, Ann Robertson said George Robertson enlisted first in the infantry in the "northern Army" and afterwards was in the light horse under Col. William Washington. She married George Robertson about March 1783, and he died March 14, 1824. (Revolutionary War Pension and Bounty-Land Warrant Application Files. National Archives Microfilm Publication M804, roll 2061.)

Robertson, Henry

Henry Robertson, 3rd Regiment of Virginia Dragoons; Bounty Land Warrant Card, Numbers 12499 and 14126, issued 5 August 1795. (Revolutionary War Pension and Bounty-Land Warrant Application Files. National Archives Microfilm Publication M804, roll 2061.)

Robertson, Reuben

Reuben Robertson "Lost while on command." Return, dated 1 March 1778, of arms and accouterments in the Third Troop belonging to Colonel George Baylor's Regiment of Light Dragoons. (Virginia Office of the Quartermaster General, Fredericksburg. Returns of Colonel George Baylor's Regiment, 1778-1779. Accession 22547, The Library of Virginia, Richmond, Va.)

Robinson, Benjamin

Benjamin Robinson, S9090. In Bedford County, Virginia, in December 1832, Benjamin Robinson, age 79, stated that he was born in Caroline County, Virginia, and enlisted January or February 1776 in the infantry with Captain Samuel Hawes in the 2nd Virginia Regiment for two years under Col. Spotswood, during which he was in the battles of Germantown and Brandywine. He then enlisted for three years as Sergeant with Captain Jones under Col. Baylor, and was in the attack at Tappan. He was discharged at the Catawba River in December 1780. (Revolutionary War Pension and Bounty-Land Warrant Application Files. National Archives Microfilm Publication M804, roll 2064.)

Rogers, John

"I do hereby Certify that John Rogers was enlisted in February one thousand seven hundred & eighty one into the 3d Regiment of Light Dragoons & that he continued in this Regiment until it was disbanded." George Baylor, Caroline County, January 29, 1784. (Virginia Governor's Office. Bounty Warrants, 1779-1860. Accession 41429, The Library of Virginia, Richmond, Va.)

Roods, William

"I do Certify that William Roods a soldier joined the third Virginia Regiment of Light Dragoons the 20th day of November 1779 for during the war & that he served a faithfully Good Soldier to the End of the same as the muster Rolls will shew given Under my hand this 24th day July 1798." John Watts, late captain, 1st Regiment. (Virginia Governor's Office. Bounty Warrants, 1779-1860. Accession 41429, The Library of Virginia, Richmond, Va.)

Rose or Rhose, Henry

Henry Rhose, corporal in Baylor's regiment of Dragoons. David Stringfellow managed to escape the attack at Tappan, but during his escape, he heard "Corporal Henry Rose" cry out for quarters. At daylight, he returned to the barn to retrieve his clothes, and "found Corporal Henry Rhose dead." (David Griffith. Letter, 20 October 1778. Accession 22789. Personal papers collection. The Library of Virginia, Richmond, Va.)

Rose, Robert

Robert Rose signed an oath of allegiance 18 August 1778 "in camp", as surgeon. (Numbered Record Books Concerning Military Operations and Service, Pay and Settlement of Accounts, and Supplies in the War Department Collection of Revolutionary War Records. National Archives Microfilm Publication M853. Roll 12: Oaths of allegiance and fidelity and oaths of office 1778-1781. Book 166, page 104.)

"I, John Champe Carter of the County of Nelson formerly of the Continental Line, do hereby Certify that the late Doctor Robert Rose did act in the capacity of a Surgeon from the Commencement to the end of the Revolutionary war." John Champe Carter, November 24, 1808. (Virginia Governor's Office. Bounty Warrants, 1779-1860. Accession 41429, The Library of Virginia, Richmond, Va.)

Ross, James

"I do Certify that James Ross enlisted as a soldier in Baylor's Dragoons March 8th 1778 for three years and served faithfully the full term of his enlistment." William Barret, undated. (Virginia Governor's Office. Bounty Warrants, 1779-1860. Accession 41429, The Library of Virginia, Richmond, Va.)

Sailor, Martin

"I do Certify that Martin Sailor enlisted in July 1777 to serve three years as saddler to Said Regiment... and did Said duty faithfully until Discharged by Col. G. Baylor April 15 1782." Robert Morrow, 14 November 1783.

"I do Certify that the above mentioned Sailor was always considered a Sergt. although he did the duty of Saddler & in that he saved the States a very considerable expense as witness my hand." William Barret, 19 December 1789. (Virginia Governor's Office. Bounty Warrants, 1779-1860. Accession 41429, The Library of Virginia, Richmond, Va.)

Sawers or Sawyers, William

William Sawyers' name appears on a list of applicants for invalid pension returned by the District Courts for the district of Kentucky, North Carolina, and South Carolina, submitted to the House of Representatives by the Secretary of War, on April 25, 1794. He is listed as a dragoon from the 3rd Regiment; badly wounded in his head, right shoulder, and having lost both thumbs at the battle of Eutaw Springs in September 1781, and currently living in the Beaufort district, South Carolina. (Revolutionary War Pension and Bounty-Land Warrant Application Files. National Archives Microfilm Publication M804, roll 2127.)

William Sawers, Private, 3d Regiment Light Dragoons, accounted $234.17, May 13, 1794. (Clark, Murtie June. 1991. The pension lists of 1792-1795. Genealogical Publishing Company, Baltimore, Md.)

Scott, Charles

"I do Certify that Mr. Charles Scott was appointed a Cornet in the 1st Regiment of Light Dragoons in July 1781 and served to the end of the war." John Watts, Captain, February 5, 1784. (Virginia Governor's Office. Bounty Warrants, 1779-1860. Accession 41429, The Library of Virginia, Richmond, Va.)

Charles Scott, W5996. Priscilla Scott, nee Read, age 64, made a declaration in 1838 that she and Captain Charles Scott were married in Charlotte County, Virginia, in December, 1790, and Charles Scott died in Halifax County, Virginia in 1818. In August 1843, in Halifax County, the widow said Charles Scott was a Cornet under Col. William Washington. According to pension papers, Priscilla Scott died 18 September 1843. (Revolutionary War Pension and Bounty-Land Warrant Application Files. National Archives Microfilm Publication M804, roll 2135.)

Shiber, Frederick

Frederick Shiber, Private, enlisted February 1779. Muster Roll of the 2nd Troop in the 3^{d} Regiment Light Dragoons in the Service of the United States commanded by Lieutenant Colonel William Washington for the Months of May, June, July August, September, October 1779. (Revolutionary War Rolls, 1775-1783. National Archives Microfilm Publication M246. Roll 115, folder 13, 3^{d} Regiment Light Dragoons, 1779, item 1.)

Shope or Shoup, William

William Shope had pistol; "Sword and Belt Lost." William Carster's sword was "given to Shope and Shope Broke it." Return, dated 1 March 1778, of arms and accouterments in the Third Troop belonging to Colonel George Baylor's Regiment of Light Dragoons. (Virginia Office of the Quartermaster General, Fredericksburg. Returns of Colonel George Baylor's Regiment, 1778-1779. Accession 22547, The Library of Virginia, Richmond, Va.)

Sergeant William Shope and Lieutenant Charles Yarbrough signed a return of clothing delivered to the 3rd Regiment Dragoons, April 23, 1782. (University of Virginia. Alderman Library Special Collections. Accession 2257, Papers of the Baylor Family of Newmarket, Caroline County, Va, in part transcripts: [manuscript],

1653-1915. Box 4: the folder is labeled "Military Papers, 1782, 1814, & n.d.," item 10: "1782 April 23, Continental Troops, Return of Clothing Delivered.")

"I Certify that Sergeant Will Shoup Enlisted as a Soldier for three Years in Colonel Baylor's Dragoons in 79 Reenlisted for the war June 5th 81 served as a good Soldier until the mutiny of 1783." William Barret, December 20, 1784. (Virginia Governor's Office. Bounty Warrants, 1779-1860. Accession 41429, The Library of Virginia, Richmond, Va.)

Simons, James

James Simons, Lieutenant; pay due him from 1 July 1780 to 25 September 1781; pay as Adjutant from 2 June to 26 December 1781; pay as Brigade Major from 27 December 1781 to 30 April 1782. (Miscellaneous Numbered Records [The Manuscript File] in the War Department Collection of Revolutionary War Records, 1775-1790's. National Archives Microfilm Publication M859. Manuscript 17638, "The United States in Account with James Simons late Lieut. in Colonel Washington's Regiment Cavalry," dated 13 August 1792.)

Sled, Seaton or Sexton

"I do Certify that Sergeant Seaton Sled enlisted himself for the war in 3 Regiment L Dragoons Decr. 1779 & has faithfully served the war as witness my hand." William Barret, April 19, 1784. (Virginia Governor's Office. Bounty Warrants, 1779-1860. Accession 41429, The Library of Virginia, Richmond, Va.)

Sexton Sled, Sergeant, 3rd troop; pay due him from 1 January 1782 to 16 November 1783. (Miscellaneous Numbered Records [The Manuscript File] in the War Department Collection of Revolutionary War Records, 1775-1790's. National Archives Microfilm Publication M859. Manuscript 17658, "The United States in a/c with Sexton Sled Sergeant 3^d Regiment light Dragons," dated 5 May 1794.)

Smith, Bouton

Bouton Smith had pistol, belt; "on Command Sword Lost." Return, dated 1 March 1778, of arms and accouterments in the Third Troop belonging to Colonel George Baylor's Regiment of Light Dragoons. (Virginia Office of the Quartermaster General, Fredericksburg. Returns of Colonel George Baylor's Regiment,

1778-1779. Accession 22547, The Library of Virginia, Richmond, Va.)

Smith, Cornet

John Aplin's arms and accouterments were given to Cornet Smith's servant. Return, dated 1 March 1778, of arms and accouterments in the Third Troop belonging to Colonel George Baylor's Regiment of Light Dragoons. (Virginia Office of the Quartermaster General, Fredericksburg. Returns of Colonel George Baylor's Regiment, 1778-1779. Accession 22547, The Library of Virginia, Richmond, Va.)

Smith, Jesse

"This is to certify that Jesse Smith has served three years as a faithful soldier in the third Regiment of Light Dragoons in the service of the United States, being the full time for which he engaged, and is hereby discharged from the Said Regiment." William Washington, Philadelphia, December 13, 1779. (Virginia Governor's Office. Bounty Warrants, 1779-1860. Accession 41429, The Library of Virginia, Richmond, Va.)

Jesse Smith, R9789. In January 1855, Lucy Smith of Henrico County, Virginia, age 82, submitted another copy of Jesse Smith's discharge from Col. William Washington, and stated that she and Jesse Smith were married 29 March 1805 in Henrico County, and that at the time, she was Lucy Cocke, widow of Robert Cocke. (Revolutionary War Pension and Bounty-Land Warrant Application Files. National Archives Microfilm Publication M804, roll 2218.)

Smith, John

John Smith "Sword Broke & belt Lost Deserted with his arms." Return, dated 1 March 1778, of arms and accouterments in the Third Troop belonging to Colonel George Baylor's Regiment of Light Dragoons. (Virginia Office of the Quartermaster General, Fredericksburg. Returns of Colonel George Baylor's Regiment, 1778-1779. Accession 22547, The Library of Virginia, Richmond, Va.)

Smith, Juby

Juby Smith, Private. Muster Roll of the 2nd Troop in the 3^{d} Regiment Light Dragoons in the Service of the United States commanded by Lieutenant Colonel William Washington for the Months of May, June, July, August, September, October 1779. (Revolutionary War Rolls, 1775-1783. National Archives Microfilm Publication M246. Roll 115, folder 13, 3ᵈ Regiment Light Dragoons, 1779, item 1.)

Smith, Richard

In 1835, Richard Smith, of Franklin County, Indiana, declared that he first enlisted under Captain Marks' company for eighteen months, but served only nine months before joining Captain Parsons' company, which formed a part of Col. William Washington's Regiment of Light horse. After the battle of Guilford, he was made an Orderly Sergeant in the same company and continued to the close of the war. (Virginia Governor's Office. Bounty Warrants, 1779-1860. Accession 41429, The Library of Virginia, Richmond, Va.)

"I do Certify that Richard Smith enlisted in the first Regiment of Light Dragoons the 1ˢᵗ of March 1781 for During the war and continued in said Regiment till furloughed by order of General Greene." Henry Bowyer, Lieutenant, December 28, 1783. (Virginia Governor's Office. Bounty Warrants, 1779-1860. Accession 41429, The Library of Virginia, Richmond, Va.)

Richard Smith, S16254. In July 1820, Richard Smith of Franklin County, Indiana, age 64, stated that he served in Captain Parsons' company under Col. William Washington. He enlisted in Prince Edward County, Virginia, in February 1780, was in the battle of Guilford Courthouse, was wounded at Eutaw Springs, and discharged June 1782 in South Carolina. In 1832, John Wynne declared that Richard Smith was an orderly-sergeant in Col. William Washington's light horse. A letter summarizing his service from the war office said that he died July 1, 1840, leaving a widow. (Revolutionary War Pension and Bounty-Land Warrant Application Files. National Archives Microfilm Publication M804, roll 2230.)

Smith, Robert

Robert Smith, Captain, Date of Commission January 9, 1777. Arrangement of Light Dragoons, 3ᵈ Regiment, undated. (Revolutionary War Rolls, 1775-1783. National Archives Microfilm Publication M246. Roll 115, folder 13, 3ᵈ Regiment Light Dragoons, 1779, item 3.)

Robert Smith, Captain, January 8, 1777. Arrangement of part of Colonel Baylor's Regiment, showing the date of Lieutenant Colonel Byrd's, Captain Smith's, Lieutenant Page's, Lieutenant Randolph's, and Lieutenant Baylor's commissions, undated. (Revolutionary War Rolls, 1775-1783. National Archives Microfilm Publication M246. Roll 115, folder 13, 3^d Regiment Light Dragoons, 1779, item 4.)

Robert Smith, Captain, January 9, 1777. A Return of Officers in the 3rd Regiment of Light Dragoons with the Dates of their Commissions, Sept. 18, 1777. (Revolutionary War Rolls, 1775-1783. National Archives Microfilm Publication M246. Roll 115, folder 13, 3^d Regiment Light Dragoons, 1779, item 6.)

Captain Smith, mentioned on a weekly return of the 3rd Regiment of Light Dragoons, dated 5 February 1778. In his troop, there was one lieutenant, two sergeants, one farrier, ten privates present, one private sick, twenty-two on command, and one on furlough, leaving them two men short. Since the last return taken, one man had been discharged, one had deserted, and two had been killed. (University of Virginia. Alderman Library Special Collections. Accession 2257, Papers of the Baylor Family of Newmarket, Caroline County, Va, in part transcripts: [manuscript], 1653-1915. Box 4: the folder is labeled "1756, 1777-1781; Military Papers," item 9: "A Weekly Return of the 3d Regiment of Light Dragoons Commanded by Col. Baylor, Feb 5th 1778.")

Smith, Wyatt

"I do Certify that Wiatt Smith was enlisted by me in April 1777 for three years which time he faithfully served as a soldier in the 3d Regiment of Light Dragoons, and was reenlisted for the war by one of the officers of the Regiment this the 25th day of April 1786." (signature not legible.) "Wyatt Smith was killed on the Attack of 96." Statement by Thomas Tinsley, who also stated that Elizabeth Jones, wife of S. Jones was the sister and heir-at-law of Wyatt Smith, 18 December 1795. (Virginia Governor's Office. Bounty Warrants, 1779-1860. Accession 41429, The Library of Virginia, Richmond, Va.)

Southard, James (see James Sudduth)

Stewart, Benjamin

"I do certify that Benjamin Stewart enlisted as a soldier in the 3d Reg Dragoons 22 Dec 1779 for the war, and is now on furlough." Robert Morrow, Captain, October 13, 1783. (Virginia Governor's Office. Bounty Warrants, 1779-1860. Accession 41429, The Library of Virginia, Richmond, Va.)

Benjamin Stewart, W6162. "I do certify that Benjamin Stuart enlisted in the 3rd Regiment L. dragoons for the war." Chiswell Barrett, Lieutenant, Richmond, October 12, 1783.

In 1843, Dorothy Stewart, nee Straugham, widow of Benjamin Stewart, and resident of Spotsylvania County, Virginia, stated that she married Benjamin Stewart December 24, 1792 in Spotsylvania County, and he died there August 15, 1842. In 1844, Dorothy Stewart recollected that he served under an officer named Barrett, and a Captain Morrow in the Dragoons, but didn't remember anything more about his service. (Revolutionary War Pension and Bounty-Land Warrant Application Files. National Archives Microfilm Publication M804, roll 2289.)

Stewart or Stuart, Philip

Philip Stewart, mentioned on a roster of officers of 3rd Regiment. (University of Virginia. Alderman Library Special Collections. Accession 2257, Papers of the Baylor Family of Newmarket, Caroline County, Va, in part transcripts: [manuscript], 1653-1915. Box 4: the folder is labeled "1756, 1777-1781; Military Papers," item 21: "ca. 1780 Continental Troops, roster of Officers, 1st & 3rd Regiments.")

"I do Certify that Lieut. Philip Stewart was assigned in the first Regiment of Cavalry & continued in the Regiment until it was disbanded." George Baylor, Caroline County, January 29, 1784. (Virginia Governor's Office. Bounty Warrants, 1779-1860. Accession 41429, The Library of Virginia, Richmond, Va.)

Philip Stuart, S20989. In Washington, DC in March 1821, where he had been living for more than two years, Philip Stuart stated that he served in the 3rd Regiment of Cavalry commanded by Colonel William Washington. He said he formerly lived in Charles County, Maryland. A letter from his physician in January 1822 mentioned that he had been wounded by a musket ball, which lodged near his backbone, and he had wounds in his right arm. In a statement made in October 1828, he said he served in Captain Parsons' troop in the 3rd regiment. (Revolutionary War Pension and

Bounty-Land Warrant Application Files. National Archives Microfilm Publication M804, roll 2317.)

Charles Stuart, a resident of Prince William County, Virginia, in August 1854, said he was one of the two surviving children of Philip Stuart, who died 14 August 1830, leaving a widow and children. An attorney's letter of the same month said Philip Stuart had eight children. (Revolutionary War Pension and Bounty-Land Warrant Application Files. National Archives Microfilm Publication M804, roll 2317.)

Stith, John

John Stith, Lieutenant, February 6, 1777. A Return of Officers in the 3rd Regiment of Light Dragoons with the Dates of their Commissions, Sept. 18, 1777. (Revolutionary War Rolls, 1775-1783. National Archives Microfilm Publication M246. Roll 115, folder 13, 3^d Regiment Light Dragoons, 1779, item 6.)

John Stith, Lieutenant, February 6, 1777, commission granted March 4, 1778. (Revolutionary War Rolls, 1775-1783. National Archives Microfilm Publication M246. Roll 115, folder 13, 3^d Regiment Light Dragoons, 1779, item 2.)

John Stith, Lieutenant, Date of Commission February 6, 1777. Arrangement of Light Dragoons, 3^d Regiment, undated. (Revolutionary War Rolls, 1775-1783. National Archives Microfilm Publication M246. Roll 115, folder 13, 3^d Regiment Light Dragoons, 1779, item 3.)

Captain Stith. A Return of the 3^d Regiment of L. D. Commanded by Captain Stith, October 23, 1778. (Revolutionary War Rolls, 1775-1783. National Archives Microfilm Publication M246. Roll 115, folder 13, 3^d Regiment Light Dragoons, 1779, item 5.)

John Stith, Captain, on command. Muster Roll of the 2nd Troop in the 3^d Regiment Light Dragoons in the Service of the United States commanded by Lieutenant Colonel William Washington for the Months of May, June, July August, September, October 1779. (Revolutionary War Rolls, 1775-1783. National Archives Microfilm Publication M246. Roll 115, folder 13, 3^d Regiment Light Dragoons, 1779, item 1.)

John Stith, cash paid him by Mr. Harrison for defraying the charges of marching his troops to South Carolina, January 1779. (Miscellaneous Numbered Records [The Manuscript File] in the War Department Collection of Revolutionary War Records, 1775-

1790's. National Archives Microfilm Publication M859. Manuscript 17584, "George Baylor's Regiment of Horse," undated.)

"John Stith has drawn 4666 2/3 acres of Mil. Land Warrants for seven years as a Captain of the Continental Line." William Price, August 14, 1807. "I do Certify that Captain John Stith of the Virginia line Continental establishment continued in Service until the final end of the war, and that his time of Service was upwards of seven years." James Wood, late Brigadier-General, November 1, 1798. (Virginia Governor's Office. Bounty Warrants, 1779-1860. Accession 41429, The Library of Virginia, Richmond, Va.)

Storm, John

John Storm, W1953. In 1831, John Storm of Green County, Indiana, who said that he was of Dutch descent, declared that he enlisted first for 18 months in August 1780 in Col. Ballard Smith's infantry. When his term was up, he next enlisted in the first troop of the Third Regiment, under Captain Robert Morrow, Major Parsons, and Col. Washington. He was discharged at the close of the war in Winchester, Virginia.

In July 1848, Ann Storm, nee Parsons, age 72, stated that she married John Storm 1 February 1788 in Carter County, Tennessee, and that John died 13 December 1835 in Green County, Indiana. In June 1849, Isaac Storm of Green County, Indiana, age 63, said that he was half-brother to John Storm by their father's first wife, and that John Storm was born 3 February 1760, in Pennsylvania, and was raised in Virginia. Ann Parsons was born 10 September 1776, and they had eleven children. Ann Storm was at the time living with her son Peter, also of Green County. (Revolutionary War Pension and Bounty-Land Warrant Application Files. National Archives Microfilm Publication M804, roll 2306.)

Story, John

John Story of Franklin County, Kentucky in July 1818, declared he was a soldier in Captain William Barret's troop of Colonel William Washington's Light Dragoons, and served in the same troop as John Casey. John Story in September 1823, aged 60, stated that he was born and raised in Culpeper County, Virginia, and enlisted in Colonel William Washington's regiment in Hillsborough, North Carolina, at the same time as John Casey, in 1779. They fought together at the battles of Cowpens, Guilford, Camden, Eutaw Springs, and others. (under John Casey, S30308.

Revolutionary War Pension and Bounty-Land Warrant Application Files. National Archives Microfilm Publication M804, roll 493; also Dorman, John Frederick. 1958. Virginia Revolutionary Pension Applications, 16:72-74.)

John Story of Franklin County, Kentucky in July 1818 stated that he enlisted in 1779 in Captain Barret's troop under William Washington, served until the close of the war, and was honorably discharged. Charles Neal of Scott County, Kentucky in October 1818, affirmed that John Story enlisted under Captain Barret's troop, served to the close of the war, and was honorably discharged. (Virginia Governor's Office. Bounty Warrants, 1779-1860. Accession 41429, The Library of Virginia, Richmond, Va.)

John Story, of Anderson County, Kentucky, in October 1833, declared that he served in the 3rd Regiment of Light Dragoons under Colonel William Washington at the battles of Cowpens, Guilford Court House, Camden, and others. (under William Cardwell, W8590. Revolutionary War Pension and Bounty-Land Warrant Application Files. National Archives Microfilm Publication M804, roll 467; also Dorman, John Frederick. 1958. Virginia Revolutionary Pension Applications, 15:69-70.)

John Story or Storey, S30721. John Story first enlisted in Virginia in the militia in 1780 under General Stevens, was marched to North Carolina, and then entered service under Col. William Washington. He was at the battles of Cowpens, Guilford, Camden, and Ninety-Six. At the battle of Eutaw Springs, he was wounded and captured and taken to Charleston, South Carolina. In June 1818, he was living in Franklin County, Kentucky, and in August 1833, he was a resident of Anderson County, Kentucky. (Revolutionary War Pension and Bounty-Land Warrant Application Files. National Archives Microfilm Publication M804, roll 2307.)

Stratton, Seth

"I do Certify that Seth Stratton of 3 Troop enlisted for the war in Colonel Baylor's Dragoons April 10th 1781 & served the full Term of his Enlistment." William Barret, April 23, 1785. (Virginia Governor's Office. Bounty Warrants, 1779-1860. Accession 41429, The Library of Virginia, Richmond, Va.)

Seth Stratton, S37473. Seth Stratton of Shelby County, Kentucky, age 58, said in June 1818 that he enlisted in 1781 in the Third Regiment of Light Dragoons under Col. William Washington, was in the battle of Camden, continued to the end of the war, and was discharged in Winchester, Virginia. He was a private in Captain William Parsons' company, and Peter Brumback affirmed his service. (Revolutionary War Pension and Bounty-Land Warrant Application Files. National Archives Microfilm Publication M804, roll 2312.)

Stribling, Talliferro

Talliferro Stribling, mentioned on a roster of officers of 3rd Regiment. (University of Virginia. Alderman Library Special Collections. Accession 2257, Papers of the Baylor Family of Newmarket, Caroline County, Va, in part transcripts: [manuscript], 1653-1915. Box 4: the folder is labeled "1756, 1777-1781; Military Papers," item 21: "ca. 1780 Continental Troops, roster of Officers, 1st & 3rd Regiments.")

Stringfellow, David

David Stringfellow, Private, enlisted May 22, 1777. Muster Roll of the 2nd Troop in the 3^d Regiment Light Dragoons in the Service of the United States commanded by Lieutenant Colonel William Washington for the Months of May, June, July August, September, October 1779. (Revolutionary War Rolls, 1775-1783. National Archives Microfilm Publication M246. Roll 115, folder 13, 3^d Regiment Light Dragoons, 1779, item 1.)

David Stringfellow, private in Colonel Baylor's regiment of Dragoons, was wounded in his attempt to get out of the barn during the attack at Tappan, but managed to hide himself behind one of the regiment's horses in a small shed, and remained there until daylight. During his escape, he heard Corporal Henry Rose cry out for quarters. At daylight, he returned to the barn to retrieve his clothes, and found Corporal Henry Rhose dead. This deposition was taken by William Livingston, Governor of New Jersey, and sent to Henry Laurens; see the letter dated Morris Town, 22 October 1778, in Papers of the Continental Congress. (David Griffith. Letter, 20 October 1778. Accession 22789. Personal papers collection. The Library of Virginia, Richmond, Va.)

"I do Certify that David Stringfellow enlisted as a Soldier in 3 Regiment LD May 1779 for 3 years and Dec. 1779 he reenlisted for the war, was appointed Corporal 1st May 1780 & a Sergeant in Oct 80, and Continued in Service until his death Oct 1781 & was paid to the 1st Aug. 1780...." William Barret, May 3, 1784.

(Virginia Governor's Office. Bounty Warrants, 1779-1860. Accession 41429, The Library of Virginia, Richmond, Va.)

Sturdivan, Jno.

"I do Certify that Jno. Sturdivan enlisted for the war April 81 in Colonel Baylor's Regiment Dragoons and has faithfully served to the end of the war." William Barret, August 11, 1784. (Virginia Governor's Office. Bounty Warrants, 1779-1860. Accession 41429, The Library of Virginia, Richmond, Va.)

Suddoth, John

"By virtue of the Order of the Honorable Major General Green, John Suddoth ... belonging to the fifth troop 1st Regiment L D Com'd by Colonel George Baylor has leave to be absent from his said Regiment Till called for to repair to such Rendezvous as shall be appointed in the State of Virginia under pain of being Considered and treated as a deserter...." John Hughes and C. Jones, Nelson's Ferry, June 12, 1783. (Virginia Governor's Office. Bounty Warrants, 1779-1860. Accession 41429, The Library of Virginia, Richmond, Va.)

Sudduth or Southward, James

James Sudduth had sword, pistol, belt, cartridge box; "Present." Return, dated 1 March 1778, of arms and accouterments in the Third Troop belonging to Colonel George Baylor's Regiment of Light Dragoons. (Virginia Office of the Quartermaster General, Fredericksburg. Returns of Colonel George Baylor's Regiment, 1778-1779. Accession 22547, The Library of Virginia, Richmond, Va.)

James Southward, 5th troop. During the attack at Tappan, he escaped injury by concealing himself in the barn where they were quartered, while five men were killed outright, and the rest bayoneted. (David Griffith. Letter, 20 October 1778. Accession 22789. Personal papers collection. The Library of Virginia, Richmond, Va.)

James Sudduth, Sergeant, 5th troop. James Sudduth stated in his deposition that he was a sergeant in the fifth troop of Baylor's Regiment. He was awakened by the cries of alarm in the barn at Herring town near Tappan. He turned out with the rest of the men, but the British killed five of the men as they came out of the barn to surrender. He stated that the regiment was in six different quarters, with the Colonel in a seventh that night. This deposition was taken by William Livingston, Governor of New Jersey, and sent to Henry Laurens; see the letter dated Morris Town, 22 October 1778, in Papers of the Continental Congress. (David Griffith. Letter, 20 October 1778. Accession 22789. Personal papers collection. The Library of Virginia, Richmond, Va.)

Henry Roberts stated that James Suddith alias James Southard enlisted in the summer of 1777 under Col. George Baylor, and marched to Fredricksberg in September 1777 with the 3rd troop, under Captain Churchill Jones, and served as Quartermaster Sergeant. After his discharge in 1780, James Suddith went to Philadelphia and enlisted as a steward's mate on board the sloop Saratoga, which was later lost at sea with all hands. (Virginia Governor's Office. Bounty Warrants, 1779-1860. Accession 41429, The Library of Virginia, Richmond, Va.)

Sutton, Joseph

Joseph Sutton, Private. Muster Roll of the 2nd Troop in the 3d Regiment Light Dragoons in the Service of the United States commanded by Lieutenant Colonel William Washington for the Months of May, June, July August, September, October 1779. (Revolutionary War Rolls, 1775-1783. National Archives Microfilm Publication M246. Roll 115, folder 13, 3d Regiment Light Dragoons, 1779, item 1.)

Swan, Charles

In Tyler County, in August 1832, Charles Swan declared that he enlisted in Fredericksburg, Virginia, with Captain Cadwallader Jones of the Third Regiment of Light Dragoons. He was in the battle at Monmouth, and later, during the attack at Tappan, was taken prisoner by the British, confined in New York for about six weeks, but then escaped and rejoined his regiment at Bristol, Pennsylvania. He served about three years before being discharged.(Virginia Governor's Office. Bounty Warrants, 1779-1860. Accession 41429, The Library of Virginia, Richmond, Va.)

Charles Swan, W19425. Charles Swan, of Tyler County, Virginia, in August 1832, stated that he enlisted in Fredricksburg, Virginia, where he was living, with Captain Cadwallader Jones.

He stated that he was born in London, England, and after the war lived in Fauquier County, Virginia and later in Middleburg, Virginia. In 1840, Charles stated that he was married to Catherine

Goyer in Fredericktown, Maryland, in December 1779. In April 1843, Catherine, age 83, wrote that Charles died 4 August 1841, in Middleburg, Virginia. (Revolutionary War Pension and Bounty-Land Warrant Application Files. National Archives Microfilm Publication M804, roll 2327.)

Swan, John

John Swan, Captain, April 26, 1777, commission granted March 4, 1778. (Revolutionary War Rolls, 1775-1783. National Archives Microfilm Publication M246. Roll 115, folder 13, 3^d Regiment Light Dragoons, 1779, item 2.)

John Swan, Captain, Date of Commission April 26, 1777. Arrangement of Light Dragoons, 3^d Regiment, undated. (Revolutionary War Rolls, 1775-1783. National Archives Microfilm Publication M246. Roll 115, folder 13, 3^d Regiment Light Dragoons, 1779, item 3.)

John Swan, Captain, April 26, 1777. A Return of Officers in the 3rd Regiment of Light Dragoons with the Dates of their Commissions, Sept. 18, 1777. (Revolutionary War Rolls, 1775-1783. National Archives Microfilm Publication M246. Roll 115, folder 13, 3^d Regiment Light Dragoons, 1779, item 6.)

John Swan signed an oath of allegiance as Captain in Baylor's Light Dragoons, at Camp White Plain on 8 September 1778. (Numbered Record Books Concerning Military Operations and Service, Pay and Settlement of Accounts, and Supplies in the War Department Collection of Revolutionary War Records. National Archives Microfilm Publication M853. Roll 12: Oaths of allegiance and fidelity and oaths of office 1778-1781. Book 166, page 113.)

Captain Swan. "There are, besides, Prisoners in New York, A Captain (Swan) two subalterns, (Randolph and Dade) a volunteer, (Kilty) and the Surgeons Mate...." (David Griffith. Letter, 20 October 1778. Accession 22789. Personal papers collection. The Library of Virginia, Richmond, Va.)

John Swan wrote from Philadelphia, October 13, 1781, to Major Richard Call with the regiment in Richmond, about the lack of progress in obtaining supplies for the regiment. (University of Virginia. Alderman Library Special Collections. Accession 2257, Papers of the Baylor Family of Newmarket, Caroline County, Va, in part transcripts: [manuscript], 1653-1915. Box 4: the folder is labeled "1756, 1777-1781; Military Papers," item 22: "1781 J. Swan to Richard Call.")

J. Swan wrote to Col. Baylor about their march to Carolina, and that part of the regiment was still unequipped. He also asked Col. Baylor, "If you mean I shall continue in your regiment be so good as to keep me a good Regimental Horse, those I have here are not worth anything, and will not undergo hard service." (University of Virginia. Alderman Library Special Collections. Accession 2257, Papers of the Baylor Family of Newmarket, Caroline County, Va, in part transcripts: [manuscript], 1653-1915. Box 4: the folder is labeled "1756, 1777-1781; Military Papers," item 26: "1781 Nov 2 [Major John] Swan to Col. George Baylor, 3rd Regiment Dragoons Hdqts.")

John Swan, subsistence due from 1 June to 28 September 1778; subsistence due while a prisoner on Long Island 28 September 1778 to 25 October 1780; subsistence and pay due as Major from 25 October 1780 to 15 November 1783. (Miscellaneous Numbered Records [The Manuscript File] in the War Department Collection of Revolutionary War Records, 1775-1790's. National Archives Microfilm Publication M859. Manuscript 17567, "The United States in Account with Major John Swan of Colonel Baylor's Dragoons," dated 14 October 1785.)

John Swan, Captain, cash paid to him 13 May 1780. Also cash paid him on account, being two months pay and subsistence, 27 November 1779. (Miscellaneous Numbered Records [The Manuscript File] in the War Department Collection of Revolutionary War Records, 1775-1790's. National Archives Microfilm Publication M859. Manuscript 17584, "George Baylor's Regiment of Horse," undated.)

John Swan; pay for rations he did not draw from 11 August 1777 to 1 June 1778. (Miscellaneous Numbered Records [The Manuscript File] in the War Department Collection of Revolutionary War Records, 1775-1790's. National Archives Microfilm Publication M859. Manuscript 17681, "The Commissary Genl to John Swan Cap^{tn} of Light Dragoons," undated.)

John Swan, Major. On 10 August 1782, John Sandford Dart, Auditor for the Army, certified that John Swan settled his accounts for traveling expenses. (Miscellaneous Numbered Records [The Manuscript File] in the War Department Collection of Revolutionary War Records, 1775-1790's. National Archives Microfilm Publication M859. Manuscript 18055, "Certificate respecting Maj^r Swans Settlement with Mr Dart," dated 10 August 1782.)

"I hereby certify that on examining the books & records in the Department of War it appears that John Swan, Esqr., now of the city of Baltimore, was a Major of Dragoons at the close of the late revolutionary war and as such received the bounty in land which was promised by Congress, to the officers and Soldiers of the late Army." H. Rogers, December 30, 1807. (Virginia Governor's Office. Bounty Warrants, 1779-1860. Accession 41429, The Library of Virginia, Richmond, Va.)

Sway, George

George Sway, S42439. In 1833, he stated that he was known as George Haley in the Revolutionary War, and that within the third day after the battle of Guilford Court House, or between 15 and 19 March 1781, he enlisted under Colonel Washington, and served with Nathan Dobbs three years. (Revolutionary War Pension and Bounty-Land Warrant Application Files. National Archives Microfilm Publication M804, roll 2329; also Dorman, John Frederick. 1958. Virginia Revolutionary Pension Applications, 30:43.)

Talley or Tolley, Thomas

Thomas Tolley, Corporal, enlisted March 4, 1777, on command. Muster Roll of the 2nd Troop in the 3^d Regiment Light Dragoons in the Service of the United States commanded by Lieutenant Colonel William Washington for the Months of May, June, July August, September, October 1779. (Revolutionary War Rolls, 1775-1783. National Archives Microfilm Publication M246. Roll 115, folder 13, 3^d Regiment Light Dragoons, 1779, item 1.)

Thomas Talley, 2nd troop. Thomas Talley got into his clothes upon hearing the alarm during the attack at Tappan, and went to the barn door to ask for quarters, but the British soldiers stripped him of his breeches, money, and silver buckles. They then stabbed him six times with their bayonets, held a candle to his face to determine if he was still alive, and then left him. This deposition was taken by William Livingston, Governor of New Jersey, and sent to Henry Laurens; see the letter dated Morris Town, 22 October 1778, in Papers of the Continental Congress. (David Griffith. Letter, 20 October 1778. Accession 22789. Personal papers collection. The Library of Virginia, Richmond, Va.)

Taylor, John (died 1778)

"...In the Month of August 1777 John Taylor enlisted as a Sergeant In Captain Cadwallader Jones Troop of light dragoons It being the 4th troop of the 3rd Regiment commanded by Colonel George Baylor. And Said Taylor died in the month April the 25 day in the year 1778. I further state that from the time of his enlistment to the time he died I belonged to the Same Troop. Given under my hand this day of Sept 1811." Voucher signed by John Walker of Roane County, Tennessee. An affidavit by Samuel Walker dated September 2, 1811, in Roane County, Tennessee, stated that Cawfield Taylor was the only surviving brother of John Taylor. (Virginia Governor's Office. Bounty Warrants, 1779-1860. Accession 41429, The Library of Virginia, Richmond, Va.)

Taylor, John (former officer)

John Taylor submitted a recommendation, possibly from his previous commanding officer and dated March 22, 1782, to Col. George Baylor beginning "The bearer Mr John Taylor informs me that he intends to apply for an appointment in your Corps of Cavalry." The letter goes on to commend John Taylor, who had previously served as a Lieutenant and Adjutant, as a diligent, active officer. (University of Virginia. Alderman Library Special Collections. Accession 2257, Papers of the Baylor Family of Newmarket, Caroline County, Va, in part transcripts: [manuscript], 1653-1915. Box 4: the folder is labeled "Military Papers, 1782, 1814, & n.d.," item 4/5.)

Taylor, John (of Lincoln County, Kentucky)

John Taylor, S17138. John Taylor, age 68, was a resident of Lincoln County, Kentucky in August 1832. He was born in Prince Edward County, Virginia, and enlisted there in December 1779 as a private under Lieutenant Clem Read and Major John Nelson. John Taylor then enlisted in Colonel William Washington's 3rd Dragoons, and was discharged in December 1781. In December 1836, he removed to Ray County, Missouri to be with his children. (Revolutionary War Pension and Bounty-Land Warrant Application Files. National Archives Microfilm Publication M804, roll 2348.)

Taylor, Jonathan

Jonathan Taylor, Private, enlisted March 9, 1777, on command. Muster Roll of the 2nd Troop in the 3^{d} Regiment Light

Dragoons in the Service of the United States commanded by Lieutenant Colonel William Washington for the Months of May, June, July August, September, October 1779. (Revolutionary War Rolls, 1775-1783. National Archives Microfilm Publication M246. Roll 115, folder 13, 3^d Regiment Light Dragoons, 1779, item 1.)

Jonathan Taylor, private; pay due him from 15 February 1777 to 9 June 1781. (Miscellaneous Numbered Records [The Manuscript File] in the War Department Collection of Revolutionary War Records, 1775-1790's. National Archives Microfilm Publication M859. Manuscript 17653, "The United States in Account with Jonathan Taylor p^t Lt Dragoons," dated 5 August 1795.)

Jonathan Taylor, W4351. Jonathan Taylor, age 58, in Edgefield County, South Carolina, in October 1818, stated that he enlisted in Cumberland County, Virginia with Captain Smith, and served in the 2nd troop of the 3rd Regiment under George Baylor. He was discharged 9 June 1781, after fighting in the battles of Brandywine and Monmouth. He died in April 1830, leaving a widow, Joanna, who died 3 May 1839. (Revolutionary War Pension and Bounty-Land Warrant Application Files. National Archives Microfilm Publication M804, roll 2349.)

Tennell, George

"I do Certify that Geo Tennell enlisted for the war 1781 in 1st Regiment Light Dragoons." William Barret, August 27, 1784. (Virginia Governor's Office. Bounty Warrants, 1779-1860. Accession 41429, The Library of Virginia, Richmond, Va.)

George Tennell, S37485. George Tennell, age 62, a resident of Madison County, Kentucky in 1818 and 1821, stated that he enlisted in 1776 for 18 months with Captain Fauntleroy in the 3rd Regiment under Colonel Baylor; he next served under Colonel White as Corporal, where he was under Captain John Watts when he received his discharge in 1783. He fought in the Battles of Cowpens and Guilford. His family consisted of his wife, age 67, two daughters and one son who was not residing with them. (Revolutionary War Pension and Bounty-Land Warrant Application Files. National Archives Microfilm Publication M804, roll 2357.)

Thomas, Jacob

Jacob Thomas had sword, pistol, belt, and cartridge box; "on Command." Return, dated 1 March 1778, of arms and accouterments in the Third Troop belonging to Colonel George Baylor's Regiment of Light Dragoons. (Virginia Office of the Quartermaster General, Fredericksburg. Returns of Colonel George Baylor's Regiment, 1778-1779. Accession 22547, The Library of Virginia, Richmond, Va.)

"I do Certify that Jacob Thomas enlisted as Soldier in the 3 Regiment L Dragoons July 8th 1777 for Three years which time he has faithfully served." William Barret, January 21, 1784. (Virginia Governor's Office. Bounty Warrants, 1779-1860. Accession 41429, The Library of Virginia, Richmond, Va.)

Jacob Thomas, S39106. Jacob Thomas, of Knox County, Tennessee, in May 1818, stated that he was age 62 as of December 1817. He said he enlisted in Richmond, Virginia, 8 July 1777 with Lieutenant William Barret, in the 3rd Virginia Regiment commanded by Colonel Baylor. He served faithfully until 6 May 1780 at Lenud's Ferry in South Carolina, when he was taken prisoner and put on a prison ship near Charleston, and then moved to Charleston. He escaped on 23 June 1780 and went to Halifax, North Carolina, where the regiment was. His term of enlistment had expired, so in Halifax, he obtained a discharge from William Barret.

In 1820, still in Knox County, Jacob Thomas stated that his total property was only worth $7.50, and his family consisted of his wife, age 67, and himself, age 64. According to the pension office, Jacob Thomas died 28 February 1831. (Revolutionary War Pension and Bounty-Land Warrant Application Files. National Archives Microfilm Publication M804, roll 2369.)

Thorn, John

In September 1819, William Hebb of Preston County, Virginia, stated that he enlisted in 1777 in the company of Captain John Thorn of the regiment commanded by Col. Baylor, the 3rd Regiment of Light Dragoons. (under William Hebb, S38022. Revolutionary War Pension and Bounty-Land Warrant Application Files. National Archives Microfilm Publication M804, roll 1245.)

Thornton, Presley

Presley Thornton, Cornet, February 21, 1777, commission granted March 4, 1778. (Revolutionary War Rolls, 1775-1783. National Archives Microfilm Publication M246. Roll 115, folder 13, 3^{d} Regiment Light Dragoons, 1779, item 2.)

Presley Thornton, Cornet, Date of Commission February 21, 1777. Arrangement of Light Dragoons, 3^d Regiment, undated. (Revolutionary War Rolls, 1775-1783. National Archives Microfilm Publication M246. Roll 115, folder 13, 3^d Regiment Light Dragoons, 1779, item 3.)

Presley Thornton, Cornet, February 21, 1777. A Return of Officers in the 3rd Regiment of Light Dragoons with the Dates of their Commissions, Sept. 18, 1777. (Revolutionary War Rolls, 1775-1783. National Archives Microfilm Publication M246. Roll 115, folder 13, 3^d Regiment Light Dragoons, 1779, item 6.)

Alexander Clough wrote that Mr. Thornton had lately written from camp, begging to be relieved. (University of Virginia. Alderman Library Special Collections. Accession 2257, Papers of the Baylor Family of Newmarket, Caroline County, Va, in part transcripts: [manuscript], 1653-1915. Box 4: the folder is labeled "1756, 1777-1781; Military Papers," item 8: "Letter from Alexander Clough to George Baylor, 4 Feb 1778 at Millsone.")

Richard Call wrote from Petersburg that Mr. Thornton "wishes to be restored to his command which appears to be agreeable to the majority of the Officers present..." and that he felt Mr. Thornton has acted with great propriety. (University of Virginia. Alderman Library Special Collections. Accession 2257, Papers of the Baylor Family of Newmarket, Caroline County, Va, in part transcripts: [manuscript], 1653-1915. Box 4: the folder is labeled "1756, 1777-1781; Military Papers," item 27: "1781 Nov 20, Maj. Richard Call to Col. George Baylor 3rd Regiment Dragoons, Caroline.")

Captain Cadwallader Jones wrote from Petersburg to Col. Baylor that he was happy with Capt. Thornton being restored to his command, saying that he never heard a word about a problem with Mr. Thornton, and believed it to be a maneuver of Col. White to discredit Thornton. (University of Virginia. Alderman Library Special Collections. Accession 2257, Papers of the Baylor Family of Newmarket, Caroline County, Va, in part transcripts: [manuscript], 1653-1915. Box 4: the folder is labeled "1756, 1777-1781; Military Papers," item 28: "1781 Nov 25, [Capt Cadwaller] Jones to Col. George Baylor.")

"I do hereby Certify that Capt. Presly Thornton was appointed a Cornet in the 3d Regiment of Light Dragoons the 17th of March 1777, he was promoted to the rank of second Lieut. the 27th of May 1778, & to the rank of first Lieut. the 15th of November

1778 & to a Captain the 15th of May 1780, which commission he resigned the 25th of November 1781." George Baylor, Caroline County, June 15, 1783.

"Captain Presley Thornton late of Baylor's Regiment of Cavalry entered into the Service of the United States prior to November 1776, and Continued in Service until the Conclusion of the war in November 1783." James Wood, Brigadier-General, March 30, 1796. (Virginia Governor's Office. Bounty Warrants, 1779-1860. Accession 41429, The Library of Virginia, Richmond, Va.)

Presley Thornton, BLWt 553-300. Captain in the Virginia Line, allowed 300 acres March 2, 1811. (Revolutionary War Pension and Bounty-Land Warrant Application Files. National Archives Microfilm Publication M804, roll 2382.)

Thornton, William

"I do hereby Certify that William Thornton enlisted as a soldier for the war in the 2st Virginia Regiment of Cavalry the [illegible] day of October 1780 – and has been in actual service as such until this year." John Perry, Cornet, October 8, 1783. (Virginia Governor's Office. Bounty Warrants, 1779-1860. Accession 41429, The Library of Virginia, Richmond, Va.)

William Thornton, W6260. William Thornton, in Spotsylvania County, Virginia, in April 1818, stated that he enlisted October 1779 with Captain William Barret in the 4th Troop of George Baylor's Third Continental Dragoons. He was wounded in his right eye at the battle of Guilford Courthouse, and discharged at Nelson's Ferry, South Carolina. In November 1839, Frances Thornton, widow of William, age about 80, said he was in several battles during which he lost his right eye, got a ball in his hip, and received a number of other wounds. She and William Thornton were married in the spring of 1787 or 1788 in Spotsylvania County, and she was a resident of Hanover County in April 1847. A declaration made by Thomas Moses, Sr. and others in 1812 mentions two children. (Revolutionary War Pension and Bounty-Land Warrant Application Files. National Archives Microfilm Publication M804, roll 2382.)

Triplett, Nathaniel

"I do Certify that Sergeant Nathaniel Triplett Enlisted in Col. Baylor's Regiment of Light Dragoons the 20th of Dec. 1779 was appointed Corporal in said Regiment in August 1780 and a Sergeant in December 1780 has Received paper money pay to the first of August 1780 since which his pay is due him from the Public, the said Sergeant belonged to the Regiment, when it was Furlough'd June 1783." C. Jones, Captain, undated. (Virginia Governor's Office. Bounty Warrants, 1779-1860. Accession 41429, The Library of Virginia, Richmond, Va.)

Trusloe or Truslow, Benjamin

Benjamin Trusloe, S7757. Benjamin Truslow, a resident of Stafford County, Virginia in October 1841, was age 85 in January 1841. He said that he went to enlist in Stafford County, Virginia, but because he was not yet 21 years old, he was refused enlistment. He went back to his home in King George County and got written permission from his father, and was then able to enlist. He served under Major Churchill Jones and Captain Victor for five years, and included marching from Falmouth in Stafford County, Virginia to Petersburg, Virginia and then to Littleton, North Carolina. He was in the battle of Cowpens, where he was wounded in his left eye and took a ball in his left leg. He then marched to South Carolina and was stationed in Charleston, where he received his discharge from Colonel William Washington. He enlisted a second time under Captain Michael Wallace and Colonel Skinner of the Virginia troops. (Revolutionary War Pension and Bounty-Land Warrant Application Files. National Archives Microfilm Publication M804, roll 2417.)

Turnham, Thomas

Thomas Turnham had sword, pistol, belt, cartridge box; "on Command." Return, dated 1 March 1778, of arms and accouterments in the Third Troop belonging to Colonel George Baylor's Regiment of Light Dragoons. (Virginia Office of the Quartermaster General, Fredericksburg. Returns of Colonel George Baylor's Regiment, 1778-1779. Accession 22547, The Library of Virginia, Richmond, Va.)

"Thomas Turnham having served faithfully three years in the 3d Regmt. L. Dragoons is hereby discharged." William Washington, 16 May 1780. (Virginia Governor's Office. Bounty Warrants, 1779-1860. Accession 41429, The Library of Virginia, Richmond, Va.)

Thomas Turnham, S36831. Thomas, age 69, a resident of Wilson County, Tennessee in 1818, claimed that he enlisted in the fall of 1775 with Captain William Taliaferro of Colonel Woodford's 2nd Virginia Regiment for one year, but after a few months transferred under Captain Walker Vowles in the 3rd Virginia Continental Regiment. After a few months with that regiment, he exchanged with a soldier in the horse services and served under Captain Churchill Jones for three years.

According to information from the Pension Bureau, Thomas Turnham was discharged 25 October 1781; moved in 1822 to Spencer County, Indiana; his wife was age 66 in 1819. (Revolutionary War Pension and Bounty-Land Warrant Application Files. National Archives Microfilm Publication M804, roll 2428.)

Tyree, William

"I do certify that William Tyree was enlisted as a private Soldier in Baylor's Regiment of Lt. Dragoons, the 11th day of January 1778 & was discharged the 30 of May 1781. Given under my hand this 9th day of April 1783." Voucher by John Stith. (Virginia Governor's Office. Bounty Warrants, 1779-1860. Accession 41429, The Library of Virginia, Richmond, Va.)

Vaden, Bradock

"I do Certify that Bradock Vaden Enlisted for the war in Baylor's Dragoons 15 January 1780 & Cont'd to serve as a good and faithful Soldier for the full term of his Enlistment." William Barret, 5 November 1783. (Virginia Governor's Office. Bounty Warrants, 1779-1860. Accession 41429, The Library of Virginia, Richmond, Va.)

Vanpelt, S.

Listed as a prisoner on a report of the Quarter Guard, May 2, 1782, confined for two days and nights for "Loseing Currycomb." (University of Virginia. Alderman Library Special Collections. Accession 2257, Papers of the Baylor Family of Newmarket, Caroline County, Va, in part transcripts: [manuscript], 1653-1915. Box 4: the folder is labeled "Military Papers, 1782, 1814, & n.d.," item 13: "1782 May 2, Continental Troops, report of Quarter Guard, 3rd Regiment Light Dragoons, Report signed by James Meriwether, Lt. Officer of the Day.")

Vaughan, Claiborne

Claiborne Vaughan signed an oath of allegiance as Surgeons Mate of 6th Virginia Regiment, "at camp", 18 May 1778. (Numbered Record Books Concerning Military Operations and Service, Pay and Settlement of Accounts, and Supplies in the War Department Collection of Revolutionary War Records. National Archives Microfilm Publication M853. Roll 12: Oaths of allegiance and fidelity and oaths of office 1778-1781. Book 166, page 108.)

"To pay as Surgeon's Mate to Colonel Baylor's Regiment Dragoons from 20 Oct 80 to 31st Dec. 1781" The United States in Account with Claiborne Vaughan, 28 April 1838. (Virginia Governor's Office. Bounty Warrants, 1779-1860. Accession 41429, The Library of Virginia, Richmond, Va.)

Claiborne Vaughan, BLWt 637-300 issued 11 November 1814 to Wilie Vaughan and the other heirs of the late Claiborne Vaughan, Surgeon's Mate, of Baylor's Dragoons. William Langley of Kershaw District, South Carolina stated in May 1814 that Claiborne Vaughan left no descendants, and that Wilie Vaughan, formerly of Virginia, now residing in Camden, South Carolina, was the brother of Claiborne. (Revolutionary War Pension and Bounty-Land Warrant Application Files. National Archives Microfilm Publication M804, roll 2455)

Victor, John

Adjutant Victor, mentioned as receiving a set of officers bridle bits on 18 October 1777. (University of Virginia. Alderman Library Special Collections. Accession 2257, Papers of the Baylor Family of Newmarket, Caroline County, Va, in part transcripts: [manuscript], 1653-1915. Box 4: the folder is labeled "1756, 1777-1781; Military Papers," item 19: "Continental Troops, Itemized Account, September 1777 to June 1779.")

Thomas Gibson, of Pittsylvania County, Virginia, declared in September 1833 that he "was well acquainted with John Victor who acted as Lieutenant and Adjutant in Col. Baylor's Regiment of Cavalry from the year 1776 to the year 1779 or 1780." (Virginia Governor's Office. Bounty Warrants, 1779-1860. Accession 41429, The Library of Virginia, Richmond, Va.)

John Victor, W5171. Sarah Victor, age 78 in May 1838, stated that John Victor was a Lieutenant in Colonel Baylor's Corps of Horse, and that he died in January 1817, at which time she moved from Fredericksburg to Lynchburg, Virginia. She said that they were married between 1777 and 1780, their oldest child was about 58 years old, and that there were only three children now living.

John Victor, Jr., a resident of Lynchburg, Virginia in August 1838, said he was the youngest of six children of John and Sarah Victor, being born 1 February 1793. He stated that John Victor served as an Adjutant from March 1777 to July 1778, and that his parents were married in Caroline County, Virginia. Sarah Victor died 1 September 1839.

In a statement made by Christian Bankhead of Caroline County, Virginia, in June 1838, she said she was acquainted with Sally Tankersley, who married John Victor probably about 1777. (Revolutionary War Pension and Bounty-Land Warrant Application Files. National Archives Microfilm Publication M804, roll 2459.)

Wade, Acra

"I do Certify that Acra Wade was enlisted as a private soldier in the 1st Virginia Continental Regiment about the last of August 1780 & Continued till the latter end of March 1781 when he was transferred to the 1st Regiment of light Dragoons & Serv'd till the end of the war. Acra Wade was enlisted for During the war. N.B. Colonel Baylor mentions in a Furlough which Acra Wade has that he is to be answerable for a Horse which Wade says is since Dead." Arch^d Dunholm, Richmond, 9 April 1784.

"I do Certify that Acra Wade enlisted in Baylor's Regiment L Dragoons April 5th 81 for the war & that he is a native of Virginia as witness my hand." William Barret, Captain, Baylor's Dragoons, December 20, 1783.

"I do Certify that Acra Wade enlisted in Baylor's Regiment L Dragoons April 5th 1780 for the war & that he has not received any part of his pay as witness my hand." William Barret, Richmond, December 20, 1783.

"For a valuable consideration I do assign a good right to the within balance of my pay to Wm Reynolds which I assign to him & my land also." Acra Wade, December 20, 1783. (all vouchers from Virginia Governor's Office. Bounty Warrants, 1779-1860. Accession 41429, The Library of Virginia, Richmond, Va.)

Walker, Jeremiah

"I do Certify that Geremiah Walker enlisted him self to serve the war 7th June 1781 in the Baylor's Dragoons & that he has not drawn any pay." William Barret, 6 January 1784. (Virginia

Governor's Office. Bounty Warrants, 1779-1860. Accession 41429, The Library of Virginia, Richmond, Va.)

Jeremiah Walker, W6399. As a soldier of Cavalry, he was granted a certificate from the Auditor's Office, Richmond, Virginia, dated 3 November 1784.

Mary Walker, age 80 in October 1845, of Grainger County, Tennessee, stated that Jeremiah Walker was a private in the Virginia troops. The Pittsylvania County Clerk's office verified that Jeremiah Walker and Mary Mallicoat were married there in 1787. Mary Walker was still alive as of May 1849, when the Pension Office issued a certificate to her. (Revolutionary War Pension and Bounty-Land Warrant Application Files. National Archives Microfilm Publication M804, roll 2474.)

Walker, John (of Tennessee)

John Walker, in 1811 stated: "...In the Month of August 1777 John Taylor enlisted as a Sergeant In Captain Cadwallader Jones Troop of light dragoons It being the 4th troop of the 3rd Regiment commanded by Colonel George Baylor. I further state that from the time of his enlistment to the time he died I belonged to the Same Troop. Given under my hand this day of Sept 2d 1811." Voucher signed by John Walker of Roane County, Tennessee. (Virginia Governor's Office. Bounty Warrants, 1779-1860. Accession 41429, The Library of Virginia, Richmond, Va.)

John Walker, S48765. In Roane County, Tennessee, in April 1818, he stated that he enlisted under Captain Matthew Arbuckle in Botetourt County, Virginia for one year and was discharged about October 1776. He next enlisted 11 August 1777 with Captain Cadwallader Jones, and was discharged from that regiment in August 1780. In October 1821, John Walker of Roane County, age 66, stated he served in the 3rd Regiment of Dragoons for three years under Captain Cadwallader Jones. An Accounting Office report said John Walker died 2 February 1830, with the last pension payment paid to John M. Walker, attorney for the heirs. It also mentions his wife Margaret, who died in August 1819. (Revolutionary War Pension and Bounty-Land Warrant Application Files. National Archives Microfilm Publication M804, roll 2475.)

Walker, John (of Virginia)

"I do certify that John Walker enlisted as a soldier for the war in 3d Regiment L D Dec 24th 1779 as witness my hand Oct 9th,

1783." William Barret. "I do certify the above mentioned soldier served in the 3 Reg L Dragoons three years." Chiswell Barrett and Robert Morrow, undated.

"John Walker having faithfully served in the 3d Regiment of Light Dragoons is discharged." William Washington, August 11, 1790. "I do hereby certify that John Walker was a citizen of Virginia when he enlisted into the 3rd Regiment of Cavalry." Samuel Walker, Lieutenant in Colonel Gist's Regiment, October 15, 1783.

"By virtue of the orders of the Honorable Major General Greene, Jno Walker the bearer belonging to the third troop of the first Regiment of Dragoons commanded by Colonel George Baylor has leave of absence from the said Regiment until call for and then to return to such rendezvous as shall be appointed in the State of Virginia under pain of being considered and treated as a deserter, the said summons being published in the Virginia newspapers three weeks successively to be considered as sufficient notice." Henry Bowyer and C. Jones, undated. (Virginia Governor's Office. Bounty Warrants, 1779-1860. Accession 41429, The Library of Virginia, Richmond, Va.)

John Walker, BLWt 2230-100. Littleton W. Walker, of Charlotte County, Virginia in July 1838, heir of John Walker, stated that John Walker served as Dragoon in the 3rd Regiment of Light Dragoons under Colonel William Washington. Littleton and William Walker were the only heirs of the late John Walker. A Halifax County court statement in June 1838 listed six children of John Walker. (Revolutionary War Pension and Bounty-Land Warrant Application Files. National Archives Microfilm Publication M804, roll 2475)

Wallace, James

James Wallace, mentioned on a roster of officers of 3rd Regiment. (University of Virginia. Alderman Library Special Collections. Accession 2257, Papers of the Baylor Family of Newmarket, Caroline County, Va, in part transcripts: [manuscript], 1653-1915. Box 4: the folder is labeled "1756, 1777-1781; Military Papers," item 21: "ca. 1780 Continental Troops, roster of Officers, 1st & 3rd Regiments.")

Richard Call wrote October 26, 1781 to Col. George Baylor, "Capt Parsons wrote for Doct^r Wallace to go to the assistance of our wounded to the Southward he is now with the sick in Hanover. I shall direct him to wait your pleasure." (University of Virginia. Alderman Library Special Collections. Accession 2257, Papers of the Baylor Family of Newmarket, Caroline County, Va, in part transcripts: [manuscript], 1653-1915. Box 4: the folder is labeled "1756, 1777-1781; Military Papers," item 24: "1781 Oct 26, Maj. Richard Call to Col. [George] Baylor.")

Cadwallader Jones wrote from Petersburg to Col. George Baylor that one of the soldiers in the Regiment broke out with smallpox, and that "Doctor Wallis (who joined us with his party two days ago)" was making preparations to inoculate the remainder of the men, but that he was in want of some medicine which he hoped to find at Fredericksburg. (University of Virginia. Alderman Library Special Collections. Accession 2257, Papers of the Baylor Family of Newmarket, Caroline County, Va, in part transcripts: [manuscript], 1653-1915. Box 4: the folder is labeled "1756, 1777-1781; Military Papers," item 28: "1781 Nov 25 Capt Cadwaller Jones to Col. George Baylor.")

James Wallace, BLWt 2425-400. Surgeon, issued 27 March 1794 to William B. Wallace, executor. (Revolutionary War Pension and Bounty-Land Warrant Application Files. National Archives Microfilm Publication M804, roll 2479.)

Ward, John

"I John Ward do upon oath Certify and declare that I enlisted as a private in the 3rd Troop of Virginia light horse in the service of the United States in the spring of the year 1781 for during the war, and that I served in the company commanded by Captain Wm Parsons in the Regiment commanded by Col. Baylor of the Virginia continental line and was honorably discharged on or about the month of November 1783." (Virginia Governor's Office. Revolutionary War Rejected Claims, 1779-1860. Accession 41986, State government records collection, The Library of Virginia, Richmond, Va.)

John Ward, W8974. "John Ward a soldier in Colonel Baylor's regiment is hereby permitted to return home until the tenth of August unless sooner ordered to repair to home place of residence." L. Hardy, Council Chambers, dated 25 July 1783. "John Ward a soldier in the first Regiment of Dragoons has leave of absence with his horse arms and accouterments until the 20th of July then to repair to the Rendezvous of the Regiment sooner if called on by the commanding officer." Robert Morrow, Captain, 25 June 1788.

John Ward, a resident of Mason County, Kentucky in September 1828, stated that he enlisted as a private in Captain Parson's company, under Lieutenant H. Bell, in the 3rd Regiment of Colonel Baylor. In 1830, John Ward, age 65, claimed he enlisted in Lunenberg County, Virginia in the summer of 1781, and was discharged in 1783 by Captain Jones at Richmond. Alberry B. Ward, and Robert Ward, both of Lunenberg County in 1829, said John Ward, who was a native of Nottoway County, Virginia, was their brother, and that he enlisted in the 3rd troop of Light Horse commanded by Colonel George Baylor.

The Amelia County Clerk's Office affirmed that John Ward and Theodosia Anderson obtained their marriage license on 30 March 1789. Pages from the Ward family Bible have family information: Richard Ward, father of John Ward, was born 1737, and married Anna Ford in 1763; Anna Ford was born 1740; John Ward was born 1766, and married Dosha Anderson 4 April 1789 and had eleven children. Theodosia Ward, age 81, a resident of Mason County in 1849, stated that John Ward died 25 October 1846. (Revolutionary War Pension and Bounty-Land Warrant Application Files. National Archives Microfilm Publication M804, roll 2488.)

Warren or Warrin, John

John Warrin had sword, pistol, belt, cartridge box; "on command." Return, dated 1 March 1778, of arms and accouterments in the Third Troop belonging to Colonel George Baylor's Regiment of Light Dragoons. (Virginia Office of the Quartermaster General, Fredericksburg. Returns of Colonel George Baylor's Regiment, 1778-1779. Accession 22547, The Library of Virginia, Richmond, Va.)

"John Worain, with Lt. Randol" (University of Virginia. Alderman Library Special Collections. Accession 2257, Papers of the Baylor Family of Newmarket, Caroline County, Va, in part transcripts: [manuscript], 1653-1915. Box 4: the folder is labeled "1756, 1777-1781; Military Papers," item 14: "A list of the men's names absent belonging to Colonel Baylor's Regiment, Fredericksburg, June 27, 1778.")

John Warren, S3458. A resident of Rutherford County, Tennessee in 1832, he stated that he was living in Petersburg,

Virginia in 1777, when he enlisted with Captain Cadwallader Jones at Fredericksburg. He survived the massacre at Tappan in 1778, saying that "all of the men who did not make their escape were put to the sword." He was discharged not far from Manigault's Ferry on the Santee River, and returned to Petersburg, where he substituted under Colonel Campbell and Major Edmiston for 18 months. He then joined Colonel Lee's infantry under Lieutenant Handy. John Warren died 26 September 1836. (Revolutionary War Pension and Bounty-Land Warrant Application Files. National Archives Microfilm Publication M804, roll 2498.)

Washington, George Augustine

Cornet Washington mentioned as receiving a sword and scabbard, and one pair of pistols April 8, 1778; a set of bits on May 11th, 1778; and another set of bits on May 31, 1779. (University of Virginia. Alderman Library Special Collections. Accession 2257, Papers of the Baylor Family of Newmarket, Caroline County, Va, in part transcripts: [manuscript], 1653-1915. Box 4: the folder is labeled "1756, 1777-1781; Military Papers," item 19: "Continental Troops, Itemized Account, September 1777 to June 1779.")

Cornet Washington is mentioned as having Jesse Blanks with him. (University of Virginia. Alderman Library Special Collections. Accession 2257, Papers of the Baylor Family of Newmarket, Caroline County, Va, in part transcripts: [manuscript], 1653-1915. Box 4: the folder is labeled "1756, 1777-1781; Military Papers," item 14: "A list of the men's names absent belonging to Colonel Baylor's Regiment, Fredericksburg, June 27, 1778.")

George Augustine Washington, BLWt 2146-200. Lieutenant George Augustine Washington was dead by April 1836, when his son George F. Washington requested his father's bounty land. George F., Churchill Thornton and Charles A. Thornton, grandsons of George A. Washington, were the only heirs. (Revolutionary War Pension and Bounty-Land Warrant Application Files. National Archives Microfilm Publication M804, roll 2502.)

Washington, William

William Washington signed oath of allegiance on 18 August 1778 as Major of Light Dragoons. (Numbered Record Books Concerning Military Operations and Service, Pay and Settlement of Accounts, and Supplies in the War Department Collection of Revolutionary War Records. National Archives

Microfilm Publication M853. Roll 12: Oaths of allegiance and fidelity and oaths of office 1778-1781. Book 166, page 110.)

William Washington, Lt. Col. Muster Roll of the 2nd Troop in the 3^d Regiment Light Dragoons in the Service of the United States commanded by Lieutenant Colonel William Washington for the Months of May, June, July August, September, October 1779. (Revolutionary War Rolls, 1775-1783. National Archives Microfilm Publication M246. Roll 115, folder 13, 3^d Regiment Light Dragoons, 1779, item 1.)

Lt. Col. Washington, cash paid to him towards the expenses of furnishing horses by Mr. Palfrey, 10 July 1779. (Miscellaneous Numbered Records [The Manuscript File] in the War Department Collection of Revolutionary War Records, 1775-1790's. National Archives Microfilm Publication M859. Manuscript 17584, "George Baylor's Regiment of Horse," undated.)

William Washington, BLWt 2421-450, issued March 7, 1798, no papers. (Revolutionary War Pension and Bounty-Land Warrant Application Files. National Archives Microfilm Publication M804, roll 2502.)

Waterfield, John

"I do certify that John Waterfield of the 4th Troop enlisted for the war in Baylor's Dragoons 18th December 1779... he continued to serve until the mutiny May 83." William Barrett, December 14, 1783. (Virginia Governor's Office. Bounty Warrants, 1779-1860. Accession 41429, The Library of Virginia, Richmond, Va.)

John Waterfield, BLWt 1978-100. According to Elizabeth Hutchinson, a resident of Northampton County, Virginia in 1833, John Waterfield never married. She stated that John was a soldier in the Virginia Line. Also in Northampton County, George D. White said that John Waterfield served as a soldier of Cavalry during the war. John was survived by two brothers, William and Richard Waterfield. (Revolutionary War Pension and Bounty-Land Warrant Application Files. National Archives Microfilm Publication M804, roll 2502.)

Webster, Richard

Richard Webster had sword, pistol, belt, cartridge box; "Present." Return, dated 1 March 1778, of arms and accouterments in the Third Troop belonging to Colonel George Baylor's Regiment of Light Dragoons. (Virginia Office of the Quartermaster General, Fredericksburg. Returns of Colonel George Baylor's Regiment, 1778-1779. Accession 22547, The Library of Virginia, Richmond, Va.)

"I do Certify that Richard Webster enlisted as a soldier in Baylor's Dragoons May 1777 for three years and Served the full term of his enlistment." William Barret, 22 October 1787. (Virginia Governor's Office. Bounty Warrants, 1779-1860. Accession 41429, The Library of Virginia, Richmond, Va.)

Welch, Richard

Richard Welch, Trumpeter or Farrier, enlisted June 5, 1777. Muster Roll of the 2nd Troop in the 3^{d} Regiment Light Dragoons in the Service of the United States commanded by Lieutenant Colonel William Washington for the Months of May, June, July August, September, October 1779. (Revolutionary War Rolls, 1775-1783. National Archives Microfilm Publication M246. Roll 115, folder 13, 3^{d} Regiment Light Dragoons, 1779, item 1.)

White, Jonathan

Jonathan White, pay due him as trumpeter from 2 June 1782 to 15 November 1783. (Miscellaneous Numbered Records [The Manuscript File] in the War Department Collection of Revolutionary War Records, 1775-1790's. National Archives Microfilm Publication M859. Manuscript 17662, "The United States in a/c with Jonathan White of the late 3^{d} Regiment of Dragoons," dated 17 April 1792.)

Jonathan White, S35115. Jonathan White, of Cecil County, Maryland in 1818, stated that he enlisted in the spring of 1776 under Captain Fauntleroy of the 1st Regiment under William Washington. He was wounded at Hillsborough, North Carolina, and afterward served as trumpeter under Captain James Gunn until the close of the war. Mrs. Cromwell of Baltimore, Maryland, said she was the daughter of Jonathan White, who died 30 October 1830 in Cecil County. (Revolutionary War Pension and Bounty-Land Warrant Application Files. National Archives Microfilm Publication M804, roll 2556.)

Wilkerson, John

"It appears from the Size Roll 3 Troop that John Wilkerson Enlisted for the war in Baylor's Dragoons 1st Oct 81 & served faithfully the term of his Enlistment." William Barret, December 15, 1784. (Virginia Governor's Office. Bounty Warrants, 1779-1860. Accession 41429, The Library of Virginia, Richmond, Va.)

Williams, William

William Williams, S36394. At age 62, and a resident of Wilkes County, Georgia, he stated that he enlisted 1 September 1781 under Major Richard Call, and served under Captain Churchill Jones until about 7 June 1783, when he was discharged at Nelson's Ferry, in South Carolina. William Williams, still in Wilkes County in 1828, said he served in the company commanded by Captain Churchill Jones under Colonel George Baylor, and was wounded during his service. He said his wife was 63, and he had two daughter, one age 14 and the other 22 years old. (Revolutionary War Pension and Bounty-Land Warrant Application Files. National Archives Microfilm Publication M804, roll 2596.)

Willson, Moore

Moore Willson, Private, enlisted April 3, 1777, absent without leave. Muster Roll of the 2nd Troop in the 3^d Regiment Light Dragoons in the Service of the United States commanded by Lieutenant Colonel William Washington for the Months of May, June, July August, September, October 1779. (Revolutionary War Rolls, 1775-1783. National Archives Microfilm Publication M246. Roll 115, folder 13, 3^d Regiment Light Dragoons, 1779, item 1.)

Moore Willson, S44078. In 1818 he claimed that he was in General Washington's Life Guards, under Captain Robert Smith, and was wounded in the battle of Monmouth. Moore Willson, age 71, living in Wayne, Steuben County, New York in October 1821, stated that he first enlisted in April 1776 in Richmond, Virginia, with Captain Richard Park, under Colonel Woodford, in the 2nd Virginia Infantry, and was discharged at Williamsburg by Lieutenant Parker. He next enlisted as a private with Captain Robert Smith, under Colonel George Baylor, in April 1777. He was discharged at Fredericksburg, Virginia by Colonel Baylor. Moore said he was by trade a house carpenter and joiner, his wife Christina was age 58 in May 1821, and they had a daughter Sarah, age 14.

"I certify that More Wilson did duty as a private Soldier in Colonel Baylor's Regiment of horse in the Winter 1779 in Frederick Town Maryland then commanded by Colonel William Washington and that the said Wilson was much estimated by his officers as a faithful Soldier and an honest man. I have no doubt but that the said Wilson continued in the said Regiment to the termination of his Enlistment." Mountjoy Bayly, Captain 7th Maryland Regiment, City of Washington, November 16, 1822. (Revolutionary War Pension and Bounty-Land Warrant Application Files. National Archives Microfilm Publication M804, roll 2602.)

Wolfenbarger, Philip

Philip Wolfenbarger. W6575. Philip Wolfenbarger, age 57 and a resident of Gallia County, Ohio in 1819 and 1820, said he enlisted first at Millerstown, in Shenandoah County, Virginia, with Captain Williams' company under Major Ridley for eighteen months. He claimed he disliked the foot service so much that he next enlisted in Captain Hughes' company under Colonel White, shortly after the Battle of Guilford. White's regiment became so reduced that it was consolidated into Colonel Washington's Corps of Cavalry, where Philip Wolfenbarger served under Captain Watts, and was discharged at Winchester, Virginia. He was at the Battles of Cowpens and Eutaw Springs.

Catherine Wolfenbarger, a resident of Pike County, Ohio in 1852, stated that her maiden name was Cooper, and that she and Philip Wolfenbarger were married in Greenbrier County, Virginia, 23 May 1791. Elizabeth Taylor, wife of Abraham Taylor, and daughter and only child of Philip and Catherine Wolfenbarger, was living in Pike County in 1855. She said her father was in Lt. Colonel William Washington's regiment, and that he died in Pike County, Ohio, October 1, 1852. She also said that her mother lived for about 40 years in Pike County, and died 14 February 1855. (Revolutionary War Pension and Bounty-Land Warrant Application Files. National Archives Microfilm Publication M804, roll 2624.)

Wood, John

John Wood had sword, pistol, belt, cartridge box; "Present." Return, dated 1 March 1778, of arms and accouterments in the Third Troop belonging to Colonel George Baylor's Regiment of Light Dragoons. (Virginia Office of the Quartermaster General, Fredericksburg. Returns of Colonel George Baylor's Regiment, 1778-1779. Accession 22547, The Library of Virginia, Richmond, Va.)

John Wood, with Mr. B. Dade. (University of Virginia. Alderman Library Special Collections. Accession 2257, Papers of the Baylor Family of Newmarket, Caroline County, Va, in part transcripts: [manuscript], 1653-1915. Box 4: the folder is labeled "1756, 1777-1781; Military Papers," item 14: "A list of the men's names absent belonging to Colonel Baylor's Regiment, Fredericksburg, June 27, 1778.")

"I do Certify John Wood enlisted in 3d Regiment Dragoons for 3 years in the war... June 1777 and Served until 15th May 1778 when he was killed." William Barret, April 15, 1787. (Virginia Governor's Office. Bounty Warrants, 1779-1860. Accession 41429, The Library of Virginia, Richmond, Va.)

Woolfolk, William (or Francis)

In August 1821, William Woolfolk, of Kentucky, declared that he was a native of Virginia and enlisted in the spring of 1777 as a private in the second troop of the 3rd Regiment of horse under Walker Baylor in Caroline County. He was sent to Fredericksburg, where he was trained and made Sergeant, then to Dumfries where he was inoculated for smallpox. After recovering from the inoculation, he was at Brandywine, then his troop was employed in blockading British supplies from Philadelphia.

After the battle of Germantown, he escorted the wounded to Reading. He survived the massacre at Tappan, and was later appointed Cornet and Quartermaster. He resigned his commission in the spring of 1780. (Virginia Governor's Office. Bounty Warrants, 1779-1860. Accession 41429, The Library of Virginia, Richmond, Va.)

"I do hereby Certify that Mr Frances [William] Woolfolk Served in the 3d Regiment of Light Dragoons as a Private from the 8th of March 1777 until the 16th of May 1778 from that time until the 9th of March 1780 he Served as a Sergeant he was appoint Quartermaster to the Regiment the 9th of March 1780 and acted in that Post until the 23d of Oct of the same year." George Baylor, Caroline County, June 1781.

"I do hereby Certify that the Bearer Mr. Wm Woolfork was enlisted as a Dragoon in the late 3^{d} Regiment of Light Dragoons to serve three years." George Baylor, late Colonel, Caroline County, January 26, 1784. (under the name Francis Woolfork. Virginia Governor's Office. Bounty Warrants, 1779-1860. Accession 41429, The Library of Virginia, Richmond, Va.)

Wooten, Thomas

Thomas Wooten, pay due him for 1782 and 1783. (Miscellaneous Numbered Records [The Manuscript File] in the War Department Collection of Revolutionary War Records, 1775-1790's. National Archives Microfilm Publication M859. Manuscript 17663, "The United States in Account with Thomas Wooten Soldier in late 3rd Regiment Light Dragoons," dated May 1792.)

Wyatt or Wiet, Francis

Francis Wyatt had sword, pistol, belt; "on Command Sword Broke and Lost." Return, dated 1 March 1778, of arms and accouterments in the Third Troop belonging to Colonel George Baylor's Regiment of Light Dragoons. (Virginia Office of the Quartermaster General, Fredericksburg. Returns of Colonel George Baylor's Regiment, 1778-1779. Accession 22547, The Library of Virginia, Richmond, Va.)

"I do certify that Corporal Francis Wiet enlisted for three years in Colonel Geo Baylor's Dragoons August 5th 1777 and served as a good and faithful soldier the full term of his enlistment." William Barret, March 25, 1785. (Virginia Governor's Office. Bounty Warrants, 1779-1860. Accession 41429, The Library of Virginia, Richmond, Va.)

Francis Wyatt, W2042. Fanny Wyatt, age 65, widow of Francis Wyatt, a resident of Caroline County, Virginia in 1848, said her husband enlisted 5 August 1777 in Caroline County and served as corporal for three years under Colonel George Baylor. He died in April 1803, and they had two children; one died a minor, and the other never married. The Caroline County Clerk's Office verified that Francis Wyatt married Frances Austin on 23 December 1799. (Revolutionary War Pension and Bounty-Land Warrant Application Files. National Archives Microfilm Publication M804, roll 2653.)

Wyllis or Wiles, George

George Wyllis, 2nd troop. Upon hearing the alarm the night of the Tappan attack, he put on his coat and boots, but on going to the door of the barn, found they were surrounded by British soldiers. The soldiers first demanded everything from his pockets, then stabbed him twelve times. After he had fallen with his wounds, they stripped him and left him for dead. This deposition was taken by William Livingston, Governor of New Jersey, and sent to Henry

Laurens; see the letter dated Morris Town, 22 October 1778, in Papers of the Continental Congress. (David Griffith. Letter, 20 October 1778. Accession 22789. Personal papers collection. The Library of Virginia, Richmond, Va.)

"I do Certify that I enlisted George Wiles as a Soldier in the late 3d Regiment of dragoons in or about the 10th June 1777 and that he Served during the war in the said Regiment agreeable to the terms of his enlistment." John Swan, former Major 1st Regiment Light Dragoons, Baltimore, 23 February 1786. (Virginia Governor's Office. Bounty Warrants, 1779-1860. Accession 41429, The Library of Virginia, Richmond, Va.)

Yarborough, Charles

Charles Yarbrough signed an oath of allegiance as Lieutenant of 1st Virginia State Regiment, 1 June 1778. (Numbered Record Books Concerning Military Operations and Service, Pay and Settlement of Accounts, and Supplies in the War Department Collection of Revolutionary War Records. National Archives Microfilm Publication M853. Roll 12: Oaths of allegiance and fidelity and oaths of office 1778-1781. Book 166, page 106.)

"Mr. Yarborough writes me from Dumfries that he & his party are sick & have got but two horses. He thinks there is little prospect of getting any more & wishes to know whether he must return to the Regiment. He is without money." (University of Virginia. Alderman Library Special Collections. Accession 2257, Papers of the Baylor Family of Newmarket, Caroline County, Va, in part transcripts: [manuscript], 1653-1915. Box 4: the folder is labeled "1756, 1777-1781; Military Papers," item 24: "1781 Oct 26, Maj. Richard Call to Col. [George] Baylor.")

William Shope, Sergeant, and Charles Yarbrough, Lieutenant signed a return of clothing delivered to the 3rd Regiment Dragoons, April 23, 1782. (University of Virginia. Alderman Library Special Collections. Accession 2257, Papers of the Baylor Family of Newmarket, Caroline County, Va, in part transcripts: [manuscript], 1653-1915. Box 4: the folder is labeled "Military Papers, 1782, 1814, & n.d.," item 10: "1782 April 23, Continental Troops, Return of Clothing Delivered.")

Chas. Yarbrough, BLWt 1923-200. "Rec'd in full from Gen[l] Isaac Huger for one thousand acres of my military Claim of Land in the Virginia Line also for two Hundred acres as Continental Given under my hand this 19th March [1797]. Chas Yarbrough, Late

Lieut. 1st Regiment LD." (Revolutionary War Pension and Bounty-Land Warrant Application Files. National Archives Microfilm Publication M804, roll 2656.)

Bibliography

Bockstruck, Lloyd DeWitt. 1990. *Virginia's Colonial Soldiers.* Genealogical Publishing Company, Baltimore, Maryland.

Brumbaugh, Gaius Marcus. 1995. *Revolutionary War Records.* Genealogical Publishing Company, Baltimore, Maryland.

Chase, Philander D. 1985. *The Papers of George Washington. Revolutionary War Series.* University Press of Virginia, Charlottesville, Virginia.

Clark, Murtie June. 1991. *The Pension Lists of 1792-1795.* Genealogical Publishing Company, Baltimore, Maryland.

Dorman, John Frederick. 1958. *Virginia Revolutionary Pension Applications.* Washington, D.C.

Eckenrode, Hamilton James. 1980. *List of the colonial soldiers of Virginia: special report of the Department of Archives and History for 1913.* Genealogical Publishing Company, Baltimore, Maryland.

Eckenrode, Hamilton James. c1989. *Virginia soldiers of the American Revolution.* 2 Volumes. Virginia State Library and Archives, Richmond, Virginia.

Godfrey, Carlos E. 1995. *The Commander-in-Chief's Guard.* 1972. Reprinted for Clearfield Company, Inc., by the Genealogical Publishing Company, Inc., Baltimore, Maryland.

Griffith, David. Letter, 20 October 1778. Accession 22789. Personal papers collection. The Library of Virginia, Richmond, Virginia.

Gwathmey, John Hastings. 1938. *Historical Register of Virginians in the Revolution: Soldiers, sailors, marines, 1775-1783.* Dietz Press, Richmond, Virginia.

Haller, Stephen E. 2001. *William Washington: Cavalryman of the Revolution.* Heritage Books, Bowie, Maryland.

Heitman, Francis B. 1997. *Historical Register Of Officers of Continental Army during War of Revolution, April 1775 to December, 1783.* Genealogical Publishing Co, Baltimore, Maryland.

Hoyt, Max Ellsworth, and Frank Johnson Metcalf. 1943-1966. *Index of Revolutionary War pension applications.* Washington D.C.

Maurer, C. F. William. 2005. *Dragoon Diary: The History of the Third Continental Light Dragoons.* AuthorHouse, Bloomington, Indiana.

National Archives and Records Administration. *Compiled Service Records of Soldiers who Served in the American Army During the Revolutionary War.* (National Archives Microfilm Publication M881, 1096 rolls.) War Department Collection of Revolutionary War Records, Record Group 93.

--------. *General Index to Compiled Military Service Records of Revolutionary War Soldiers.* (National Archives Microfilm Publication M860, 58 rolls.) War Department Collection of Revolutionary War Records, Record Group 93.

--------. *Miscellaneous Numbered Records (The Manuscript File) in the War Department Collection of Revolutionary War Records, 1775-1790's.* (National Archives Microfilm Publication M859, 125 rolls.) War Department Collection of Revolutionary War Records, Record Group 93.

--------. *Numbered Record Books Concerning Military Operations and Service, Pay and Settlement of Accounts, and Supplies in the War Department Collection of Revolutionary War Records.* (National Archives Microfilm Publication M853, 41 rolls.) War Department Collection of Revolutionary War Records, Record Group 93.

--------. *Revolutionary War Pension and Bounty-Land Warrant Application Files*. (National Archives Microfilm Publication M804, 2,670 rolls.) Records of the Department of Veterans Affairs, Record Group 15. National Archives, Washington, D.C.

--------. *Revolutionary War Rolls, 1775-1783*. (National Archives Microfilm Publication M246, 138 rolls.) War Department Collection of Revolutionary War Records, Record Group 93.

--------. *Special Index to Numbered Records in the War Department Collection of Revolutionary War Records, 1775-1783*. (National Archives Microfilm Publication M847, 39 rolls.) War Department Collection of Revolutionary War Records, Record Group 93.

Papers of the Baylor Family of Newmarket, Caroline County, Va., 1653-1915. Alderman Library Special Collections. Accession 2257. University of Virginia.

Sanchez-Saavedra, E.M. 1978. *A Guide to Virginia Military Organizations in the American Revolution, 1774-1787*. Library of Virginia, Richmond, Virginia.

Sellers, John R. 1978. *The Virginia Continental Line*. Virginia Independence Bicentennial Committee, Williamsburg, Virginia.

Virginia Governor's Office. *Bounty Warrants, 1779-1860*. Accession 41429, The Library of Virginia, Richmond, Virginia.

------. *Revolutionary War Rejected Claims, 1779-1860*. Accession 41986, State government records collection, The Library of Virginia, Richmond, Virginia.

Virginia Office of the Quartermaster General. *Return, dated 1 March 1778, of arms and accouterments in the Third Troop belonging to Colonel George Baylor's Regiment of Light Dragoons*. Virginia Office of the Quartermaster General, Fredericksburg. Returns of Colonel George Baylor's Regiment, 1778-1779. Accession 22547, The Library of Virginia, Richmond, Virginia.

Index

*Names in bold indicate a soldier in Baylor's Regiment
and his service information.*

*The officers of the Third Light Dragoons, including George Baylor,
William Barret, John Belfield, Richard Call, Francis Dade, Griffin
Fauntleroy, Cadwallader Jones, Churchill Jones, Robert Morrow, Carter
Page, William Parsons, John Perry, John Stith, John Swan, Presley
Thornton and William Washington were mentioned on almost every page,
so the index shows only their service information.*

Adams, Francis 1
Adams, John 1
Adams, Nancy 1
Allen, Daniel 2
Alison, John, Capt. 79
Amey, James 2
Anderson, Alex 4
Anderson, David 2-3 28
Anderson, Jordan 3-4 28
Anderson, Leonard 4
Anderson, Rosanna 4
Anderson, Theodosia or Dosha 181
Andrews, Adam 4-5 115
Aplin, John 5 111
Arbuckle, Capt. 107 178
Armistead, Captain 39
Armstrong, Mary or Polly 119
Arnold, Anthony 6

Arnold, John 5-6
Austin, Catherine 150
Austin, Frances 188

Bachelor, Cornelius 6
Bailey, Peirce 6
Ball, Samuel H. 8
Ball, William 6-7 53 87
Ballew, David 8 93
Ballieu, David 8 92
Baird, James 8
Bankhead, Christian 177
Barnes, James 8
Barnes, John 8-9
Barnes, Milly 8
Barret, William 9-10
Barrett, Chiswell 10-11 15 72
Barrett, Churchill 11

Barry, Michael 11
Bassett, Elizabeth 76
Bassett, Peggy 12
Bassett, William 11-12
Bayard, James A. 76
Baylor, Captain 4 38
Baylor, George, Col. 12-16
Baylor, John, Lt. 3 **16-17**
Baylor, John W. 14
Baylor, Walker 17-19 72 81
Bayly, Mountjoy, Capt. 186
Beall, Nathaniel 19-20
Beatty, Col. 55
Beatty, Thomas 109
Bechenbaugh, Mary Anne 64
Belfield, Capt. 114
Belfield, John, Major 20
Bell, Henry 20-21 91 120 181
Bell, Sergeant 21 47
Bell, William 22
Benam, John, Capt. 6
Bennett, Caleb P. 22
Benson, Thomas 23
Bentley, Capt. 116
Betsill, John 23 57
Betsill, Sarah 23
Bidgood, Margaret 24
Bidgood, Philip 23-24
Bird, Benjamin 24 34
Bishop, Charlotte 25
Bishop, Robert 24
Bishop, Stephen 24-25
Biswell, John 25 65
Bland, Theodorick, Col. 13 77 86 90 100
Blanks, Jesse 26 182
Blocksome, Arthur 26
Bloxom, Arthur 26
Bolling, Robert 100
Bourn, Elizabeth 66 67
Bowers, George 26

Bowmer, _____ 26-27 43
Bowyer, Agatha 27
Bowyer, Henry 5 **27** 44 46 157
Boyd, Thomas 28
Boyd, William 27-28
Bragg, Joel 3,4 **28**
Branham, William 28-29
Bridgeman, Boswell 29
Bridges, Jane 30
Bridges, John 29-30 32
Bridges, Richard 30
Brooking, Samuel 30-31
Brown, Samuel 31
Browning, John Capt. 6
Brumback, Peter 31-32 96 163
Brumbly, Robert 32
Brumly, Robert 32
Bryant, John 32-33
Bryant, William 33 130
Buckley, Abrim 33
Buford, Abraham, Col. 143
Buford, George, Col. 21
Bumback, Peter 31-32
Bunn, Daniel 34
Burges, James 43
Burnly, Garland, Capt. 68
Burruss, Sally 126
Byrd, Anna Munford 34
Byrd, Francis Otway, Lt. Col. 34-35
Byrd, William 35
Byrde, James M. 124
Byrns, Thomas 35

Caffrey, Charles 35
Calfrey, Charles 35
Call, Richard 36-37
Callaway, Captain 37
Callaway, Major 105
Calo, Major 50

Index

Camp, Marshall 37
Camp, Thomas 37
Campbell, Col. 39 120 146 182
Campbell, William, Capt. 123 127
Canaday, _____ 37
Cannon, L., Lt. 82
Carbell, Rebecca 142
Carden, Edwin or Youen 37-38
Carden, Judith 38
Carden, Mary 38
Carden, William 38
Cardwell, Famariah 39
Cardwell, William 38-39 42 96 135
Carrington, Ed, Lt. Col. 71 117
Carroll, Joseph 39-40
Carster, William 41-42 154
Carter, Captain 4
Carter, John Champe 153
Carter, John Hill 40
Carter, Obadiah 40-41
Carter, William 41-42 130
Casey, John 26 32 **42-43** 135 161
Catlett, Thomas. Ensign 95
Chambers, Francis 43
Chambers, James 43
Chandler, Jesse 44
Chapman, John 44
Chapman, William 44-45
Charles, Fred 45
Chew, Elizabeth 69
Christy, Lt. Col. 124
Clack, Moses 45-46
Clay, Mr. 79
Clearwater, Benjamin 46 146
Clemens, John 46
Clift, William 46-47

Clough, Alexander 3 9 14 17 21 **47** 63 142 172
Cocke, Lucy 156
Cocke, Robert 156
Colbert, Elisha 48
Colgan, William 48
Colley, Charles 48-49
Collins, John 49
Collins, Margaret 49
Conner, John 73
Connor, Edward 49-50 85 **147**
Cookes, Michael 50
Cookers, Michael 50
Cooper, Catherine 186
Cooper, Samuel 50-51
Corning, Richard 51
Cosby, Sydnor 51
Cosby, William 52
Cox, Bartlett 52
Cox, Presley 52
Crane, Captain 38
Craton, Capt. 106
Crenshaw, Nathaniel 52-53
Cromwell, Mrs. 184
Cross, John 53
Crump, Abraham, Capt. 75
Culverson, Captain 45
Cummins, Susannah 1
Curtis, James 53-54
Custis, Lieutenant 12 **54**

Dade, Baldwin 54-55 186
Dade, Francis 55-56
Dade, Laurence 56
Dade, Polly 56
Dailey, Dennis 56 106
Dandridge, Alexander S. 90
Dangerfield, William, Col. 5
Dangerfield, William 23 **56-57**
Dart, John Sandford 167

Davidson, John, Major 108
Davis, Col. 43 45 145
Davis, Henry 57
Davis, Thomas 57-58
Davis, Thompsand 57-58
Davis, William 58
Dawson, James 58-59 145
Dawson, Jane 59
Deadman, Ann 45
Deal, Joseph 59
Dishman, James 59-60
Dishman, Nancy 59
Dobbs, Nathan 60 168
Dotson, Nancy 147
Drake, Thomas 60-61
Duke, Susan 73
Dunholm, Archd. 177
Dunn, Major 83

East, David 61
Ebb, William 61
Ebbs, James 61
Ebbs, John 61
Edmiston, Major 182
Eggleston, Jos. 144
Elb, William 61
Ellison, Major 127
Emerson, Henry 62
Emet, George 62
Emmert, George 62 110
Emmons, John 62
English, Charles 62-63
English, Samuel 62
Esbell, Benjamin 63
Eslong, Captain 1
Etter, John 63
Evans, George, Dr. 3 14 47 **63**
Evans, Thomas 64
Everhart, Lawrence 64
Everheart, Lawrence 64

Fauntleroy, Eliza F. 65
Fauntleroy, Griffin 65-66
Fauntleroy, Thomas 65 66
Ferrill, Zephaniah 66
Finley, Samuel, Major 27
Finney, John 86
Finney, Reuben 66-67
Fitzgerald, Bartlett Hawkins 67-68
Fitzgerald, Benjamin Hawkins 68
Fitzhugh, Elizabeth Chew 69
Fitzhugh, Peregrine 68-70
Fitzhugh, William 69
Fitzhugh, William, Col. 69
Fitzhugh, William, Lt. 70-71
Fitzpatrick, John 71 130
Fletcher, James 71-72
Foote, Gilson 115
Ford, Anna 181
Fortune, John 72
Foss, Captain 4
Foster, Anderson 73
Foster, Cosbey 72-73
Foushee, W. 58
Fox, Nathan, Capt. 130
Franklin, Elizabeth 74
Franklin, John 73-74
Frey, John 75
Fry, Benjamin 75
Fry, John 75
Fugler, William 75

Gale, John 75
Garner, Nancy 130 131
Garnett, Ann 76
Garnett, Benjamin 37
Garnett, Benjamin, Lt. 76
Garrett, John 76
Gatewood, Grafton 76

Index

Gee, Charles 24
Gerard, John 76
Geter, Andrew 104
Gibbs, Mary 105
Gibson, Col. 79 127
Gibson, Gen. 92
Gibson, George, Col. 121 127
Gibson, Thomas 65 77-78 176
Gillison, John Capt. 141
Gist, Nathaniel, Col. 5 129 179
Glason, Patrick 78
Glayson, Patrick 78
Gleason, Patrick 78
Goatley, John 78-79
Good, Capt., Flying Camp 64
Goode, Frank, Capt. 2
Goodwyn, L. 109
Gordon, Ambrose or Ambrus 38 67 76 **79-80**
Gordon, William 122
Goyer, Catherine 165-166
Grady, John 80
Graves, Francis 2
Gray, Daniel 80
Gray, David A. 97
Grayson, Col. 129
Green, Charles 80-81
Green, Col. 90
Green, Jesse 81-82
Green, John 82 124
Green, John, Capt. 124
Green, Lucy P. 100 101
Greene, Nathaniel, Gen. 4 50 60 67 92 105 143 164 179
Gresham, Lieutenant 33 **82**
Griffin, Reuben 82-83
Griffin, Sherrod 83
Griffith, David 2 23 31 **83-84**
Grimes, Capt. 107
Groves, Berthena 31
Guillams, William 84

Gulley, Richard 84
Gunn, James, Capt. 184
Gunn, Jane 59 60
Gunn, Lieutenant 145
Gunnell, John 84-85
Gwelliams, Williams 84

Hale, Samuel 85
Haley, Daniel 88
Haley, George 85 168
Hambrick, David 85-86
Hambright, Frederick 86
Hamer, Mary 97
Hamilton, Thomas, Capt. 78 127
Hamilton, William 86-87
Hammond, Samuel, Col. 113
Hampton, John 87
Hamrick, David 85-86
Hamrick, Lettice 86
Handy, Lieut. 182
Hardy, L. 180
Harris, Henry 87 88 89
Harris, John, Lt. 98
Harrison, Col. 13
Harrison, Mr. 36 160
Hart, Benjamin 88
Hawes, Samuel, Capt. 41 95 151
Hawes, Col. 116
Hawkins, Bartlett 67-68 88
Hawkins, Benjamin 29 **68** 88
Hawkins, Martin 15
Hays, John, Capt. 93
Healey, Daniel 88
Healey, David 88
Hebb, William 88-89 171
Henderson, Nancy 72
Hendren, William 89
Henry, Patrick, Col. 124

Herndon, Mr. 16
Hert, F. 89
Heth, Col. 30
Hickman, Hannah 90
Higg, John 89
Hight, George 91-92
Hill, George 90
Hill, John 90-91
Hite, George 7 91-92
Holland, Thomas 22
Holms, Col. 58
Hood, Catherine 92
Hood, Charles 92
Hood, George 8 92-93
Hood, James 93
Hood, John 93
Hood, Mary 92
Hood, William 92
Hopkins, Samuel, Capt. 52
Horn, Christopher 93
Horn, Elizabeth 93
Horsley, Lucy 3
Howze, Lucy 113
Hubbard, James 94
Hudgins, Samuel 94
Hudgins, Thomas, Capt. 25
Hudson, Ann 95
Hudson, Rush 88 94-95
Huger, Isaac, Gen. 189
Hughes, George 95
Hughes, John, Capt. 49
Hughes, John, QM 114
Hull, Beecham 95
Hulse, William 95-96
Hutchinson, Elizabeth 183
Hutchinson, Thomas 96

Innis, James, Col. 6

Jack, Susan 122
Jacobs, Ann 97
Jacobs, John 32 96-97
Jacquet, Peter 22
Jameson, John, Lt. Col 13 15
Jarman, William 97
Javes, Thomas 97
Jenkins, Edward, Capt. 60
Jenkins, John 97-98
Jesse, William 9 98
Jeves, Thomas 97
Johnson, James 98
Johnson, John 99
Johnson, Thomas, Capt. 48
Jones, Cad. 100 101
Jones, Cadwallader 99-101
Jones, Captain 43 44 60 99-102
Jones, Catesby 43
Jones, Churchill 101-102
Jones, Cornet 144
Jones, Elizabeth 158
Jones, George 103
Jones, Griffith 103
Jones, James 103-104 115
Jones, Mary 106
Jones, Molly 103
Jones, Patsey 104
Jones, Richard 104
Jones, S. 158
Jones, Samuel 104
Jones, Solomon 104-105
Jones, Stephen 37 105
Jones, William, brother of
    Churchill Jones 102
Jones, William 105-106

Keen, John 106
Kelly, James 106-107
Kerney, John 48

Index

Kesterson, Nancy 90
Kidd, Deborah 144
Kile, Elizabeth 50
Kilty, John 55 64 **107-109**
King, Charles 109
King, Elijah 125
King, Elisha 109
King, G. H. S. 102
King, George 110
King, James 110
King, Julian or Julius 111
King, Margaret 111
King, Snelling 5 111

Lafayette, Gen. 100
Land, Benjamin 111-112
Langford, Joseph 112
Langford, Peter 112
Langley, William 112-113 176
Langsdon, Charles 113
Langsdon, Eda or Edith 113
Langsdon, Samuel 113-114
Laurens, Henry 23 31
Lawes, William 114
Lawson, Captain 43
Lawson, Col. 119 128
Leaner, George 114
Lee, Col. 120 182
Lee, General 34
Lee, Henry 10 120
Legear, Henry 114
Leonard, George 114
Level, Henry 114
Lewis, Charles 95
Lewis, Charles, Col. 109
Lewis, Eleanor 115
Lewis, Fielding 5 115
Lewis, George 115-116
Lewis, James 116
Lewis, Joseph 116

Lewis, Lucinda 115
Lewis, Robert 115
Lightfoot, John, Capt. 6
Linnard, John 116-117
Linton, John 30 32 46 61 85 **117**
Livingston, William, Gov. 23 31
Locket, Benjamin 117-118
Lockhart, William 72
Lockhert, William 118
Logen, Hugh 118
Long, John 118-119
Long, Levi 119
Lovell, James 119
Loyd, Mary 120
Loyd, William 120
Luallen, Daniel 120
Lucas, James Capt. 94 128
Lunsford, William, Sergt. 105 **120-121**
Lynch, Charles, Col. 105

Mackelroy, James 126
Macklin, James 121
Madison, William 71
Major, Humphrey 71
Mallicoat, Mary 178
Mann, Claiborne 121
Mann, Olive 121
Marion, Gen. 60 99
Marks, Capt. 157
Marshall, Richard 121
Martin, Boling 122
Mason, Nathaniel, Capt. 24 25 119
Massey, John 122
Massey, John Henry 122
Massey, Robert 122
Massey, William 122
Matthews, Col. 6 60

Matthews, George, Col. 80
May, Benjamin 123
May, Molly 123
May, Polly 123 124
May, Thomas 122-123
May, William 123-124
McBryde, James 124
McClanahan, Thomas 124-125
McCraw, Francis 125-126
McCraw, Francis 125
McCraw, George 125
McCraw, Jacob 125
McCraw, Samuel 125
McClanahan, William 125
McDonnaugh, Jonathan 126
McElroy, James 126
McGuire, William, Lt. 90
McHaney, William 127
McIntosh, _____ (officer) 105
McKay, Jesse 65
McKinney, Reuben 124
McLanahan, Thomas 124-125
McLaughter, Thomas 126
McMahan, Andrew 127
McMahan, Polly 127
McMahan, William 127
Mercer, Col. 48
Mercer, Gen. 22
Meredith, Jesse 127-128
Meriwether, James 73 128
Merryweather, Capt. 121
Metheany, Eleander 129
Metheany, Joshua 129
Metheany, Luke 128-129
Metheany, William 129
Miller, Ann 134
Miller, Elizabeth 142
Million, Haman 8
Min, David, Capt. 120
Minerich, Susanna 114
Minor, John Capt. 51

Minton, Abnezor or Ebenezer 129-130
Minton, Elizabeth 130
Montague, George 35
Moody, William 38
Moon, Capt. 105
Moore, Capt. 105
Moore, David 130-131
Moore, Nancy 130 131
Morgan, Gen. 59 92 141
Morrow, David 132
Morrow, Robert 131-132
Moses, Thomas, Sr. 173
Moxley, George 132
Muhlenberg, P., Gen. 92
Mullen, Anthony 132-133
Mullen George 133
Mullen, William 133
Muse, Caroline 133
Muse, Francis 133
Muse, George 133
Muse, Lawrence 133

Neal, Charles 42 96 118 **133-135** 162
Neilson, John 136
Nelson, George 136
Nelson, Gov. of Virginia 70
Nelson, John, Major 169
Nelson, Roger 136
Nelson, Thomas Gen. 140
Nevil, John, Capt. 76
Nevil, Zachariah 136
Newland, Mathew 136-137
Newlin, Mathew 136-137
Newton, George 137
Nixon, Andrew 137-138
Nixon, John 138
Norfleet, William 119
Norris, Bezeled 138

Norwood, Joseph 138
Nowell, Richard 138-139

Oast, George 139
Ogg, John B. 142
Owens, Ephraim 139
Owens, Evan 139

Page, Baylor 140
Page, Carter 139-141
Page, Jack 140
Page, John 140
Page, Lucy 14 140
Page, Mann 15
Palfrey, Col. 69 137
Palfrey, Mr. 183
Pamplin, Unity 52
Park, Richard, Capt. 185
Parker, Col. 86 90
Parker, Lieut. 185
Parsons, Abizah 142
Parsons, Ann 161
Parsons, George 141 145
Parsons, James 142
Parsons, William 141-142
Parsons, Willoughby 142
Peak, Jesse 143
Peek, Jesse 143
Perkinson, James 143
Perry, John 143-144
Pierce, Mr. 69 137 148
Plunkett, James 144
Plunkett, Reuben 130 144-145
Porterfield, Richard 58 59 141 145
Preston, Col. 125
Price, Frederick 100 101
Price, William 161
Pritchard, James 145-146

Pritchard, Phebe 146
Pritchard, Thomas 146
Pritchett, James 145-146
Pucket, Josiah 146
Pucket, Martha 146
Pullen, George 147
Pulling, George 147
Putnam, Gen. 92

Quynn, Catherine 108

Rambles, Sarah 133
Randall, (officer) 2
Randolph, Charles 147
Randolph, Robert 55 64 107 147-148
Rankins, Benjamin 149
Read, Clem 169
Read, Priscilla 154
Reason, Reuben 149-150
Reynolds, William 74 177
Rhose, Henry 152 163
Rice, George 5
Rider, Jesse 150
Riding, Jesse 150
Ridley, Major 186
Riley, Elizabeth 8
Robbins, Elenor or Elender 46
Roberts, Capt. 60
Roberts, Henry 26 42 150 165
Robertson, Ann 151
Robertson, Benjamin 150-151
Robertson, George 151
Robertson, Henry 151
Robertson, Reuben 151
Robinson, Benjamin 151-152
Rogers, H. 168
Rogers, John 152
Roods, William 152

Rose, Henry 152 163
Rose, Louisa 145
Rose, Robert 152-153
Ross, James 153
Rugely, Col. 25 58
Rutherford, Deborah 91

Sailor, Martin 153
Sawers, William 153-154
Sawyers, William 153-154
Scott, Captain 43
Scott, Charles 154
Seigncourt, Judy 41
Sheppard, David 11
Sherer, Keziah 121
Shiber, Frederick 154
Shope, William 154-155 189
Shoup, William 154-155
Simmons, Col. 107
Simons, James 155
Simpson, Elizabeth 32
Skinner, Col. 174
Sled, Seaton or Sexton 155
Smith, Ballard, Col. 161
Smith, Bouton 155-156
Smith, Cornet 5 156
Smith, Jesse 156
Smith, John, deserter 35 156
Smith, John 36
Smith, Juby 156-157
Smith, Richard 157
Smith, Robert, Capt. 87 150 **157-158** 170 185
Smith, Wyatt 158
Southard, James 158 164
Spotswood, Alexander, Col. 124 151
Spotswood, William, Col. 95
Stagg, John, Lt. 119
Stephens, Edward, Col. 141

Stephens, Gen. 24
Steuben, Gen. 98 143
Stevens, Gen. 162
Stewart, Benjamin 159
Stewart, Philip 159-160
Stith, John 160-161
Storm, Isaac 161
Storm, John 161
Storm, Peter 161
Story, John 39 42 135 **161-162**
Stratton, Seth 32 **162-163**
Straugham, Dorothy 159
Stribling, Talliferro 163
Stringfellow, David 152 **163-164**
Stringfellow, Henry 6
Stuart, Charles 160
Stuart, Col. 105
Stuart, Philip 159-160
Stubblefield, Robert 1
Sturdivan, Jno. 164
Suddoth, John 164
Sudduth, James 164-165
Sutton, Joseph 165
Swan, Charles 89 **165-166**
Swan, John 166-168
Sway, George 168

Taliaferro, William, Capt. 175
Talley, Thomas 168
Tankersley, Sally 177
Tapsley, Samuel, Capt. 5
Taylor, Abraham 186
Taylor, Cawfield, 169
Taylor, Elizabeth 186
Taylor, Francis, Capt. 124
Taylor, James 132
Taylor, Joanna 170
Taylor, John 169 178
Taylor, Jonathan 169-170

Index

Tennell, George 65 **170**
Thomas, Jacob 170-171
Thorn, John, Capt. 89
Thorn, John 171
Thornton, Charles A. 182
Thornton, Churchill 182
Thornton, Frances 173
Thornton, Presley 171-173
Thornton, William 173
Thorp, John 115
Tinsley, Thomas 158
Tolley, Thomas 168
Towles, Oliver, Capt. 8
Triplett, Nathaniel 173-174
Troyman, William 71
Trusloe, Benjamin 174
Truslow, Benjamin 174
Turnham, Thomas 174-175
Tyree, William 175

Vaden, Bradock 175
Valentine, Edward 74
Vanpelt, S. 175
Vaughan, Catherine 60
Vaughan, Claiborne 176
Vaughan, Wilie 176
Victor, John, Capt. 174 176-177
Victor, Sarah 176

Wade, Acra 177
Wagoner, Andrew, Capt. 76
Walker, Jeremiah 177-178
Walker, John 169 178-179
Walker, John M. 178
Walker, Littleton 179
Walker, Margaret 178
Walker, Mary 178
Walker, Samuel 169

Walker, Samuel, Lieut. 179
Walker, William 179
Wallace, James 179-180
Wallace, Michael, Capt. 174
Wallace, William B. 180
Ward, Alberry B. 181
Ward, John 180-181
Ward, Richard 181
Ward, Robert 181
Warman, Thomas, Capt. 54
Warren, John 181-182
Warrin, John 181-182
Washington, Cornet 26 182
Washington, George A. 182
Washington, George F. 182
Washington, William, Col. 182-183
Waterfield, John 183
Waterfield, Richard 183
Waterfield, William 183
Watts, John, Capt. 21 59 170
Watts, John, Cornet 77
Wayne, Gen. 68 129
Webster, Richard 183-184
Welch, Richard 184
Weedon, Gen. 69 70 137 149
Whitby, John, Capt. 145
White, Col. 60 113 143 170 172 186
White, George D. 183
White, Jonathan 65 184
Wiet, Francis 188
Wiles, George 188-189
Wilkerson, John 184-185
Williams, Capt. 186
Williams, Tabitha 125
Williams, William 185
Willis, Francis, Capt. 128
Wills, Nathaniel 23-24
Willson, Moore 185-186
Willson, Christina 185

Wolf, Morris, Capt. 4
Wolfenbarger, Catherine 186
Wolfenbarger, Philip 186
Woolfolk, Francis 187
Woolfolk, William 187
Woolfork, Francis 187
Wood, James, Brig-Gen. 10 161
    173
Wood, James, Capt. 125
Wood, James, Col. 91
Wood, John 54 186
Woodford, Col. 175 185
Woodford, William, Gen. 123
Wooten, Thomas 188
Worain, John 148 181-182
Wyatt, Frances 188
Wyatt, Francis 187
Wyllis, George 188-189
Wynne, John 157

Yarborough, Charles 38 46
    154 **189-190**
Young, Richard 15 16

About the Author

Christine Langner finds it amusing and ironic that, even though history was her least favorite subject as a child, she has become very aware of, and knowledgeable about, the Revolutionary War, and in particular, the Third Continental Light Dragoons.

She started researching her family history years ago, after hearing stories about an ancestor who, according to family tradition, fought for the British in the Revolutionary War, liked the area around Camden, South Carolina, and decided to settled there after the war. When she found a letter from this ancestor to the Governor of Virginia, in which he stated that on the first day of May in 1777 he enlisted in Petersburg, Virginia as a Soldier in the 3rd Virginia Regiment of Light Dragoons, commanded by Col. George Baylor, she wanted to find out if it was true. And thus began the project to identify Baylor's men.

Christine Langner works in Information Technology Services at Longwood University in Virginia, and continues her research to help others find out more about their family history.

www.ingramcontent.com/pod-product-compliance
Lightning Source LLC
Chambersburg PA
CBHW050146170426
43197CB00011B/1977